THE PENALTY IS DEATH

Barry Jones (1932-) edited the first edition of *The Penalty is Death* in 1968 while secretary of the Victorian Anti-Hanging Committee (later Council) from 1962 to 1975. He has been a teacher, lawyer (briefly), academic, politician, and author. He was a Labor member of the Victorian Parliament 1972-77 and of the Commonwealth Parliament 1977-98. The Minister for Science in 1983-90, he represented Australia at UNESCO in Paris 1991-96 and carried out research in Cambridge 2000-01. His books include *Sleepers, Wake!* (1982), *A Thinking Reed* (2006), *The Shock of Recognition* (2016), *What Is To Be Done* (2020), and *Dictionary of World Biography* (latest edition 2021). A Fellow of four of Australia's five learned Academies, Barry Jones was awarded an AC in 2014.

THE PENALTY
IS DEATH

state power, law, and justice

Edited by Barry Jones

SCRIBE
Melbourne • London

Scribe Publications
18-20 Edward St, Brunswick, Victoria 3056, Australia
2 John St, Clerkenwell, London, WC1N 2ES, United Kingdom
3754 Pleasant Ave, Suite 100, Minneapolis, Minnesota 55409, USA

First published as *The Penalty is Death: capital punishment in the twentieth century* by Sun Books, in association with the Anti-Hanging Council of Victoria, in 1968

This edition published by Scribe in 2022, in association with the Capital Punishment Justice Project

Typeset in Bembo by the publishers

Printed and bound in Australia by Griffin Press

Scribe is committed to the sustainable use of natural resources and the use of paper products made responsibly from those resources.

Scribe acknowledges Australia's First Nations peoples as the traditional owners and custodians of this country. We recognise that sovereignty was never ceded, and we pay our respects to their elders, past and present.

978 1 922585 77 6 (Australian edition)
978 1 922586 75 9 (ebook)

A catalogue record for this book is available from the National Library of Australia.

scribepublications.com.au
scribepublications.co.uk
scribepublications.com

For politicians, judges, lawyers, journalists,
teachers, and opinion leaders in retentionist nations

A note on grammar and punctuation

A collection such as this, containing diverse historical material, inevitably features a range of grammatical and punctuation styles. Throughout, we have retained what were contemporary conventions, making changes only in order to remove ambiguity and improve clarity.

Contents

Part III
The Case for Retention

Part IV
The Reality

Part V
The Decline and Fall of the Death Penalty
in the English-speaking World

Acknowledgments

The second edition of *The Penalty is Death*, fifty-four years after the first, is entirely due to the initiative, drive, and encouragement of Stephen Keim, SC, chair of the Capital Punishment Justice Project (CPJP), who wanted its publication to mark the centenary of the abolition of the death penalty in Queensland on 1 August 2022. He has been enthusiastically supported by Dr Sarah Pritchard, SC, Nick Cowdery, AM, QC, and Lex Lasry, AM, QC.

Forewords have been written by Justice Michael Kirby, AC, CMG, Richard Bourke, an Australian barrister, now director of The Justice Center in Louisiana, and Julian McMahon, AC, a Melbourne barrister with extensive overseas experience in death-penalty cases.

Mike Richards, author of *The Hanged Man* (2002), has been a great resource and has contributed a new chapter. (See Appendix D.)

Brian Walters, AM, SC, made valuable suggestions.

The Queensland Parliamentary Library was very helpful.

Russ Radcliffe has been an inspired choice as publishing editor.

The Penalty is Death, while essentially retaining the 1968 format, has been updated and extensively rewritten.

In the 1968 edition, there was grateful acknowledgment of permission to reprint texts and extracts from the following:

Professor Thorsten Sellin for *The Death Penalty*; Sir Ernest Gowers and Chatto & Windus for *A Life for a Life?*; Lord Gardiner of Kittisford for *Capital Punishment as a Deterrent*.

Reflections on the Guillotine by Albert Camus (1957), reprinted in the *Evergreen Review*, vol. 4, no. 12 (March–April 1960) by courtesy of Grove Press Inc, NY. The John Howard Assoc., Chicago and Hans

W. Mattick for *The Unexamined Death*; *The Herald*, Melbourne and Sir Eugene Gorman for 'The Victims of a Hanging are You and Me'; Sir John Barry for 'Views on the Alternative to Capital Punishment and the Commutation of Sentences'; *The Australian* and Stanley W. Johnston for 'Why Can't We Be Reasonable About Hanging?'; 'Statements in Favour of the Death Penalty' by J. Edgar Hoover are from the *FBI Law Enforcement Bulletins*; 'Capital Punishment: Your Protection and Mine' by Edward J. Allen from *The Police Chief*, vol. 27, June 1960; *The Wimmera Mail-Times* for 'Crime increase a threat to all citizens' by P.R. Biggin; the editor of the *Geelong Advertiser* for 'Crime and Punishment'. The authors and Penguin Books for extracts from *Hanged by the Neck* by Arthur Koestler and C.H. Rolph. 'A Hanging' by George Orwell by kind permission of Mrs Sonia Orwell; 'An Execution' by Peter Lewis by the editor of the *New Statesman*; 'Death of Ronald Ryan' by Patrick Tennison and *The Australian*. The chart 'Hangings in Australia 1901–67' has been adapted (and corrected) from Stanley W. Johnston's *Criminal Homicide Rates in Australia*.

FOREWORD
Michael Kirby

The original version of *The Penalty is Death*, edited by Barry Jones, was published in 1968 in the aftermath of the hanging of Ronald Ryan at Pentridge Prison, Melbourne on 3 February 1967. Ronald Ryan was the last person in Australia to be executed.

The State of Queensland had its last execution in 1913. However, capital punishment remained in South Australia and Western Australia until 1964. It lingered on in Victoria until the hanging of Ronald Ryan, carried out on the insistence of Premier Henry Bolte, who was strong and successful on 'law and order' politics. He won six elections in succession in Victoria. He was not interested in criminology, theology, or philosophy. He pandered to a majority of electors who then supported capital punishment in Victoria, amongst other causes. It was only when he was replaced by his younger Liberal successor, Dick Hamer, that it became possible to get abolition of capital punishment through the Victorian Parliament. The editor of this book, Barry Jones, played an important part in securing the majority that achieved that objective.

Virtually from its start, abolition of capital punishment had been a policy of the Australian Labor Party (ALP). State governments in Victoria and other states, formed by the ALP, played a major part in securing the fruits of abolition, but, admittedly were slower in Western Australia and South Australia. They did so by removing the punishment from state legislation but, also, earlier by narrowing the crimes to which it would apply and commuting the carrying out of the punishment where they could not gather enough parliamentary votes for abolition. There always remained (and still is) a lobby in Australia that supports capital punishment for so-called extreme crimes. It was to counteract and rebut that residual pressure that Barry Jones first published this book in 1968. As he points out in his 'Overview' for this book, there is always a risk of restoration in any jurisdiction.

The hundredth anniversary of the formal abolition of capital punishment by the Parliament of Queensland on 1 August 1922 is an event worth celebrating. We should reflect on the fact that it was Queensland that was the first jurisdiction in the then British Empire to take that step. Breaking the logjam of inaction was a crucial move that led the way for others to follow. Now, more than half of the 200 members of the United Nations have abolished capital punishment However, that still leaves almost as many nations that cling on to this form of punishment. In 2021, perhaps 3,000 people were executed in retentionist countries, many kept secret. Of these, astonishingly, probably more than 2,000 were executed in China.

There was a time when Australia pioneered reforms that led the way in other countries: votes for women; industrial arbitration; testamentary justice; and even abolition of capital punishment. It has now disappeared from all Australian states and territories. Australia has signed on to the Second Optional Protocol to the International Covenant on Civil and Political Rights of 1976. However, there remain political leaders in Australia who, occasionally, try to tap the wellsprings of electoral popularity sometimes to be found in this idea. It is therefore timely to see this book republished, especially by its original editor. Although the first printing was fifty years ago, Barry Jones is still happily energetic, committed, and persuasive on multiple ethical causes. Including this. Truly, he is a national treasure.

Barry Jones identifies the theories that kept capital punishment alive in our own land after many others had earlier embraced repeal.

Nobel Laureate John Coetzee, in *Waiting for the Barbarians* (1980), adapting an idea by Nathaniel Hawthorne, referred to 'the black flower of civilisation', essentially the coercive power of the state, which would include the death penalty, torture and wrongful imprisonment.

Essentially, there are two black flowers: the barbarity of state involvement in the premeditated extinguishing of a human life, and the overwhelming objective proof that doing so did not have the suggested practical merit of reducing the incidence of serious crimes.

Yet, there is a third bloom, a golden flower that can be identified in the advance of civilisation in our world. It is the golden flower of universal human rights that has enhanced civilisation since the Queensland abolition of capital punishment in 1922.

Increasingly, lawyers, theologians, philosophers, politicians, and other citizens see capital punishment as incompatible with the universal values of the world after the United Nations Charter of 1945 and the Universal Declaration of Human Rights of 1948, even without subscription to the Second Optional Protocol. At a time in history when such universal values are being endangered by a few, it is all the more important to restate and reaffirm the arguments assembled in this book. The days when nation states could suppress and destroy their own citizens and others have been replaced by a time when universal human rights are at the core of national and international law and policy, and human commitment. There is a unity in this. Without the central wellspring of civilisation that includes respect for universal human rights, the risks of destruction of civilisation are ever-present and evermore dangerous.

As I read this book again, so long after my first reading of it in 1968, I was reminded of an assertion by a judicial colleague who declared that the loss of the power of Australia's judges over the lives of its citizens had resulted in lamentable damage to the rule of law and respect for the judiciary as the arbiter of all things legal, including to the right of some to live or to die. I protested against this notion. Was he joking? No, I am sure that my colleague was serious about this thesis. Yet if he could embrace such an idea, how seductive such notions must be to others, of narrower education and experience.

For my own part, I continue to watch the international news reports of the continuing moves to abolish capital punishment. Simon Locodo, a former Ugandan government minister, remarkably for ethics and integrity, died in January 2022, unrepentant over legislation introduced by him that imposed the death penalty for acts of homosexuality in his country. Fortunately, his enactment was struck down on a technicality by the courts. But his violent beliefs still live in many countries. In February 2022, Iran was once again reported to have executed two gay men. It is not the only country that has executed LGBT people and others for victimless crimes. Happier news has recently been welcomed from Papua New Guinea. Ironically, it inherited capital punishment in the original form of its criminal code borrowed from Queensland. Now, forty-five years after independence, it has decided to repeal the death penalty. As new evidence gathered in this book reveals, during World War II, death sentences were imposed in grossly disproportionate numbers on 150 Indigenous people (often for collaboration with the enemy). This is a shocking fact, still largely redacted, that demonstrates the special vulnerability of the poor, uneducated, and vulnerable to this form of punishment. And the tendency of autocratic government to hide such wrongs from the people.

So these are some of the reasons for reprinting and updating Barry Jones's book and its collection of ageless writings on capital punishment by Cesare Beccaria, Charles Dickens, Albert Camus, Arthur Koestler, George Orwell, and other greats. Certainly, it is still relevant to Australia. Clearly, it is timely for the wider world. The true foundation for the authority of the judiciary and other governmental institutions of Australia rests not on executions but on the adherence of its judges and people to constitutionalism and its respect for the human dignity of all people. No exceptions—even those convicted of grave crimes. This is the message of this book. It remains relevant and timely in Australia, 100 years after the first abolition of capital punishment in Queensland. It is more than ever a timely message for a wider world in which violence by states and their agencies is never far from human deeds and imagination.

Hon. Michael Kirby AC CMG (1939–)was a justice of the
High Court of Australia (1996–2009); president of the International
Commission of Jurists (1995–98); and co-chair, Human Rights Institute,
International Bar Association (2018–21). See M.D. Kirby, 'The High Court
and the Death Penalty' (2003) 77 *Australian Law Journal* 811, Foreword

FOREWORD

Richard Bourke

I was born in Melbourne, Australia, three years after Ronald Ryan, the last person executed in Australia, met his death. My father, a staunch abolitionist and a Kellyphile, attended the vigils outside Pentridge Prison.

I grew up to be a criminal lawyer, and, while practising with Peter Clarebrough in St Kilda, had the pleasure of representing a man who had been sentenced to death as a teenager and had been on death row at Pentridge when Ryan was hanged. My client's sentence was commuted, and he was eventually released to lead a shattered but mainly harmless life, punctuated by periods of drug use and hopeless shoplifting.

I am not sure how many times I stood up for him in court and watched the magistrate frown at his list of priors, only to have me direct the court's attention to the conviction and sentence at the start of the list and assure the court there was nothing it could say that was worse than what my client had heard, previously, from a judge.

Each magistrate's eyes would, invariably, widen and they would look up from the paperwork and really look at my client for the first time—a piece of history and a link to a barbaric judicial past.

I remember, from when I joined the Victorian Bar, some of the other more savvy junior barristers pointing out Philip Opas QC, Ryan's trial counsel, by then in his seventies, and explaining that he was the last Victorian barrister to represent a client facing the death penalty. He was another, more noble, link to the past, and one that was rightly humbling as we fumbled along at the start of our careers, trying our best on much more minor briefs, the prospect of capital defence happily unimaginable.

I did not know much about Barry Jones's work as an abolitionist then and had no idea this book existed. If someone had handed it to me, I would have thought it a publication whose time had passed.

In 1998, still working as a criminal lawyer, I travelled to New Orleans to volunteer for a couple of months at the Louisiana Capital Assistance Center, a non-profit law office representing poor people facing the death penalty in the Deep South. The experience left an indelible mark on me.

I returned to New Orleans in 2002 and have been here ever since, working exclusively for poor folks, usually people of colour, whom the government is trying to kill. For twenty years, I have had the best job in the world. I wake up every day and go to work, and my job is, in a thousand different ways, to try to persuade people not to kill. It can be a very difficult and demanding job, but it has given far more than it has taken from me.

Twenty years of death-penalty work has taught me a deep appreciation of the texts Barry has gathered in this book and an ever-deeper appreciation that the questions they ask and the insights they share are timeless, and that this is a publication whose time has most definitely not passed.

A strength of the book is that it does not shy from an attempt to reflect the views of those who support capital punishment, though Barry's lament at the difficulty in gathering material of sufficient quality to merit publication makes its own point.

Here, in Louisiana, in 2015, Dale Cox, one of the lead death prosecutors in the state, made the argument, succinctly, declaring that revenge is the only justification for the death penalty and that it is a good justification. Cox opined, 'I think we need to kill more people … I think the death penalty should be used more often.'.In 2020-21, starting in the run-up to the presidential election, the United States government executed thirteen prisoners in a six-month period, more people than it had executed in the preceding seventy years.

In the face of this vision of a society built on a core of vengeance and killing, it is a comfort to read the words of others who have come before who have believed in and fought for a better way.

When I stood witness to the execution of our client, Jackie Elliott, in Texas, in 2003, I experienced not only the horror and sadness one might expect, but a profound, soul-deep sense of how wrong capital punishment was, a sense far deeper than simply vehement opposition. To realise that Tolstoy had experienced this same feeling, though expressing it more eloquently than I ever could, is a powerful affirmation.

Reinhold Niebuhr declared that, 'Nothing that is worth doing can be achieved in our lifetime; therefore, we must be saved by hope.' Barry's collection serves to connect us across generations, working hand in hand in a shared belief and in the hope that one day that belief will prevail. Barry began this work long before I was born and continues it even now with the republication of *The Penalty is Death*.

It has become a bit of a cliché to talk about standing on the shoulders of giants. But as I look at Barry's work in this field and the writings he has gathered here, it seems more apt for me to say that I take great comfort in toiling in their shadows.

Richard Bourke (1970–) was born and educated in Melbourne, and a barrister and co-founder of Reprieve Australia. He has worked in the United States on death-penalty cases since 2002, and is an eloquent and passionate advocate.

FOREWORD
Julian McMahon

In September 2008, Luke Davies wrote an extended essay for *The Monthly* on Myuran Sukumaran and Andrew Chan, the condemned prisoners from the so-called Bali Nine. The editor at the time, Sally Warhaft, entitled the cover of that edition 'The penalty is death'.

The article was strategic, intended to reintroduce the two prisoners into the public eye after a long hiatus, to show them as humans deserving of dignity and understanding and not merely as criminals to be shot. It is remarkable to think that, forty years after its publication, both the very title of the book we here introduce and, of course, its content would still shape Australian thinking in 2008. Remarkable, too, that the man who compiled this book would be an important supporter, five decades later, of the younger people fighting the death penalty.

It is an honour to write this short foreword. I write as a lawyer with twenty years' involvement in death-penalty work, in Asia and beyond. This foreword gives me a chance to note the importance of mentors, scholarship, and activism.

Most readers of this will know that two of the noblest and most significant voices in Australia on matters of human rights, in the last forty years and more, have been Barry Jones AC and Michael Kirby AC CMG. They share, inter alia, a passionate opposition to the death penalty. Barry was a key player in the final struggle that led to the abolition of the death penalty in Victoria (and was, of course, the moving force for this book).

Michael, who has also provided a foreword, has written numerous scholarly articles on the topic. Both have spoken to audiences, large and small, whether to dignitaries, students, or quietly interested members of the public, on innumerable occasions. They give their time. They do the work. Both continue to influence the debate, here in Australia, and, in Michael's case, abroad through the International Bar Association and the UN.

Importantly, both have given generous support, publicly and privately, to younger people now engaged in the fight. They are uplifting. Their writings, their advocacy, their mentorship and leadership have shaped and guided the next generations of advocates. It is no accident that the death-penalty debate in this country has been for decades conducted variously in a respectful, scholarly, hopeful, and fearless way. Such is the fruit of their labours.

The other foreword written here is by Richard Bourke. In its early days he was a key part of Reprieve Australia. As a young Melbourne lawyer, Richard came to the Victorian Bar in May 1998. We were on the same Bar admission course of three months' intensive training. Many barristers on that course have reached eminent positions, but none was so powerful a presence or mighty a talent as Richard. He was an unforgettable whirlwind of personality and brilliant advocacy. For him, in Australia, the sky was hardly the limit. With that future open to him, he has spent his entire career in the southern states of the US fighting death-penalty cases. With a low income and working in a hostile and badly resourced environment, he has persevered, fighting to save the most helpless and forgotten and unwanted from the worst excesses of the US's penal systems.

For many years, the patron of what was Reprieve Australia, now the Capital Justice Punishment Project Inc, has been Michael Kirby. He has often travelled to speak at functions, to warmly encourage young lawyers and activists, with great effect. One of the young lawyers who heard such talks is Matt Goldberg. In 2008, as one of the newest young lawyers at Reprieve Australia, Matt went to Louisiana to work over the summer with Richard Bourke in fighting the death penalty. After years at the Melbourne Bar, while simultaneously working against the death penalty, Matt is now the president of the World Coalition Against the Death Penalty, working from London across the world and at the UN on this debate.

Those engaged in this debate know that perseverance is required. As many of the authors within the following pages attest, they argued knowing that, at the time, they would fail. But they knew, too, that their arguments would fall on soil that might, eventually, prove to be fertile. Camus fought against the death penalty, his whole life, and, twenty-one years after his death, it was abolished in France. His brilliant polemic, here, makes the point that many governments fear: 'If you think it is right to execute, why do it so shamefully, hidden and darkly secret?' He exposes their shame.

Others write of the essential dignity of each person, its centrality to society. Where the dignity of each person is not valued, where the violence of killing by the state is accepted, there we often find other senseless brutality. There, all too often, you will find prisons of torture and horror. It is not a coincidence, just as it is not a coincidence that the keenest executing states in the US have histories drenched in slavery and lynching. The fight against such conduct requires perseverance. As this book has a very Victorian history, I should note that, on fifteen occasions between 1956 and 1974, a local MP, Jack Galbally, introduced a bill to abolish the death penalty into the Victorian Parliament. He failed to have it passed every time. Finally, his political opponents abolished it in 1975. Perseverance is part of this struggle.

We were fortunate in Australia that in 2015, in the lead-up to the executions of Sukumaran and Chan, the then foreign minister and the then shadow foreign minister, Julie Bishop and Tanya Plibersek, had the capacity to work together, to put aside other political differences and lead parliament to a universal opposition to all executions, everywhere.

Australia now does play a real role in this debate, internationally. Locally, these steps have led to the creation at Monash University Law School of Eleos Justice, an academic centre solely focussed on the death penalty, in research, training, and other areas. The leading anti-death penalty NGO, the Capital Punishment Justice Project Inc, plays an important role in the region. The Department of Foreign Affairs and Trade maintains a keen interest and willingness to engage, to lend its support in multiple forums.

It is not an exaggeration to say that all these developments stand upon the shoulders of those who have done the hard yards over decades. This book is not only a testament to such a long history. It remains an invaluable resource, filled with wisdom and powerful writing to make us all think more deeply.

Julian McMahon, AC, SC (1963–) is a Melbourne barrister who has chaired Reprieve Australia. He was awarded the AC in 2017 for 'eminent service to the law and the legal profession, through pro bono representation of defendants in capital punishment cases overseas, as an advocate for the abolition of the death penalty, and to human rights and social justice reform'.

Part I

The Death Penalty:
an overview

1

The penalty is death: an overview and update

Barry Jones

The first edition of this book was published in 1968, in the aftermath of Ronald Ryan's hanging at Pentridge on 3 February 1967. He was the last of 2,140 people to be executed in Australia since 1629, 187 of them in Victoria.

In 1968 capital punishment had been abolished as the penalty for murder in only thirty nations, although there was a moratorium on its use in many more.

In 2022 the number of abolitionist nations has risen to 108, and fifty-four more have a long-standing moratorium.[1] In 2021, among retentionist states, there were no recorded executions in India, Bangladesh, Singapore, Pakistan, Indonesia, Japan, Nigeria, Taiwan, Belarus, and South Korea.

What is the relevance of debating the death penalty in 2022?

Capital punishment is a central metaphor/analogy about the problems of state power, the fallibility of human judgment, flaws in rigid institutions, the use of special pleading, and the danger of making decisions that are irreversible.

The World Coalition against the Death Penalty reported the number of recorded executions internationally in 2021 at 2,397, with at least 2,000 in China. The total figure is probably far higher, because China keeps details of its executions a state secret. An estimated 33,000 people are currently under sentence of death, globally.

---

1   See Appendix E.

China executes for murder, drug trafficking, official corruption, financial crimes, and robbing ancient cultural sites. However, the number of executions fell significantly from 12,000 in 2002 to 6,500 in 2005. Many of those convicted (and acquittal is very rare) may be sentenced to death, subject to a reprieve.

Iran, with a population of 83 million, has a higher execution rate per capita than China. In addition to murder, treason, and drug-trafficking it is enforced for a far wider range of offences, including sodomy, rape, incest, paedophilia, adultery (for repeat offenders), producing pornography, political dissidence, apostacy, blasphemy, some economic crimes, and 'enmity against God'. There were 977 executions in 2015, when Hassan Rouhani, regarded as a moderate, was president; 507 in 2017; and 365 in 2021.

Egypt ranks third among executing states. In the decade 2011-21 the Muslim Brotherhood sentenced to death 2,182 people, including children, mostly for political offences. In 2020 there were 152 executions, which was a record, and more than 100 in 2021.

Vietnam executed 429 people in the period 2013-16, but capital punishment is a state secret, and recent figures have not been released.

Saudi Arabia executed sixty-seven prisoners in 2021, but there have been some reforms: an indication that juveniles will not be executed, and that penalties for drug-related crimes will be reduced. In March 2022 there were eighty-one executions, mostly political, including Yemeni nationals and members of al-Qaeda.

In Australia, the Criminal Code Amendment Bill, providing for the abolition of capital punishment, was introduced into the Queensland Legislative Assembly in September 1916, during the premiership of Thomas Joseph Ryan[2] (1876-1921), by the assistant minister for justice, John Fihelly[3].

He modestly argued that his Bill 'was by no means a novel enactment', contending that the death penalty was on the way out everywhere. 'In the United States it has been practically abolished', he said and drew attention to Italy, the Netherlands, and Belgium. Oddly, he did not refer to the United Kingdom or the other Australian states.

---

2   *Australian Dictionary of Biography*, vol. 11, 1988, by Ross Johnston and Denis Murphy.
3   Ibid., vol. 8, 1981, by Betty Crouchley.

The 1916 Bill was carried 37–14 in the Legislative Assembly, but was blocked by the conservative Legislative Council, a body that was then entirely appointed.

In 1921 Premier Edward Granville ('Red Ted') Theodore,[4] later Commonwealth treasurer, persuaded the governor of Queensland, Sir Matthew Nathan, to appoint enough new members (soon dubbed 'the suicide club') to vote the Legislative Council out of existence.

On 1 August 1922 capital punishment was abolished in Queensland for all crimes, the first jurisdiction in the then British Empire to do so. The Criminal Code Amendment Act, moved by attorney-general John Mullan,[5] was passed by the Legislative Assembly 33-30.

The centennial in 2022 is an appropriate time for reflection and celebration.

Queensland had its last execution in 1913, New South Wales in 1939, Tasmania in 1946, the Northern Territory (under Commonwealth law) in 1952, South Australia and Western Australia in 1964, and Victoria in 1967. Between 1901 and 1964 Western Australia executed more than any other Australian state, and was the last to abolish the death penalty for murder.

First Nations people in Australia had strict codes of punishment, some of which may have resulted in death, but execution as a ritual begins in Australia with European intervention.

In October 1629, seven Dutch mutineers (and murderers), survivors of the sinking of *The Batavia*, were hanged by the Dutch East India Company (VOC) on Seal Island, on the Houtman Abrolhos Islands, off the coast of Western Australia.

The First Fleet began the occupation/settlement of Australia in January 1788. The first execution took place in Sydney just one month later, when Thomas Barrett, aged seventeen, was hanged for theft. The first twenty-four executions in New South Wales were for stealing or burglary.

In Australia (and Norfolk Island) there were seven hangings in the seventeenth century, 380 in the eighteenth, 1,630 in the nineteenth, 118 in the twentieth, and none in the twenty-first.

---

4   Ibid., vol.12, 1990, by Neville Cain.
5   Ibid., vol. 10, 1986, by Joy Guyatt.

Not all executions took place in, or outside, Australian prisons. There were extra-judicial killings of Aboriginal people—probably thousands.

Arguments for abolition

The death penalty is deeply embedded in our culture, and probably our psyches. It was inextricably linked with imperialism, colonialism, and Christianity, too. The crucifixion of Jesus, by a Roman method, is central to the Church's history and teaching, to its liturgy and art. For millennia the practice of execution was virtually unchallenged.

Michel de Montaigne, the great French essayist—and magistrate—neatly set out his reasons for opposing the death penalty:

> Judgments normally inflame themselves towards revenge out of horror for the crime. That is precisely what tempers mine: my horror for the first murder makes me frightened of committing a second, and my loathing for the original act of cruelty makes me loath to imitate it. (*On Physiognomy*, 1588).

The Milanese economist Cesare Beccaria in *On Crimes and Punishments* (*Dei delitti e delle pene*), published in 1764, argued for the abolition of the death penalty with a classic simplicity: there is no demonstrable correlation between the severity of punishment and the crime rate; all punishment deters, but there is no statistical evidence that execution, or torture, deters uniquely. Essentially, there have been no new arguments for abolition since Beccaria.

Leo Tolstoy, the pre-eminent Russian novelist, observed the guillotining of a murderer, Francis Richeux, in Paris on 6 April 1857, and the image haunted him all his life.[6]

> I witnessed many atrocities in the war and in the Caucasus, but I should have been less sickened to see a man torn to pieces before my eyes than

---

6   Tolstoy recorded his observation in his diary, and published it in his essay *What is To Be Done?* (1886). I quoted it in my 1975 speech in the Victorian Parliament on the abolition of the death penalty. (See Appendix C.)

I was by this perfected, elegant machine by means of which a strong, clean, healthy man was killed in an instant. In the first case, there is no reasoning will, but a paroxysm of human passion; in the second, coolness to the point of refinement, homicide-with-comfort, nothing big.

When I saw the head part from the body and each of them fall separately into a box with a thud, I understood—not in my mind, but with my whole being—that no rational doctrine of progress could justify that act, and that if every man now living in the world and every man who had lived since the beginning of time were to maintain, in the name of some theory or other, that this execution was indispensable, I should still know that it was not indispensable, that it was wrong.

Ultimately, all executions are political. Their exercise is arbitrary, often capricious, and irrevocable. It depends on geography, too, as Blaise Pascal noted in his *Pensées,* no. 434:

Three degrees of latitude upset the whole of jurisprudence and one meridian determines what is true ... It is an odd sort of justice whose limits are marked by a river, true on this side of the Pyrenees, false on the other.

The Canadian philosopher Ronald Wright argues:

States arrogate to themselves the power of coercive violence: the right to crack the whip, execute prisoners, send young men to the battlefield. From this stems that venomous bloom which J.M. Coetzee has called 'the black flower of civilisation'—torture, wrongful imprisonment, violence for display—the forging of might into right. States employ 'various styles of human sacrifice' as forms of 'the ultimate political theatre'.

Executions and the 'war on drugs'

By the mid-1980s in Australia, de facto abolition had become de jure. However, the death penalty returned to the news when Australians Kevin Barlow and Brian Chambers were hanged in Penang, Malaysia, in July 1986 for drug offences. Prime Minister Bob Hawke called the act 'barbaric'. There were strong diplomatic representations, bipartisan political protests, and a surprising degree of media coverage, all of which reinforced the intransigence of the Malaysian authorities. Chambers' sister talked to me, but there was no more I could do as a minister because the Hawke government had already offended Prime Minister Mahathir Mohamad by its strong protests. The ALP's national conference was meeting in Hobart on the morning of the hangings, and I read John Donne's words, 'No man is an island …'. The atmosphere was electric.

A Queenslander, Michael McAuliffe, was hanged in Penang in June 1993, also for drug-trafficking, but the event passed virtually unnoticed, and without protest, because the victim apparently accepted his fate.

Nguyen Tuong Van, aged twenty-five, an Australian citizen of Vietnamese origin, was hanged in Singapore in December 2005 for carrying drugs for his brother from Cambodia to Australia and being caught in transit. Under Singapore's mandatory death penalty, a system applied with equal inflexibility in China, mitigating circumstances were irrelevant. It would be impossible to characterise Van Nguyen as the criminal of the year, or the century, but his penalty would have been no greater if he had been. Execution is the ultimate demonstration of state power; there are no chance factors, and the victim becomes a passive object, even before he/she dies. In some jurisdictions, cost is a major factor: execution is far cheaper than lifelong imprisonment.

Indonesia's execution by firing squad on 29 April 2015 of eight people convicted of drug offences, among them the Australians Andrew Chan and Myuran Sukumaran, revived domestic concerns about capital punishment to higher levels than any time since the 1960s, although public opinion polls suggested that Australians were evenly divided about their case.

In 1991 Australia ratified the Second Protocol of the International Convention on Civil and Political Rights (ICCPR), which binds nations to oppose the death penalty and has been adopted by the UN General Assembly.

Australia has been monumentally hypocritical about the death penalty abroad. We will not extradite persons held here to death-penalty jurisdictions, even to our close ally the United States. But we are also highly selective. We empathise with our fellow citizens, and will campaign to save them, but fail to argue strongly enough for the general principle of opposition to the death penalty. Chan and Sukumaran had good reasons to expect clemency. They were exporting drugs from Indonesia, not taking them in. If the Australian Federal Police had waited to arrest them on returning with drugs to Australia, they might well have received only short prison terms. There was no contesting the evidence that they had been dramatically rehabilitated during their decade in prison.

Andrew Colvin, the AFP commissioner, in an organisation-serving press conference, complained that attacks on the AFP's involvement in the execution of Chan and Sukumaran had been in 'very bad taste'. One's heart went out to him. Colvin's justification for the AFP's role in ensuring that Chan and Sukumaran were arrested in a death penalty jurisdiction was that between 2007 and 2011 some 4,100 Australians had died from heroin overdoses.

His logic was dubious.

In Australia, drugs of addiction fall into two categories: legal and illegal. Which kills more of our citizens? Legal drugs. While there are restrictions on how tobacco products are sold, advertised, and packaged, cigarettes remain a legal product. The Australian Bureau of Statistics estimates that in 2021 smoking killed 20,500 Australians, which represented 13 per cent of deaths in that year. In 2020 alcohol-related deaths in Australia totalled 6,000. While nobody in the AFP recommends death or even imprisonment for tobacconists or alcohol retailers, or the corporations behind them, we should reflect on the monstrous hypocrisy of the 'war on drugs'.

The AFP's conduct was immoral and indefensible. As Brian Walters, SC, observes:

Under the Extradition Act, or under the Mutual Assistance in Criminal Matters Act, provision of assistance to a foreign country that might result in the imposition of the death penalty is illegal. The provision of information in this instance was not caught by either of those pieces of legislation, but the principle ought to be the same, and it ought to be a crime for Australian law enforcement authorities to provide intelligence or assistance to foreign countries in the absence of an undertaking that no death penalty would be imposed as a result. Such an undertaking should be sought in advance on a generic basis.

One of the sickening aspects of execution for drug offences is that only mules are caught. Those who control the drug syndicates just read about the executions on Facebook.

With murder, there can be no crime, no conviction, without an identifiable victim or victims.

Executions and the 'war on terror'

There are disturbing similarities between having a 'war on drugs' and a 'war on terror'. Each punishes the potentiality for death and destruction, and challenges, even undermines, the basis of how law and justice ought to be administered. Evaluation of evidence, deep analysis, rationalit,y and causality may be discarded or suffer collateral damage.

In the case of the execution of Amrozi and two other Bali bombers, in 2008—after an appalling act of terrorism in October 2002, killing 202 people, eighty-eight of them Australian—Kevin Rudd and John Howard both declined to make representations to Indonesia on the general principle of opposition to the death penalty. Simon Crean, as Labor leader, had been equivocal at the time of the Bali bombing. Mark Latham, his successor, had supported John Howard on the execution of Saddam Hussein in 2006.

Saddam's hanging was very important to older neoconservatives in the US, eager to draw parallels between Hitler and Saddam, the Nuremberg Trials, and the Baghdad Trials. Brutal as Saddam's crimes were over a long period, it was a supreme irony that he should be sentenced for a massacre that occurred in 1982 in Dujail, when he was being supported by the US in his war against Iran and was a valued customer for weapons of mass destruction.

Executions and changing public opinion

Capital punishment is a clear example of where elites—political, legal, judicial, medical, philosophical, and creative—are usually well ahead of public feeling.

The case of Ronald Ryan in 1967 had been an important factor in recruiting young people to political activism, perhaps second only to the Vietnam War, Steve Bracks being a prime example. Nevertheless, Sir Henry Bolte cruised to victories in the Victorian elections in 1967 and 1970. But Bolte's successor, Dick Hamer, was a convinced abolitionist and, following the long campaign by Jack Galbally, Labor's Upper House leader, worked with me to repeal the death penalty in 1975.

Public opinion polling by Roy Morgan Research indicated that support for capital punishment in Australia fell from 68 per cent in 1953 to 23 per cent in 2009, although in a 2014 poll this figure rose to 52.5 per cent for 'a deadly terrorist attack'. The only political leaders currently advocating restoration of the death penalty are One Nation leaders Pauline Hanson and Mark Latham.

Wartime executions by the AIF in Papua New Guinea

The numbers of executions in Papua New Guinea under colonial rule (first Germany in New Guinea, then Queensland, and then the Commonwealth in Papua) are elusive, but there may had been almost sixty until hangings ceased in 1954.

In Papua New Guinea in 1943 and 1944, the Australian Imperial Force (AIF) tried, convicted and hanged about 150 indigenous people in remote areas, mostly for murder, but often for collaboration with Japanese forces. These punishments, carried out in public, but not reported to the Australian government, now seem inexplicable.

In 1959 I was told about these extraordinary executions by Alf Conlon, a consummate networker who advised both John Curtin and Sir Thomas Blamey as head of the army's Directorate of Research and Civil Affairs (DORCA).

In May 1978 I delivered a speech in the House of Representatives about what I had been able to glean from the mutilated files in the Australian National Archives (ANA) about the hanging of thirty-four New Guineans at Higaturu by the AIF in September 1943:

> The New Guineans all lived in a small area to the east of the Owen Stanley Ranges, near the point of cultural 'interface' where territory was successively occupied by Germans [before 1918], Australians and Japanese. If there was any lesson that these people and their families must have learned, it was that foreigners—whether German, Australian or Japanese—wearing a uniform and an air of authority were in a position to enforce their wishes and had to be obeyed without question. Treason is a highly conceptual crime involving an understanding of legal obligations to the Australian State or the British Crown, and the significance of breaching them. In the first batch of trials the sentences were referred to and apparently confirmed by the General Officer Commanding (GOC) the 1st Australian Army, Lieutenant General Sir Edmund Herring, later Chief Justice of Victoria, in his capacity as Administrator of the Australia–New Guinea Administration Unit (ANGAU).[7]

I received more hate mail after this speech than on any other issue in my career. Some of the angriest letters contained important new evidence. I didn't know what I was talking about, my informants wrote; the hangings had not been at Higaturu, but at Samarai/Milne Bay, Aitape, Lae, Rabaul, Port Moresby, and in the Sepik, where they had been witnesses. The numbers began to rise sharply, to more than 100.

---

7   Commonwealth House of Representatives Debates (Hansard), 8 May 1978, vol. 109, p. 1941. http://historichansard.net/hofreps/1978/19780505_reps_31_hor109/#debate-33

It is clear that the Australian Army was very careful *not* to tell the Australian government what it was doing, and when Prime Minister John Curtin found out in April 1945 he ordered the executions stopped.

The few files remaining in the ANA reveal that after cabinet directed the then GOC, Lieutenant General V.A.H. (later Sir Vernon) Sturdee not to proceed with hanging about fifty Papua New Guineans, in July 1945 he sought legal advice from the director of Army Legal Services, Brigadier Alan S. Lloyd (later a judge in New South Wales) as to whether he was bound to follow cabinet's direction. Lloyd replied, drily, that while the GOC might not be legally compellable, a reading of history suggested a certain caution: had he failed to comply, 'the consequences might not have been happy', because 'Cabinet enforces compliance ... by removing from office any public servant who flouts its instructions'. The oddest feature of the incident was to find a GOC urging execution as a matter of military necessity within weeks of Japan's surrender.

Because the official files had been gutted, it is impossible to form a judgment about:

1. How many indigeneous Papua New Guineans were executed, and where and when.
2. The precise nature of the charges—was it murder, rape, treason, collaborating with the Japanese?
3. The nature and quality of the evidence.
4. How the trials were conducted and by whom.
5. Whether the accused had the benefit of defence counsel.
6. Whether prosecution witnesses were subject to cross-examination.
7. What languages the trials were conducted in, and whether translators were available.
8. The average duration of each trial.
9. Whether there was a right of appeal against conviction and sentence.
10. How much time elapsed between conviction and execution?
11. Whether there were any commutations.

12. Whether full records were kept.
13. Who was the driving figure behind the trials and executions.
14. Why, if the aim of the hangings was deterrence, they were kept secret.
15. Why Canberra was not briefed.
16. Why the military historians ignored the hangings.
17. Who mutilated the national memory?

There are other disturbing issues. Significantly, the executions were, in effect, redacted from *The Australian Official War History*. These trials and executions had occurred at the same time as action on the Kokoda Track, when indigeneous Papua New Guineans received very sympathetic press coverage in Australia as 'the fuzzy-wuzzy angels', so savage punishments, carried out in public, but unreported, are inexplicable. Was it to encourage enthusiasm for the Allied cause?

And there is also the question of proportionality.

The number of AIF executions in Papua-New Guinea over two years was about 150—thirty-five more than all executions in Australia between 1901 and 1967.

American exceptionalism

In the United States, the death penalty has now been abolished in twenty-three states and retained in twenty-seven, but with a moratorium in force in California, Ohio, Oregon, and Pennsylvania.[8]

The penalty remains under military law and for some federal crimes, although a moratorium is in force under Joe Biden's presidency. Donald Trump had been an enthusiast.

Capital punishment is more likely to be abolished in the US by executive order (moratorium) or by judicial activism than by legislation: it would be hard to pass in the Senate.

The twenty-three retentionist states are all in the Old South, the

---

8   See Appendix E.

sparsely populated Midwest, and the border states of Oklahoma and Missouri.

The death penalty has been abolished in Europe, South America, many African states, and in every other nation in the English-speaking world. It is subject to a moratorium in Russia, and generally remains throughout Asia.

Support for the death penalty is one of the few social policies that the US has in common with China, Iran, Egypt, Iraq, Saudi Arabia, and North Korea.

Religious fundamentalism is a powerful force in the US, and Christian fundamentalists are among the most zealous supporters of judicial execution. They rely on a highly selective reading of the Bible. On my reading of the New Testament, it is hard to see Jesus, a victim of execution himself, as a hard-line retentionist.

Fundamentalists rely on the Mosaic code, which provided death for many crimes, including murder, witchcraft, and cursing parents—although the last two are no longer insisted on. It is worth recalling that as an expression of the prevailing thinking of the Hebrews when they were nomads without penitentiaries, the Mosaic law expressly endorsed slavery. Those who insist that capital punishment is 'God's law' still read that law selectively.

Eleven executions were carried oun the US in 2021, the lowest number since 1988. Three of them were federal, in the last week of Donald Trump's presidency, as a farewell gesture; three in Texas, maintaining its record as the state ranking first for executions; two in Oklahoma; and one each in Alabama, Mississippi, and Missouri.

All five states had been in the old Confederacy or on the border, with a history of slavery, racism, and lynching.

A common factor was the very long period between the crime and execution in 2021. The shortest period was eleven years, in Texas and Mississippi; the longest, thirty-seven years, in Oklahoma.

Only eighteen death sentences were imposed in 2021 in the US.

Paradoxically, in California, referenda to abolish the death penalty were defeated in 2012 and 2016, just when Barack Obama and Hillary Clinton won large majorities in the presidential elections.

Lethal injection is the method of choice for most retentionist states. It is more palatable for the squeamish and may have weakened some objections to execution because it resembles a medical procedure that always results in the patient's death, without screaming or struggling. It is less grisly or shocking than other methods, with their images of blood, mutilation, sparks, burning flesh, the *coup de grace*, and the occasional decapitation.

The US Supreme Court is less preoccupied with the moral issue of whether to execute or not, but with techniques: how best to execute, especially when pharmaceutical companies have qualms about providing lethal drugs, as it would be unthinkable to challenge intellectual property rights.

President Obama used to campaign against the death penalty, and it has been abolished in his home state of Illinois. However, President Trump was a death-penalty enthusiast. President Biden declared himself an opponent of capital punishment, and all current death sentences under federal law are subject to a moratorium.

But there are puzzling inconsistencies. The bombings at the Boston Marathon in April 2013 resulted in three deaths and 280 injuries. Dzhokhar Tsarnaev, a Kyrgyz-American, aged nineteen at the time, the surviving bomber, was tried under federal law in 2015, convicted of using a weapon of mass destruction and murder of a policeman, and sentenced to death. In July 2020 the US Circuit Court of Appeal overturned the death penalty in Tsarnaev's case. The Trump administration appealed to the US Supreme Court to reinstate the death penalty, and judgment was expected later in 2022.

Massachusetts had abolished the death penalty in 1984.

The way ahead

There is much to reflect upon.

Seeking security is understandable. Reacting to fear is another.

But fear is a bad driver for public policy. We live in deeply troubling times. It is easy to understand why people in many countries are gripped by insecurity. The ready access to lethal weapons and mood-changing drugs and the risk of attack, from internal or imported terrorism, in schools, churches, mosques, heritage sites, public transport, shopping malls, and offices are horrors seen every day on television and the internet. As a defensive reaction, many citizens would like to see the return of retributive punishments. Desperation may push them to rely on subjective opinion rather than objective evidence.

We need to think deeply about how we define our humanity. In the final analysis, do we make judgments coolly and calmly on the basis of evidence that is capable of being weighed and objectively analysed? Or is it the case that, in dealing with human nature, objective analysis is useless and we are forced into *terra incognita* and must decide blindly, on the basis of instinct or gut reaction? We stand, I hope, against darkness, against obscurantism, against instinct, against pessimism about society and the capacity that individuals have for moral regeneration.

Campaigners for abolition have to be prepared to argue for the tough cases, repulsive as they are: Julius Streicher, Adolf Eichmann, Saddam Hussein, Osama bin-Laden, Timothy McVeigh, Amrozi, John Wayne Gacy, Ted Bundy, Eric Cooke. The moral high ground does not allow campaigners to be selective.

A former archbishop of Paris, Cardinal François Marty, wrote:

> If a man does no longer act like a man, the community must refrain from following him. Each time a human being is treated as a non-human being, then every human being is threatened. Any individual who commits an act of violence against another individual is degrading mankind. If we want to safeguard the concept of human beings now being threatened, we must resist the temptation of retributive anger.
>
> Can man, that imperfect being, be expected to render perfect justice? In that respect, could capital punishment give a notion of perfection to the justice of human beings?

State killing is not only brutal and destructive, but also pointless. In the world of an eye for an eye and a tooth for a tooth, we can all be blind and toothless, but it will not preserve our lives or maintain our values. The evidence for abolition is compelling, as we face the challenges of violence, drug dependence, and jihadism. We cannot rely on an instinct for vengeance. As we fight against darkness, we need rationality, evidence, values ,and compassion at the highest level.

If the senseless executions of Sukumaran and Chan in 2015 taught us anything, it is this: Australia must be much more active in advocating abolition of the death penalty internationally. This is not merely to protect and preserve its own nationals, but as part of a campaign with universal application, without picking and choosing, and with the moral force that earlier generations worked with to end slavery, liberate women, and eliminate torture and punishments for heresy or witchcraft.

2

Capital punishment:
the moral issues

Max Charlesworth, AO

Max Charlesworth, AO (1925–2014) was an outstanding Australian philosopher, with an exceptional range of interests, including bioethics, the interaction between religion and civil society, indigenous issues, and education generally. Professor of Philosophy at Melbourne University, he became foundation Dean of Humanities at Deakin University 1975–90. He was Senior Lecturer in Philosophy at Melbourne when he wrote the essay below.

Brian Walters, SC, commented:

> The dignity of the human person accords with Charlesworth's analysis of the Christian position, but would also fit with pretty much every other religious (and non-religious) philosophy. It was, after all, the founding idea behind the Universal Declaration of Human Rights, support for which crossed national, ethnic and religious lines.

* * *

A plea for a dispassionate, rational approach

The debate over capital punishment has aroused the most violent passions on both sides. Many who advocate the abolition of capital punishment look on their opponents as vengeful sadists demanding a life for a life, while those who favour the retention of punishment by death tend to view the abolitionists as irresponsible sentimentalists who have no concern for justice or for the peace and order of society. Neither side is willing to admit that the other has a rational case based on principle: the abolitionist just cannot see how any intelligent and honest man who realised the value of human life could possibly favour capital punishment, and equally the retentionist cannot see how any one with any sense of justice at all could deny that the gravest crime, murder, should be punished by the ultimate sanction, death.

And so the debate drags on—all the more emotionally in that it is doomed to inconclusiveness. It seems to me, that both sides do have a rational and principled case, and that it is quite possible to be an abolitionist or a retentionist, and at the same time intelligent and honest man. It is only if we recognise the element of truth in both positions and, after removing those elements from the confused and misleading formulations they have been given, harmonise them with each other, that we can get an adequate view of this whole question of capital punishment. My view, if I may oversimplify a little, is that the abolitionist has reached the right conclusion about capital punishment for the wrong reasons, while the retentionist has the right reasons about punishment in general but has reached the wrong conclusion about capital punishment.

Those who offer to reconcile warring parties usually find themselves distrusted and fired on by both sides, and I have no illusion that the present effort at conciliation will at once produce sweetness and light in this area of contention. However, removing the debate to a philosophical plane, as I have tried, may have a soothing effect on the emotions of both sides and lead to that calmness of mind of which Milton speaks and which is the necessary condition for dispassionate and rational reflection on this whole question.

The philosophy of punishment

No area of moral philosophy is more confused than that concerned with the justification of punishment, and this same confusion is of course reflected in the subsidiary question of capital punishment.

The confusions that beset this question criss-cross each other, but the central confusion consists in the mixing up of two quite different arguments: *pragmatic* arguments on the one hand and *moral* arguments on the other. Thus punishment is often justified in terms of its practical effects—for example, in terms of its deterrent effect on the offender and other would-be offenders, or even in terms of its curative or therapeutic effects on the offender. From this point of view the justification of a given form of punishment becomes a straight-out empirical, quasi-scientific matter of ascertaining whether or not the punishment is effective in producing the end desired. This kind of argument is what I call a pragmatic justification of punishment. On the other hand, a given form of punishment is often justified because of some moral principle—for example, that immoral and anti-social acts should always be visited with retribution regardless of whether such retribution has any practical effects. Or it may be rejected because of some moral principle—for example, most people would reject torture as a licit means of punishment because they think that, whatever its effectiveness or practical value, it offends against human dignity in some way. Such arguments are moral arguments.

It is obvious that the two kinds of arguments are quite different. For the pragmatist it is the usefulness and effectiveness of the punishment that determines whether or not it is to be employed, and since this is a matter depending on circumstances and social and other conditions, no particular form of punishment will ever be deemed to be necessarily (or 'in principle') appropriate or inappropriate. For one who appeals to moral principle, on the other hand, the usefulness or effectiveness of a given form of punishment will be quite irrelevant. Even if it could be shown, for instance, that public torture had a very effective deterrent effect, such a form of punishment could never be justified, the moralist would say, because it offends against a moral principle, namely that human beings have a certain 'dignity' which cannot ever be violated. And yet, different as they are, the two arguments are often mixed up together in the most inconsistent way; the pragmatist supporting his case by surreptitiously introducing issues of moral principle, and the moralist supporting his case by appeal to utilitarian evidence.

Confusion of arguments

This confusion and inconsistency can be seen quite flagrantly both in the arguments of those who favour the abolition of capital punishment, and of those who favour its retention. The retentionist often argues that capital punishment is justified because it is the only effective deterrent against certain forms of homicide, but he is at the same time unwilling to allow this to be wholly determined by empirical evidence, and when evidence to the contrary is produced (showing, for example, that there is no real factual proof that capital punishment does function as a better deterrent than life imprisonment) he then falls back on an argument of moral principle. Capital punishment, he will say, is demanded by a principle of strict justice, namely that a crime be visited with proportionate retribution. He will claim that to say 'This man has murdered another, i.e., has committed the greatest crime, but he should not be visited with the severest form of punishment (namely, death)' is to contradict the very principle of justice itself. And now, of course, the argument has become a moral one and considerations of the pragmatic effectiveness of capital punishment are completely irrelevant.

On the other hand, the abolitionist frequently pleads his case against capital punishment in pragmatic terms, alleging that the factual evidence shows that capital punishment is no more effective than less drastic forms of punishment. But it is obvious enough that he is not willing fully to accept the logical consequences of the pragmatist's position. As we have seen, for the pragmatist the effectiveness of capital punishment is a contingent or open question; in other words, the pragmatic abolitionist must at least admit the *possibility* that capital punishment could prove to be the most effective deterrent in certain circumstances, so that his rejection of capital punishment cannot be an *absolute* one. He can never say, at least on these grounds, that capital punishment can *never* be justified; the best that he can say is that in a society of a certain degree of civilisation and moral and political maturity, capital punishment is not, as a matter of fact, uniquely effective as a deterrent against murder, while admitting that in other circumstances, capital punishment might possibly be more effective as a deterrent than other forms of punishment, and so be justified.

In parenthesis it might be noted that the abolitionists' use of what empirical evidence there is about the relative deterrent value of capital punishment is not always as scrupulous as it might be. As one writer has put it, the figures available are very unsatisfactory:

> There are far too few of them to admit of any statistical inferences, in the strict sense: they admit in almost all cases of a wide variety of causal interpretations: they contain no break-downs of different types of murder, in relation to break-downs of relatively comparable crimes.'[1]

Again, while the figures available do not confirm the retentionist case for capital punishment, they are not therefore positively against it. And it does not follow, as some abolitionists claim, that if the statistics neither confirm nor deny the uniquely deterrent effect of capital punishment, they may therefore be used in support of the abolitionist case 'since all the moral arguments are on that side'. As the same writer remarks:

> This is simply to beg the moral question. Retentionists will naturally retort that they have a moral case also … They can advance genuine and important moral claims, which favour retention of the death penalty for *some* types of murder anyhow. [2]

At all events, it is obvious, as I have said, that the abolitionist does not really view the question of capital punishment as a contingent or open question to be settled solely by appeal to the empirical evidence in the context of a particular set of circumstances. The tone of moral indignation and passion that the abolitionist typically uses indicates that for him issues of principle are at stake and that he is not concerned with contingent and particular issues but with absolute and universal ones. In so far as he does this he has ceased to be a pragmatist and is appealing implicitly to moral principles.

---

1   W.B. Gallie, 'The Lords' Debate on Hanging', July 1956; 'Interpretation and Comment', in *Philosophy*, XXXII, 1957, p. 146.
2   Ibid.

Moral arguments: the abolitionists

It is this oscillation on both sides between the two kinds of argument that gives to the whole debate on capital punishment its very unsatisfactory character, for the fundamental arguments (the moral ones) are rarely brought out clearly and unequivocally into the open and discussed as such. Again, the debate has often been clouded by the irresponsible use of emotive language on both sides: the retentionist describes the abolitionist as a sentimentalist with a selective sympathy for the criminal at the expense of the victim and his kin, and some abolitionists describe the retentionist as a sadist. Not unnaturally, neither side recognises these descriptions as applying to it, for the retentionist sees his position as dictated by a concern for justice (criminal acts must be punished proportionately), while the abolitionist sees his position as dictated by a concern for human dignity or some other moral principle. Perhaps, then, we can bring some light to the debate by insisting that it is a debate over strictly moral issues and by examining exactly what these moral issues are.

What, first of all, is the moral principle that animates the abolitionist? This is not an easy question to answer, because abolitionists put forward a variety of principles which are often inconsistent with each other. There is, for example, which might be called the 'determinist' principle, namely that the criminal, and in particular the murderer, is not really responsible for his criminal acts and so should not be punished (since punishment presupposes responsibility) but rather given curative treatment or therapy. The idea behind this position is often expressed as: 'There are no criminals, there are only mentally sick people'. Sometimes this thesis is put forward as a general philosophical argument; since all our actions are determined by our biological make-up, our psychological conditioning and our environment, there is no such thing as free will and therefore no such thing as responsible action for which we may be either morally praised or blamed. Thus punishment (presupposing free will and responsibility and moral blameworthiness) can never be justified. This is obviously an extreme and paradoxical position and it is not one that many abolitionists have held consistently and explicitly, though some rely upon it in a surreptitious way. Sometimes, however, this thesis is put forward in a weaker quasi-scientific form, it being claimed that as matter of scientific fact there is a general correlation between criminality and mental illness and consequent lack of moral responsibility. The number of deliberate and fully responsible (and so fully blameworthy) murderers, it is claimed, is so few as not to warrant punitive measures (including capital punishment). Instead we should replace punishment by therapeutic treatment of various kinds. If this view is being put forward as a scientific one, we have a right to expect that it will be supported by empirical evidence of the alleged fairly strict correlation between criminality and mental illness (and diminished responsibility). But it must be said that the abolitionists have done very little to produce such evidence; instead they have for the most part relied upon a *prima facie* presumption that those who engage in such grossly anti-social acts as murder *must* be unhinged or psychologically abnormal.

Quite apart from these kinds of argument, there is what can be called 'pacifist' arguments. Thus some abolitionists speak as though the use of force or the infliction of pain on others can never be justified because it is intrinsically evil. *A fortiori* the taking of another life, as in capital punishment, is intrinsically evil and can never be justified. Tolstoy[3] has expressed this view in its most uncompromising form:

> I understand that under the influence of momentary irritation, hatred, revenge, or loss of consciousness of his humanity, a man may kill another in his own defence or in defence of a friend; or that under the influence of patriotic mass-hypnotism and while exposing himself to death he may take part in collective murder in war. But that men in full control of their human attributes can quietly and deliberately admit the necessity of killing a fellow man, and oblige others to perform that action so contrary to human nature, I never can understand.

For Tolstoy, then, capital punishment is tantamount to judicial murder. Once again, it is not easy to hold such an extreme position

---

3   Leo Tolstoy, *Essays and Recollections*, Worlds Classics, p. 59.

of absolute pacifism completely denying the possibility of the justified taking of a human life. However, a good many abolitionists who are not willing to adopt the position of absolute pacifism, nevertheless make covert use of this position. For example, those who speak about the brutalising effect of capital punishment on the executioner implicitly rely upon this argument. So the Bishop of Manchester, in the Lords' debate on hanging, claimed, for example, that it is 'unnatural … to ask a man in cold blood to kill one of his fellows, no matter how deserving of death that man or woman may be'.[4]

And another abolitionist cites a former prison governor as saying:

> I can never help asking myself why, when one is called upon to superintend an execution, one should have been affected with such an acute sense of personal shame. There must be something fundamentally wrong with a law which has the effect of lessening the self-respect of those whose duty it is to carry it out.[5]

These arguments have, no doubt, very powerful emotional force, but in their assumption that capital punishment is a form of judicial murder (all the more heinous for being deliberate, calculated, and cold-blooded) they simply beg the question at issue. For the question is precisely whether capital punishment is judicial murder (unjustified homicide) or whether it can, on the contrary, be justified in certain well-defined circumstances. As we have said, only those who espouse the position of absolute pacifism, with all its consequences, can assume that capital punishment is judicial murder. Obviously, if capital punishment can be *justified*, then the act of the executioner, no matter how unpleasant and horrible it may be to him, is not an immoral act and cannot be classed as conniving at murder.

There is, however, a weak or moderate form of the pacifist position, namely, that although the taking of another person's life may in certain circumstances be justified *theoretically* as a form of punishment, it ought not *in practice* be resorted to in civilised societies. For capital

---

4   Cited in Gallie, p. 138.
5   Cited in *Capital Punishment as a Deterrent; and the Alternative*, Gerald Gardiner, London 1961, p. 14.

punishment, so the argument goes, is a form of punishment that offends against (or at least is not consistent with) human dignity. It involves treating a human being as an animal, a 'mad dog'.

We reject torture for this reason, even though perhaps severe torture might be an even more stringent form of punishment than death itself, so *a fortiori* why not reject capital punishment? There is thus, so the argument proceeds, a powerful *prima facie* case against taking a person's life, so that the onus is on the one who wants to take a life to justify it. And since the taking of a human life is a matter of the utmost gravity this onus itself is of the gravest kind.

It seems to me that this latter position is the only viable one for an abolitionist to take up. If the statistics show, in addition, that capital punishment does not work effectively as a deterrent, then well and good. But the deterrent or nondeterrent effect of capital punishment does not really touch upon the moral principle that is the basis of the abolitionist's case, *namely that capital punishment is a form of punishment (like severe torture) that offends against the dignity of a human person.* Just because a person is a murderer does not mean that he forfeits his dignity as a human being, so that he becomes liable to *any* kind of punishment we may like to inflict upon him. As we have said, we do as a matter of fact exclude certain forms of punishment as not being fit or proper to apply to a human being, and the argument is that capital punishment is one of these improper forms of punishment.

Moral arguments: the retentionists

Let us now look at the retentionist position, trying to discern once again the moral principle behind it. The retentionist, as we have seen, is not committed to a position of revenge or vindictiveness—the criminal has done wrong, therefore he must be visited with harm himself: the murderer has taken a life, therefore he must have his life taken in return. Rather the retentionist bases his case on the principle of justice. Justice means that one pays to another what is due to him, or that one treats him according to his deserts. What is the due or desert of the criminal? It is obviously, so the retentionist's argument goes, that he should not benefit or be rewarded or made happy by society on account of his anti-social acts, but rather that he should be made unhappy or deprived of some benefit, i.e. that he should be punished. There is a connexion between virtue and happiness, and vice and unhappiness; it would be paradoxical to say that a wrongdoer ought to be allowed to gain some benefit from his wrongdoing and ought not to suffer any unhappiness on account of it. Justice demands, then, that the criminal ought to suffer unhappiness as a result of his crime, or in other words that he should be punished for it.

This same principle of justice, again, does not only indicate that crimes should be punished, but that they should be punished proportionately. This does not mean, of course, that the crime should be punished in exactly the same terms—stealing by dispossessing the criminal of his goods, sexual assault by sexually assaulting the criminal etc. All that the principle demands is that there be some proportion between crime and punishment—light punishment for lesser crimes, stringent punishment for serious crimes. It is, no doubt, impossible to fix an exact equivalence between crime and punishment, but we can nevertheless find rough and ready equivalences. Everyone would, for example, think it unjust if a traffic offence were punished by death. Similarly, it would be unjust if a grave crime such as murder were punished by too mild a punishment. In fact, the only proportionate punishment for murder is punishment by death. This, then, is the moral principle on which the retentionist's case rests.

No doubt the retentionists are often confused and do not always present their case as it should be presented. Like the abolitionists, they often obscure their real argument, based on moral principle, by appealing to the supposed deterrent effect of capital punishment. As we have said before, this has really nothing to do with their case, for their argument is that, regardless of its effectiveness, capital punishment is justified by what we have called the principle of justice itself. It is in fact to this principle that a good many men in the street implicitly appeal to justify capital punishment: 'He murdered another man, so he has to pay the price—that's justice'. This attitude is not necessarily an attitude of primitive revenge; it is rather based on the claim that to abolish capital punishment would be to impugn the principle that the retribution for crimes should be proportionate punishment, the principle on which the legal system of any society rests.

Legal punishment and private morality

So far we have discussed punishment in very general terms, but we must now make a distinction between legal punishment and non-legal forms of punishment. By legal punishment I mean the punishment employed by the State in the context of a legal system, as compared with the punishment that a person's own conscience may visit upon him, or the punishment that a parent or a teacher may visit upon a child, or that a religious body may visit upon its members. Capital punishment, it is obvious, only comes up (at least in civilised societies) within the context of legal or State punishment, and to get clear about the former we have first to define the function and the limits of the State's use of punishment. One's attitude to punishment will in fact depend very largely upon one's view of the function of the State *vis-à-vis* morality.

There are, broadly speaking, two main views that can be taken up here. First, there is the view that sees the State as a moral agency whose purpose is to make its members morally virtuous people. In this view the State is directly concerned with morals and the law is seen as the means by which morality is enforced.[6] No doubt the State through the agency of law, cannot train or educate its members in morality in any very complete or detailed way, but it is nevertheless concerned with a minimum morality, that is to say with the inculcation of the basic moral standards necessary for any civilised living.

As against this, there is the view that sees the State as concerned solely with the provision of a framework of peace and order within which the members of society may make their own moral choices for themselves and work out their own moral destinies. In this view the area of private morality is not the business of the law at all. It is only

---

6   See Patrick Devlin, *The Enforcement of Morals*, Oxford 1966, for an intelligent defence of his view.

in so far as the acts of the individual affect other members of society that the State and the law can take an interest in those acts. Thus an individual may engage in the grossest acts of immorality, but if those acts do not harm others the law has no purchase on him. Once again, the State and the law are not—and cannot be—interested in matters of private morality as such, for what the individual does with his own conscience is his own affair. If a person is to be a moral agent in the full sense he must have freedom to make up his own mind and conscience for himself. There is, the argument continues, a kind of self-contradiction involved in speaking of the State 'enforcing' morals, for if a person is forced to be moral by the sanctions of the law, then, precisely, he ceases to be an autonomous moral agent. In so far as he is forced to be moral his acts lack a specifically moral character. This is the position of J.S. Mill in the celebrated essay *On Liberty* which has been the charter of political liberalism, and it is, in a sense, the basis of democratic society itself.

If we adopt this latter view of the function of the State and of the law, then the State will be concerned to punish only those acts that harm other members of society. It may well be that the members of society commit many private immoralities and that these, according to the principle of justice, deserve to be punished; but the State does not concern itself with punishing them. In other words, it is not the function of the State to exact retribution for *all* immorality and to adopt, so to speak, the role of God. It is important to make this point because some Christians connect the case for capital punishment with the Christian theology of expiation and atonement, according to which the sinner must atone and do penance for his sins before they are forgiven by God. However, while it is true that for the Christian the wrongdoer must atone and do penance for his sins and ask forgiveness of God for them, it does not follow that the State has the right to force the wrongdoer to atone and do penance, even to the extent (in the case of capital punishment) of taking his life from him. It is God's sole prerogative, so the Christian believes, to exact full *moral* retribution from the sinner, and the State has no right to put itself in God's place. Put in another way, legal punishment is not the only form of retribution, not the only way in which the principle of justice can be satisfied. As we have seen, it is not because an act is immoral that the State has a right to punish the person who does that act; rather it is because that act harms other members of society and so disrupts the peace and order of society, that the State has a right to punish. The distinction may appear a fine one, but it is fraught with very large consequences for the way in which we view capital punishment.

Justice without capital punishment?

Within this context let us now look at the question of capital punishment. What I hope to show is that there is a valuable element in both the abolitionist and retentionist positions, when we clear away the confusions and the emotionalism from both of them. More specifically, I hope to be able to show that one can do full justice to the central intuition behind the retentionist's position while denying that, as a matter of fact, capital punishment is the properly proportionate retribution for murder. In other words, justice can be done in the case of punishing the murderer, without resorting to capital punishment.

The retentionist's case, we said before, rests upon the principle that justice demands retribution for wrongdoing by some proportionate punishment, and he argues that the gravest form of wrongdoing, murder, must accordingly require punishment of the most stringent kind. It is obvious, as we also remarked before, that it is not required by this principle that the punishment should *exactly resemble* the crime. No one holds that if a man wounds another the only proportionate punishment is to wound the wrongdoer, or if one person sexually violates another, that the only proportionate punishment is that he himself be sexually violated. Similarly if one man murders another, it does not *necessarily* follow that the only proportionate punishment is death. Certainly a very stringent form of punishment is required to satisfy the principle of justice in the case of murder, but one cannot conclude immediately that capital punishment is the only form of stringent punishment that meets this requirement.

As we saw before, some forms of punishment are excluded because they are not consistent with human dignity. In other words, the criminal does not forfeit all his rights as a human being by virtue of his crime, so that we can treat him as an 'outlaw' in the old sense of the word and visit any kind of punishment (torture, maiming, brainwashing, medical experimentation in the manner of the Nazis and so on) upon him. So also the murderer does not forfeit *all* his rights as a man so that he comes to assume the status of an animal (a 'mad dog') that must be destroyed. We recognise this in civilised societies by rejecting torture as a means of punishment for murder. The murderer, we say, is still a human being and cannot be treated like an animal. *A fortiori*, then, we ought to admit the same point regarding punishment by death, for if punishment by torture offends against the rights the criminal still retains as a human being, punishment by death must offend against these rights all the more. The same point has been made in a slightly different way by Professor G.E. Hughes:

In general, I may be held to have forfeited my right to pursue a certain activity when I have given evidence that I cannot be trusted to pursue it without serious danger or inconvenience to others. But justice requires that we should decide what rights a man has forfeited by reference to just those activities which he has shown himself to have abused and to be likely to abuse. It would be unjust to deprive me of my driving licence because I have destroyed library books. Now the man who has committed a murder has certainly misused a very important right — the right to move freely among other people as a trusted member of society — in a particularly flagrant way; and we may even grant that he has thereby shown himself likely to misuse it in the future. He may therefore be said to have forfeited some important right or rights. But the right to *life*? His life, after all, is the totality of all his activities; and to forfeit his right to life he must, I think, have shown himself to have misused and to be likely to misuse *all* his activities. That is something I do not think we are ever entitled to assume about anyone. And therefore justice seems to me to require that when we deprive him of the rights he has misused, we still secure to him as far as possible the rights to pursue activities which he has not misused.[7]

My conclusion is, then, that the valuable element in the retentionist case (viz., its insistence on the principle of justice, with all that that entails) can be harmonised with the valuable element in the abolitionist case, namely, that capital punishment is a form of punishment that is, like torture, not consistent with human dignity or with a respect for the other rights that the murderer as a human being retains.

Put in another way, in the case of murder the principle of justice must be satisfied by another alternative form of stringent punishment such as permanent deprivation of freedom. In determining an alternative to capital punishment we have, as the writer just cited puts it, to ask something like this: 'Here is a situation in which someone has committed the serious crime of murder; what is the most appropriate treatment of him in view of the whole situation, including his past crime, his relations to the rest of the community, his abilities, his outlook and the possibilities of change in that outlook and so on? And when I ask myself that question, I cannot help replying that, provided the interests of public security are secured, a penalty which affords him the opportunity of changing his attitudes for the better and of doing something useful with the rest of his life "fits" the total situation better than one which precludes these things.'[8]

The argument advanced here has been on a purely rational or philosophical level and no reference has been made to religious considerations. It seems to me, however, that the Christian view of man not only accords with the conclusion that capital punishment offends against the dignity of man but that it powerfully reinforces the conclusion. For no Christian with any sense of the worth and dignity of man as a creature brought into being by a pure and gratuitous act of God's love and redeemed by His mercy through Jesus Christ; no Christian with a sense of the preciousness of human

---

7   G.E. Hughes, 'Capital Punishment: a moral discussion', in *Landfall*, New Zealand, vol. II, 1957, p. 250.
8   Ibid., p. 250.

life — that same life that God himself shared — can accept punishment
by death as a fitting form of punishment for human beings. Again,
while the Christian may accept the fact that murder should be
punished by some stringent penalty, he cannot rest content with mere
retribution; he must also be concerned with the moral rehabilitation
of the criminal. If God does not despair of any man, neither can the
Christian despair of any man, no matter how apparently vicious and
'beyond redemption'. For the Christian it is (or ought to be) the evil
of murder that is the object of our hate and aversion and indignation
and outrage, and not the evil-doer. As the traditional saying has it;
we must hate the sin and love the sinner. In other words, we must
hate the evil of murder and work against the social conditions etc.
that make it possible; but we must love the murderer and see the
retribution that is justly visited upon him in the wider context of
rehabilitation.

Part II

The Case
for Abolition

3

The punishment of death

Cesare Beccaria

Cesare Bonesana Beccaria, Marchese di Gualdrasco e Villareggio (1738–1794) was born in Milan to an aristocratic family. He studied law and economics at the University of Pavia, and became a pioneer of economic and sociological analysis, anticipating Adam Smith, Jeremy Bentham, and Thomas Malthus.

The modern scientific-analytical approach to crime and punishment begins with his *On Crimes and Punishments* (*Dei delitti e delle pene*), which was written between March 1763 and January 1764, and published anonymously in Livorno (then known as Leghorn in English) in July 1764, when Beccaria was twenty-six.

With a preface by Voltaire (widely assumed to be the author), it was translated into French (1766), English (1767), and more than twenty other languages. A Chinese translation was published in 2014.

On Crimes and Punishments appeared at a time when criminal law was marked by corruption, savage and arbitrarily variable penalties, secret accusations, and confessions extorted by torture. Savage punishments failed to reduce crime rates—the Papal States had 13,000 homicides in a population of 3 million in the years 1758–69, and in Venice 73,000 were executed or sent to the galleys for life in the period 1741–62. Britain had 200 capital offences on its books, and France 115. Mutilation and branding were commonplace, especially in Italy. Montesquieu, in *The Persian Letters* (the work that turned Beccaria to penology), criticised the merciless and futile laws against suicide, ignorant judges who purchased their appointments, and the capricious infliction or lifting of penalties, and argued that punishments ought

35

to be varied according to the nature of the crime and the comparative degree of civilisation in the community.

Montesquieu went further in *The Spirit of the Laws* by rejecting the theological basis of criminal law—punishment, he wrote, is designed to protect society, not to execute the wrath of God, therefore religious crimes are best left to God alone. Penalties ought to be moderate and relate to the nature of the crime, and in order to deter the penalties for particular crimes, ought generally to be predictable. He opposed torture and thought that fines, public infamy, or expulsion from society were to be preferred to imprisonment but, if necessary, 'as a remedy, as it were, of a sick society', execution might be used for offences affecting the security of the subject.

Jean Jacques Rousseau's *The Social Contract* (1762) lays down that 'each of us puts his person and all his power in common under the supreme direction of the general will, and, in our corporate capacity, we receive each member as an indivisible part of the whole'.

In joining society we give up some of our freedom of action in return for security—if we breach that security we consent, in effect, to be punished. Rousseau argued (in Book II, chapter 6) that the state has the right to inflict the death penalty because 'it is in order that we may not fall victims of an assassin that we consent to die if we ourselves turn assassins'—and on the basis of this sentence he has been claimed as a retentionist. But he goes on with words that must have struck Beccaria: 'There is not a single ill-doer who could not be turned to some good. The State has no right to put to death, even for the sake of making an example, any one whom it can leave alive without danger'.

Rousseau insisted that laws must reflect the general will and not just the arbitrary caprice of a sovereign. Voltaire, 'the sage of Ferney', took a similar position. He campaigned to secure a posthumous pardon for Jean Calas, a French Protestant judicially murdered in Toulouse in 1762, and compensation for the persecuted Sirvan family, but he did not attempt a general critique of the criminal law.

Beccaria, on the other hand, was the first writer to treat crimes and punishments as a scientific study, where causes, effects, preventions, and cures were to be subject to cool and exhaustive analysis.

In his introduction to *On Crimes and Punishments* he introduces the utilitarian test into law:

> If we look into history we shall find that laws which are, or ought to be, conventions between men in a state of freedom, have been for the most part the work of the passions of a few, or the consequences of a fortuitous or temporary necessity; not dictated by a cool examiner of human nature who knew how to collect in one point the actions of a multitude and had only this end in view, the greatest happiness shared by the greatest number (*la massima felicità divisa nel maggior numero*) [adopting the formulation by the Scottish philosopher Francis Hutcheson].

The following extract is Chapter XXVIII of *On Crimes and Punishments*. This vital chapter has been reprinted in full.[1]

* * *

Of the punishment of death

The useless profusion of punishments, which has never made men better, induces me to enquire whether the punishment of death is really just or useful in a well governed state. What right, I ask, have men to cut the throats of their fellow creatures? Certainly not that on which the sovereignty and laws are founded. The laws, as I have said before, are only the sum of the smallest portions of the private liberty of each individual, and represent the general will which is the aggregate of that of each individual. Did anyone ever give to others the right of taking away his life? If it were so, how shall it be

---

1   Several English translations have been based on the fifth Italian edition: Henry Paolucci (Macmillan, 1963), Kenelm Foster & Jane Grigson (Oxford, 1964), Richard Davies (Cambridge, 1995), Aaron Thomas & Jeremy Parzen (Toronto, 2007), Graeme R. Newman & Pietro Marongiu (Routledge, 2016). The translation used in the 1968 edition of *The Penalty is Death* was by Edward D. Ingraham (1793–1854), an extraordinarily productive lawyer from Philadelphia, first published in 1819. I have made modest changes to punctuation and wording.

    The entire book can be downloaded from the University of Texas (https://www.laits.utexas.edu/poltheory/beccaria/delitti/delitti.c28.html).

reconciled to the maxim which tells us that a man has no right to kill himself? Which he certainly must have, if he could give it away to another.[2]

But the punishment of death is not authorised by any right, for I have demonstrated that no such right exists. It is therefore a war of a whole nation against a citizen, whose destruction they consider as necessary, or useful to the general good. But if I can prove that capital punishment is neither necessary nor useful, I shall have achieved the triumph of mankind.

The death of a citizen cannot be necessary except when, though deprived of his liberty, he has such power and connexions as may endanger the security of the nation; when his existence may produce a dangerous revolution in the established form of government. But even in this case, it can only be necessary when a nation is on the verge of recovering or losing its liberty; or in times of absolute anarchy, when the disorders themselves hold the place of laws. But in a reign of tranquillity in a form of government approved by the united wishes of the nation; in a state well fortified from enemies without, and supported by strength within, and opinion, perhaps more efficacious; where all power is lodged in the hands of a true sovereign; where riches can purchase pleasures and not authority, there can be no necessity for taking away the life of a subject.

If the experience of all ages is not sufficient to prove that the punishment of death has never prevented determined men from injuring society; if the example of the Romans; if the twenty years reign of Elizabeth, empress of Russia, in which she gave the fathers of their country an example more illustrious than many conquests bought with the blood of their sons; if, I say, all this is not sufficient to persuade mankind, who always suspect the voice of reason, and who prefer to be led by authority, let us consult human nature to prove my assertion.

It is not the intensity of pain that has the greatest effect on the mind, but its continuation. Our sensibility is more easily and more

---

2   Editor's note: This argument is a fallacy—it ignores the state's right to action in self defence, in cases of necessity, which clearly do not rely on the consent of the malefactor.

powerfully affected by weak but repeated impressions, than by a violent but momentary impulse. The power of habit is universal over every sensible being. It is by habit that we learn to speak, to walk, and to satisfy our necessities; so the ideas of morality are stamped on our minds by repeated impressions. The death of a criminal is a terrible but momentary spectacle, and therefore a less efficacious method of deterring others, than the continual example of a man deprived of his liberty, condemned as a beast of burden to repair by his labour, the injury he has done to society. If I commit such a crime, says the spectator to himself, I shall be reduced to that miserable condition for the rest of my life. A much more powerful preventative than the fear of death, which men always behold in distant obscurity.

The terrors of death make so slight an impression, that it has not force enough to withstand the forgetfulness natural to mankind, even in the most essential things; especially when assisted by the passions. Violent impressions surprise us, but their effect is momentary; they are fit to produce those revolutions which instantly transform a common man into a Lacedemonian or a Persian; but in a free and quiet government they ought to be rather frequent than strong. The execution of a criminal is, to the multitude, a spectacle which in some excites compassion mixed with indignation. These sentiments occupy the mind much more than that salutary terror which the laws endeavour to inspire; but in the contemplation of continued suffering, terror is the only, or at least predominant, sensation. The severity of a punishment should be just sufficient to excite compassion in the spectators, as it is intended more for them than for the criminal.

A punishment, to be just, should have only that degree of severity which is sufficient to deter others. Now there is no man, who upon the least reflection, would put in competition the total and perpetual loss of his liberty, with the greatest advantages he could possibly obtain in consequence of a crime. Perpetual slavery, then, has in it all that is necessary to deter the most hardened and determined, as much as the punishment of death. I say it has more. There are many who can look upon death with intrepidity and firmness; some through fanaticism, and others through vanity, which attends us even to the grave; others from a desperate resolution, either to get rid of their misery, or cease to live: but fanaticism and vanity forsake the criminal in slavery, in chains and fetters, in an iron cage; and despair seems rather to be the beginning than the end of their misery. The mind by collecting itself and uniting all its force, can, for a moment, repel assailing grief; but its most vigorous efforts are insufficient to resist perpetual wretchedness.

In all nations where death is used as a punishment every example supposes a new crime committed. Whereas in perpetual slavery every criminal affords a frequent and lasting example; and if it be necessary that men should often be witnesses of the power of the laws, criminals should often be put to death; but this supposes a frequency of crimes; and from hence this punishment will cease to have its effect, so that it must be useful and useless at the same time.

I shall be told that perpetual slavery is as painful a punishment as death, and therefore as cruel. I answer, that if all the miserable moments in the life of a slave were collected into one point, it would be a more cruel punishment than any other; but these are scattered through his whole life, whilst the pain of death exerts all its force in a moment. There is also another advantage in the punishment of slavery, which is, that it is more terrible to the spectator than to the sufferer himself; for the spectator considers the sum of all his wretched moments, whilst the sufferer, by the misery of the present, is prevented from thinking of the future. All evils are increased by the imagination, and the sufferer finds resources and consolations, of which the spectators are ignorant; who judge by their own sensibility of what passes in a mind, by habit grown callous to misfortune.

Let us, for a moment, examine the reasoning of a robber or assassin, who is deterred from violating the laws by hanging or breaking on the wheel. I am aware that to develop the sentiments of one's own heart is an art which education only can teach: but although a villain may not be able to give a clear account of his principles, principles nevertheless influence his conduct. He reasons thus:

What are these laws, that I am bound to respect, which make so great a difference between me and the rich man? He refuses me the farthing I ask of him, and excuses himself, by ordering me to labour, with which he is unacquainted. Who made these laws? The rich and the great, who never deigned to visit the miserable hut of the poor; who have never seen him dividing a piece of mouldy bread, amidst the cries of his famished children and the tears of his wife.

Let us break those ties, fatal to the greatest part of mankind, and only useful to a few indolent tyrants. Let us attack injustice at its source. I will return to my natural state of independence. I shall live free and happy on the fruits of my courage and industry. A day of pain and repentance may come, but it will be short; and for an hour of grief I shall enjoy years of pleasure and liberty.

I will lead a group of men as determined as I am to 'correct' the mistakes of fortune. Tyrants will grow pale and tremble at the sight of men whom, with insulting pride, they would treat worse than their dogs and horses.

Religion then presents itself to the mind of this lawless villain, and promising him almost a certainty of eternal happiness upon the easy terms of repentance, contributes much to lessen the horror of the last scene of the tragedy. But if a man realises that he must pass a great number of years, perhaps his whole life, in pain and slavery; imprisoned by those laws which formerly protected him in sight of his fellow citizens, with whom he lived in freedom and society; he can make a useful comparison between those evils, the uncertainty of his success, and the shortness of the time in which he can enjoy the fruits of his transgression. The example of those wretches continually before his eyes makes a much greater impression on him than a punishment, which, instead of correcting, makes him more obdurate.

The punishment of death is pernicious to society, from the example of barbarity it affords. If the passions (or the necessity of war) have taught men to shed the blood of their fellow creatures, the laws, which are intended to moderate the ferocity of mankind, should not increase it by examples of barbarity, made more horrible by the formal pageantry of execution.

Is it not absurd, that the laws which detest and punish homicide, should, in order to prevent murder, publicly commit murder themselves? What are the true and most useful laws? Those compacts and conditions which all would propose and observe, in those moments when private interest is silent, or combined with that of the public. What are the natural sentiments of every person concerning the punishment of death? We may read them in the contempt and indignation with which every one looks on the executioner, who is nevertheless an innocent executor of the public will; a good citizen, who contributes to the advantage of society; the instrument of the general security within, as good soldiers are without.

What then is the origin of this contradiction? Why is this sentiment of mankind indelible, to the scandal of reason? It is, that in a secret corner of the mind, in which the original impressions of nature are still preserved, men discover a sentiment, which tells them, that their lives are not lawfully in the power of any one, but of the iron sceptre of necessity which alone rules the universe.

What must men think when they see wise magistrates and grave ministers of justice, with indifference and tranquillity, dragging a criminal to death, and whilst a wretch trembles with agony, expecting the fatal stroke, the judge, who has condemned him, with the coldest insensibility, and perhaps with no small gratification from the exertion of his authority, quits his tribunal to enjoy the comforts and pleasures of life? They will say:

> Ah! those cruel formalities of justice are a cloak of tyranny, they are a secret language, a solemn veil, intended to conceal the sword by which we are sacrificed to the insatiable idol of despotism. Murder, which they would represent to us as an horrible crime, we see practised by them without repugnance, or remorse. Let us follow their example. A violent death appeared terrible in their descriptions, but we see that it is the affair of a moment. It will be still less terrible to him, who not expecting it, escapes almost all the pain.

Such is the fatal, though absurd reasoning of men who are disposed to commit crimes; on whom, the abuse of religion has more influence than religion itself.

It is objected that almost all nations in all ages have punished certain crimes with death; I reply that the force of these examples vanishes, when opposed to truth, against which long usage is urged in vain. The history of mankind is an immense sea of errors, in which a few obscure truths may here and there be found.

But human sacrifices have also been common in almost all nations. That some societies only, either few in number, or for a very short time, abstained from the punishment of death, is rather favourable to my argument. For such is the fate of great truths, that their duration is only as a flash of lightning in the long and dark night of error. The happy time is not yet arrived, when truth, as falsehood has been hitherto, shall be the portion of the greatest number.

I realise that the voice of one philosopher is too weak to be heard amidst the clamours of a multitude, blindly influenced by custom; but there is a small number of sages, scattered on the face of the earth, who will echo me from the bottom of their hearts. If these truths should happily force their way to the thrones of princes, let them know that they come attended with the secret wishes of all mankind. Tell the sovereign who gives them a gracious reception that his fame shall outshine the glory of conquerors, and that equitable posterity will exalt his peaceful trophies above those of a Titus, an Antoninus, of a Trajan.

How happy mankind would be if their laws could now be rewritten, as if there had never been laws before! We can now see on the thrones of Europe benevolent monarchs, friends to peace, the arts and sciences, fathers of their people, citizens as well as crowned heads; the increase of whose authority increases the happiness of their subjects, by destroying that *intermediate despotism*[3] which intercepts the prayers of the people to the throne. If these humane princes have allowed old laws to remain it is doubtless because they are deterred by the numberless obstacles which oppose the rectification of errors established by the sanction of many ages. Therefore every wise citizen will wish for the increase of the authority of these princes.

* * *

---

3   Editor's note: presumably, outdated laws.

Commentary

One can extract fifteen novel and clear-cut principles on crime and punishment from Beccaria's great book.

1. Crime is a social malady, not the Devil's work, and its punishment is the task of society.
2. The aims of punishment are purely civil. Divine vengeance is left to God.
3. Accordingly, the aims of punishment are deterrence (discouraging the criminal from repeating his crime, and dissuading others from imitating him) and reformation.
4. The 'appropriate penalty' can be worked out statistically. It is the lowest penalty consistent with public safety.
5. There is a 'critical point' in punishment beyond which increasing severity is unnecessary because it has no demonstrable effect on the crime rate. For example a 50c parking fine in a big city will have no deterrent effect on the incidence of parking offences, because paying the fine is probably cheaper than parking the vehicle in a garage. A minimum fine of $50 will drive all would-be parking offenders from the streets—and raising this minimum penalty to $75 or $100 would be pointless. If, in modern style, Beccaria had drawn a graph, it would have looked like this:

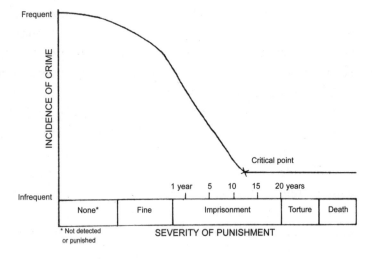

6. Thus, while imposing heavier sentences for car-stealing might effectively deter—and be statistically provable, evidence suggests that once a critical point of severity is passed any excessive punishment is 'tyrannical' and pointless. Accordingly torture or death, in practice, are unlikely to have any demonstrably superior deterrent effect than a sentence of between ten and fifteen years in prison.

7. No penalty should be imposed that is neither necessary nor useful. Since capital punishment cannot be equated with self-defence (contrary to the popular fallacy), there is never any necessity to execute—although it may well be essential to have tighter prison security. If governments don't say, 'I kill you because I must' (that is, where there is no possibility of an alternative penalty), they are in fact saying, 'I kill you because I prefer to.' (That is, there is a positive element of choice—preference.)

8. The use of torture, especially to extract information or confessions, is not only bad but stupid. 'Of two men, equally innocent or equally guilty, the robust and courageous will be acquitted, the weak and the timid will be condemned.'

9. Prevention of crime, for example by education, a proper police force, or encouragement of factors promoting social stability, is far preferable to punishment after commission.

10. Certainty of detection and conviction are better deterrents than severity of punishment. 'The certainty of a small punishment will make a stronger impression than the fear of one more severe, if there is a reasonable chance of escaping it.'

11. Penalties should not be varied arbitrarily—the law must show itself to be firm and consistent.

12. The power of pardon is undesirable. 'Clemency is a virtue that belongs to the legislator, and not to the executor of the laws; a virtue which ought to shine in the code, and not in private judgement.' Constant use of the pardoning power demonstrates a basic flaw in the law. Thus if, as had been the case in Victoria between 1955 and 1967, the death penalty was pronounced forty times and commuted thirty-eight times, it

is impossible to defend a law which is inappropriate in 95 per cent of the time.

13. All religious crimes—apostasy, heresy, blasphemy—should be struck from the statute books.

14. In sentencing prisoners it is important not to destroy 'hope' in their minds—for the absence of hope may make them desperate, or reduce them to vegetables.

15. 'Equal severity of punishment will lead to more crimes by one man.' If death were the penalty for sheep-stealing, why should the criminal not shoot the policeman who arrests him?

16. Justification for retaining criminal sanctions must always be the result of rational analysis.

Beccaria's ideas were disseminated in England by Jeremy Bentham, John Howard, Sir Samuel Romilly, and William Eden.

The Tsarina (Empress) Elizabeth of Russia enacted a moratorium on the death penalty in 1745–56, before On Crimes and Punishments. Catherine the Great quoted Beccaria in her Instruction (Nakaz) of 1767, indicating her distaste for capital punishment, but it was not abolished.

Beccaria's ideas were taken up by Leopold, the Grand Duke of Tuscany (1747–1792), who abolished capital punishment in Tuscany in 1786. His brother, Kaiser (Emperor) Joseph II (1741–1790,) followed in 1787 for the entire Holy Roman Empire (Austria-Hungary-Bohemia-Croatia-modern Belgium). Joseph was succeeded by his brother, who became Kaiser Leopold II.

Beccaria has been criticised for preferring perpetual imprisonment on the basis that it was a greater and more painful deterrent than death, but he lived in a savage age when the abolition of executions would have been thought inconceivable unless a savage alternative was provided, and he knew that he could not move too far in advance of 'opinion, that tormentor of the wise and the ignorant, [which] exalts the appearance of virtue above virtue itself'. His opposition to torture was based not on moral or aesthetic considerations, but on the fear that it makes truth dependent on the strength of a man's body and the sensitivity of his nerves. Under torture the innocent weak will confess to crime before the guilty strong—and what becomes of justice then? Secret torture is bad because it cannot deter, and the use of torture to extract a confession before trial is shocking because the accused has not been convicted by his judges. Beccaria does not deal with torture as a punishment after conviction, although he rejects the theological argument that the pain helps the guilty to purge away their infamy.

Beccaria and the classical school of penologists generally can be attacked for their principle of 'equal punishment for equal crime'. The possibility of reforming first (or other young) offenders will disappear if inexorable slot-machine justice determines the penalty with reference only to the crime and not the criminal. Beccaria's treatment of the reformative purposes of punishment is brief, but he deplored the waste of potentially useful lives by execution. There is something amazingly modern, however, in his emphasis on preventing crime, the need to reform society, education, the police, and the environments which produce criminals.

One conclusion by Beccaria feels uncomfortable in the twenty-first century: he supported the right of citizens to bear arms, and his ideas were drawn on by Thomas Jefferson and John Adams. He wanted citizens to be able to defend themselves, and resisted the idea of a standing army as a demonstration of overarching state power. He would, however, have been contemplating a slow-firing musket, and not AK–47s, rapid-fire assault rifles that can kill on an industrial scale within minutes.

4

Speech on the death penalty

Sir Samuel Romilly

The ideas of Beccaria were disseminated in England through the writings of John Howard (1726–1790), who, in travelling incessantly, acquired enormous experience of prison conditions in Europe. Another was Jeremy Bentham (1748–1832), who adopted Beccaria's test for utilitarianism as if it had been his own invention, and applied it to penology.

Others expounding Beccaria's ideas were William Eden (1745–1814), the author of *Principles of Penal Law* (1771); Basil Montagu QC (1770–1851), who in 1809 organised the 'Society for the Diffusion of Knowledge upon the punishment of Death'; and Sir Samuel Romilly KC (1757–1818). Romilly, a Whig MP (1806–18), was Solicitor-General from 1806 to 1807, and strove for modification of the death penalty and the abolition of slavery.

In 1810 a Bill was introduced into the House of Commons to provide that the punishment for high treason should be either hanging or beheading instead of the then punishment, which was:

> that the offender be dragged to the gallows; that he be hanged by the neck and then cut down alive; that his entrails be taken out and burned while he is yet alive; that his head be cut off; that his body be divided into five parts, and that his head and quarters should be at the King's disposal.

The Bill to introduce the new punishment was lost by twelve votes, largely because of the determined opposition of Lord Chancellor Eldon and Lord Chief Justice Ellenborough. In the debate, Romilly addressed the following words to his fellow MPs.

*   *   *

I call upon you to remember, that cruel punishments have an inevitable tendency to produce cruelty in the people. It is not by the destruction of tenderness, it is not by the exciting of revenge, that we can hope to generate virtuous conduct in those who are confided to our care. You may cut out the heart of a sufferer and hold it up to the view of the populace, and you may imagine that you serve the community; but the real effect of such scenes is to torture the compassionate and to harden the obdurate.

In times of tranquillity you will not diminish offences by rendering guilt callous; by teaching the subjects to look with indifference upon human suffering; and in times or turbulence, fury will retaliate the cruelties which it has been accustomed to behold. From the spirit which I have seen I shall not be surprised, and I certainly will not be deterred, by any vote of this night. I am not so unacquainted with the nature of prejudice as not to have observed that it strikes deep root; that it flourishes in all soils and spreads its branches in every direction. I have observed also, that flourish as it may, it must, by laws sacred and immutable, wither and decay after the powerful and repeated touch of truth. It was my lot to hear in parliament a negative upon that Bill which was intended to deliver this enlightened nation from the reproach of the cruel and disgusting punishment of burning women alive. It was my lot again and again to witness in this house the defeat of those wise and humane exertions which were intended to rescue Englishmen from the disgrace of abetting slavery. But the punishment of burning is no more, and Africa is free.

No resistance, no vote of this night shall prevent my again appealing to the good sense and good feeling of the legislature and of the country. If I live another year, I will renew this Bill, with the Bill for repealing the punishment of death for stealing a few shillings; and, whatever may be my fate, the seed which is scattered has not fallen upon stony ground.

5

A letter to the *Daily News*

Charles Dickens

Charles Dickens (1812–1870), the greatest English novelist of the nineteenth century, wrote many works revealing a preoccupation with sociology and the need for legal reform.

The letter below was published in the *Daily News* of 28 February 1846, and was reprinted in the Pilgrim edition of the *Letters of Charles Dickens*.

* * *

Gentlemen, In the very remarkable Report made to the State Assembly of New York, in 1841, by a select committee of that body, who arrived at the conclusion, 'that the punishment of death, by law, ought to be forthwith and for ever abolished' in that part of America, there is the following suggestion:

> Whether there sleep within the breast of man, certain dark and mysterious sympathies with the thought of that death, and that futurity which await his nature, tending to invest any act expressly forbidden by that penalty, with an unconscious and inexplicable fascination, that attracts his thoughts to it, in spite of their very shuddering dread; and bids his imagination brood over its idea, 'till out of those dark depths in his own nature, comes gradually forth a monstrous birth of Temptation.

Strongly impressed by this passage when I first read the report; and believing that it shadowed out a metaphysical truth, which, however wild and appalling in its aspect, was a truth still; I was led to consider the cases of several murderers, both in deed, and in intent, with a reference to it; and certainly it gathered very strong and special confirmation in the course of that inquiry. But, as the bearing, here, is on capital punishment in its influences on the commission of crime; and as my present object is to make it the subject of one or two considerations in its other influences on society in general; I, for the present, defer any immediate pursuit of the idea, and merely quote it now, as introducing this lesser and yet great objection to the punishment of death.

That there is, about it, a horrible fascination, which, in the minds—not of evil-disposed persons, but of good and virtuous and well-conducted people, supersedes the horror legitimately attaching to crime itself, and causes every word and action of a criminal under sentence of death to be the subject of a morbid interest and curiosity. Which is odious and painful, even to many of those who eagerly gratify it by every means they can compass; but which is, generally speaking, irresistible. The attraction of repulsion being as much a law of our moral nature, as gravitation is in the structure of the visible world, operates in no case (I believe) so powerfully, as in this case of the punishment of death; though it may occasionally diminish in its force, through strong reaction.

When the murderers Hocker and Tawell had awakened a vast amount of this depraved excitement, and it had attained to an unusually indecent and frenzied height, one of your contemporaries, deploring the necessity of ministering to such an appetite, laid the blame upon the caterers of such dainties for the Press, while some other newspapers, disputing which of them should bear the greater share of it, divided it variously. Can there be any doubt, on cool reflection, that the whole blame rested on, and was immediately and naturally referable to, the punishment of death?

Round what other punishment does the like interest gather? We read of the trials of persons who have rendered themselves liable to transportation for life, and we read of their sentences, and, in some few notorious instances, of their departure from this country, and arrival beyond sea; but they are never followed into their cells, and tracked from day to day, and night to night; they are never reproduced in their false letters, flippant conversations, theological disquisitions with visitors, lay and clerical: or served up in their whole biography and adventures—so many live romances with a bloody ending. Their portraits are not rife in the print-shops, nor are their autographs stuck up in shopwindows, nor are their snuff-boxes handed affably to gentlemen in court, nor do they inquire of other spectators with eyeglasses why they look at them so steadfastly, nor are their breakfasts, dinners, and luncheons, elaborately described, nor are their waxen images in Baker Street (unless they were in immediate danger, at one time, of the gallows), nor are high prices offered for their clothes at Newgate, nor do turnpike trusts grow rich upon the tolls that people going to see their houses, or the scenes of their offences, pay. They are tried, found guilty, punished; and there an end.

But a criminal under sentence of death, or in great peril of death upon the scaffold, becomes, immediately, the town talk; the great subject; the hero of the time. The demeanour in his latter moments, of Sir Thomas More—one of the wisest and most virtuous of men—was never the theme of more engrossing interest, than that of Hocker, Tawell Greenacre, or Courvoisier. The smallest circumstance in the behaviour of these, or any similar wretches, is noted down and published as a precious fact. And read, too—extensively and generally read—even by hundreds and thousands of people who object to the publication of such details, and are disgusted by them. The horrible fascination surrounding the punishment, and everything connected with it, is too strong for resistance; and when an attempt is made in this or that gaol (as it has been sometimes made of late), to keep such circumstances from transpiring, by excluding every class of strangers, it is only a formal admission of the existence of this fascination, and of the impossibility of otherwise withstanding it.

Is it contended that the fascination may surround the crime, and not the punishment? Let us consider whether other crimes, which have now no sort of fascination for the general public, had or had not precisely the gross kind of interest which now attaches to Murder alone, when they were visited with the same penalty. Was Forgery interesting, when Forgers were hanged? And is it less interesting now when they are transported for life? Compare the case of Dr Dodd, or Fauntleroy, of the Reverend Peter Fenn, or Montgomery, or Hunton, or any other generally known, with that of the Exchequer-Bill forgery in later times, which: with every attendant circumstance but death, or danger of death, to give it a false attraction, soon dwindled down into a mere item in a Sessions' Calendar. Coining, when the coiner was dragged (as I have seen one) on a hurdle to the place of execution; or Burglary, or Highway Robbery—did these crimes ever wear an aspect of adventure and mystery, and did the perpetrators of them ever become the town talk, when their offences were visited with death? Now, they are mean, degraded, miserable criminals; and nothing more.

That the publication of these Newgate court-circulars to which I have alluded, is injurious to society, there can be no doubt. Apart from their inevitable association with revolting details, revived again and again, of bloodshed and murder (most objectionable as familiarising people's minds with the contemplation of such horrors), it is manifest that anything which tends to awaken a false interest in great villains, and to invest their greatest villainies and lightest actions with a terrible attraction, must be vicious and bad, and cannot be wholesome reading. But it is neither just nor reasonable to charge their publication on the newspapers, or the gleaners for the newspapers. They are published because they are read and sought for. They are read and sought for: not because society has causelessly entered into a monstrous and unnatural league on this theme (which is would be absurd to suppose), but because it is in the secret nature of those of whom society is made up, to have a dark and dreadful interest in the punishment at issue.

Whether public executions produce any good impression on their habitual witnesses, or whether they are calculated to produce any good impression on the class of persons most likely to be attracted to them, is a question, by this time, pretty well decided. I was present, myself, at the execution of Courvoisier. I was, purposely, on the spot, from midnight of the night before; and was a near witness of the whole process of the building of the scaffold, the gathering of the crowd, the gradual swelling of the concourse with the coming-on of day, the hanging of the man, the cutting of the body down, and the removal of it into the prison. From the moment of my arrival, when there were but a few score boys in the street, and those all young thieves, and all clustered together behind the barrier nearest to the drop—down to the time when I saw the body with its dangling head, being carried on a wooden bier into the gaol—I did not see one token in all the immense crowd; at the windows, in the streets, on the house-tops, anywhere; of any one emotion suitable to the occasion. No sorrow, no salutary terror, no abhorrence, no seriousness; nothing but ribaldry, debauchery, levity, drunkenness, and flaunting vice in fifty other shapes. I should have deemed it impossible that I could have ever felt any large assemblage of my fellow-creatures to be so odious. I hoped, for an instant, that there was some sense of Death and Eternity in the cry of 'Hats off' when the miserable wretch appeared; but I found, next moment, that they only raised it as they would at a Play—to see the Stage the better, in the final scene.

Of the effect upon a perfectly different class, I can speak with no less confidence. There were, with me, some gentlemen of education and distinction in imaginative pursuits, who had, as I had, a particular detestation of that murderer; not only for the cruel deed he had done, but for his slow and subtle treachery, and for his wicked defence. And yet, if any one among us could have saved the man (we said so, afterwards, with one accord), he would have done it. It was so loathsome, pitiful, and vile a sight, that the law appeared to be as bad as he, or worse; being very much the stronger, and shedding around it a far more dismal contagion.

The last of the influences of this punishment on society, which I shall notice in the present letter, is, that through the prevalent and fast-increasing feeling of repugnance to it, great offenders escape with a very inadequate visitation. Only a few weeks have elapsed since the streets of London presented the obscene spectacle of a woman being brought out to be killed before such a crowd as I have described, and, while her young body was yet hanging in the brutal gaze, of portions of the concourse hurrying away, to be in time to see a man hanged elsewhere, by the same executioner. A barbarous murderer is tried soon afterwards, and acquitted on a fiction of his being insane—as any one, cognisant of these two recent executions, might have easily foreseen.

I will not enter upon the question whether juries be justified or not justified in evading their oaths, rather than add to the list of such deeply degrading and demoralising exhibitions, and sanction the infliction of a punishment which they conscientiously believe, and have so many reasons for believing, to be wrong. It is enough for me that juries do so; and I presume to think that the able writer of a powerful article on Johnstone's trial in the *Daily News*, does not sufficiently consider that this is no new course in juries, but the natural result and working of a law to which the general feeling is opposed. Mr Abercrombie, five-and-thirty years ago, stated it in the House of Commons to have become a common practice of juries, in cases of Forgery, to find verdicts 'contrary to the clearest and most indisputable evidence of facts'; and cited the case of a woman who was proved to have stolen a ten-pound note, which the jury, with the approbation of the judge, found to be worth only thirty-nine shillings. Sir Samuel Romilly, in the same debate, mentioned other cases of the same nature; and they were of frequent and constant occurrence at that time.

Besides — that juries have, within our own time, in another class of cases, arrived at the general practice of returning a verdict tacitly agreed upon beforehand, and of making it applicable to very different sets of facts, we know by the notable instance of Suicide. Within a few years, juries frequently found that a man dying by his own hand, was guilty of self-murder. But this verdict subjecting the body to a barbarous mode of burial, from which the better feeling of society revolted (as it is now revolting from the punishment of death), it was abrogated by common consent, and precisely the same evasion established, as is now, unfortunately, so often resorted to in cases of murder. That it is an evasion, and not a proceeding on a soundly proved and established principle, that he who destroys his own life must necessarily be mad — the very exceptions from this usual course in themselves demonstrate.

So it is in cases of Murder. Juries, like society, are not stricken foolish or motiveless. They have, for the most part, an objection to the punishment of death: and they will, for the most part, assert such verdicts. As jurymen, in the Forgery cases, would probably reconcile their verdict to their consciences, by calling to mind that the intrinsic value of a bank note was almost nothing, so jurymen in cases of Murder probably argue that grave doctors have said all men are more or less mad, and therefore they believe the prisoner mad. This is a great wrong to society; but it arises out of the punishment of death.

And the question will always suggest itself in jurors' minds — however earnestly the learned judge presiding, may discharge his duty — 'which is the greater wrong to society? To give this man the benefit of the possibility of his being mad, or to have another public execution, with all its depraving and hardening influences?' Imagining myself a juror, in a case of life or death: and supposing that the evidence had forced me from every other ground of opposition to this punishment in the particular case, as a possibility of irremediable mistake, or otherwise: I would go over it again on this ground; and if I could, by any reasonable special pleading with myself, find him mad rather than hang him — I think I would.

6

On capital punishment

Clarence Darrow

Clarence Darrow (1857–1938), the most brilliant US defence counsel of his time, appeared in many notable criminal trials such as the Debs, Loeb and Leopold (1924), and Scottsboro' Boys cases. He also appeared for J.T. Scopes in the famous Tennessee 'Monkey Trial' of 1925.

The following extract is from Darrow's speech in a public debate in New York on 23 September 1924 on the subject 'That capital punishment is a wise public policy'.

* * *

Every human being that believes in capital punishment loves killing, and the only reason they believe in capital punishment is because they get a kick out of it. Nobody kills anyone for love, unless they get over it temporarily or otherwise. But they kill the one they hate. And before you can get a trial to hang somebody or electrocute him, you must first hate him and then get a satisfaction over his death ...

We teach people to kill, and the State is the one that teaches them. If the State wishes that its citizens respect human life, then the State should stop killing. It can be done in no other way, and it will perhaps not be fully done that way. There are infinite reasons for killing. There are infinite circumstances under which there are more or less deaths. It never did depend and never can depend upon the severity of the punishment ...

I don't want to dispute about the right of the State to kill people. Of course, they have got a right to kill them. That is about all we do.

57

The great industry of the world for four years was killing. They have got a right to kill, of course, that is, they have got the power. And you have got a right to do what you get away with. The words power and right, so far as this is concerned, mean exactly the same thing. So nobody who has any knowledge of philosophy would pretend to say that the State had not the right to kill.

But why not do a good job of it? If you want to get rid of killings by hanging people or electrocuting them because these are so terrible, why not make a punishment that is terrible? This isn't so much. It lasts but a short time. There is no physical torture in it. Why not boil them in oil, as they used to do? Why not burn them at the stake? Why not sew them into a bag with serpents and throw them out to sea? Why not take them out on the sand and let them be eaten by ants? Why not break every bone in their body on the rack, as has been done for serious offenses as heresy and witchcraft?

Those were the good old days in which the judge should have held court. Glorious days, when you could kill them by the millions because they worshipped God in a different way from that which the State provided, or when you could kill old women for witchcraft! There might be some sense in it if you could kill young ones, but not old ones. Those were the glorious days of capital punishment. And there wasn't a judge or a preacher who didn't think that the life of the State depended upon their right to hang old women for witchcraft and to persecute others for worshipping God in the wrong way.

Why, our capital punishment isn't worth talking about, so far as its being a preventive is concerned. It isn't worth discussing. Why not call back from the dead and barbarous past the hundred and sixty- or seventy-odd crimes that were punishable by death in England? Why not once more re-enact the Blue Laws of our own country and kill people right? Why not resort to all the tortures that the world has always resorted to to keep men in the straight and narrow path? Why reduce it to a paltry question of murder? …

There is just one thing in all this question. It is a question of how you feel, that is all. It is all inside of you. If you love the thought of somebody being killed, why, you are for it. If you hate the thought of somebody being killed, you are against it …

Gradually, the world has been lopping off these punishments. Why? Because we have grown a little more sensitive, a little more imaginative, a little kindlier, that is all.

Why not re-enact the code of Blackstone's day? Why, the judges were all for it — every one of them — and the only way we got rid of these laws was because juries were too humane to obey the courts.

That is the only way we got rid of punishing old women, of hanging old women in New England — because, in spite of all the courts, the juries would no longer convict them for a crime that never existed. And in that way they have cut down the crimes in England for punishment by death from one hundred and seventy to two. What is going to happen if we get rid of them? Is the world coming to an end? The earth has been here ages and ages before man came. It will be here ages and ages after he disappears, and the amount of people you hang won't make the slightest difference with it.

Now, why am I opposed to capital punishment? It is too horrible a thing for a State to undertake. We are told by my friend, 'Oh, the killer does it; why shouldn't the State?' I would hate to live in a State that I didn't think was better than a murderer.

But I told you the real reason. The people of the State kill a man because he killed someone else — that is all — without the slightest logic, without the slightest application to life, simply from anger, nothing else!

I am against it because I believe it is inhuman, because I believe that as the hearts of men have softened they have gradually gotten rid of brutal punishment, because I believe that it will only be a few years until it will be banished forever from every civilised country — even New York; because I believe that it has no effect whatever to stop murder ...

In the end, this question is simply one of the humane feelings against the brutal feelings. One who likes to see suffering, out of what he thinks is a righteous indignation, or any other, will hold fast to capital punishment. One who has sympathy, imagination, kindness and understanding, will hate it and detest it as he hates and detests death.

7

The death penalty

Thorsten Sellin

Thorsten Sellin (1896–1994), an American criminologist, was born in Sweden and migrated to Canada in 1923. He turned from teaching to sociological casework in America, taught sociology at the University of Pennsylvania from 1922, and was Secretary General of the International Penal and Penitentiary Foundation 1949–51. Sir Ernest Gowers wrote that Sellin's 'study of capital punishment qualifies him to speak with perhaps unrivalled authority'. In submitting evidence to the UK Royal Commission on Capital Punishment 1949–53, Sellin concluded:

> The question of whether the death penalty is to be dropped, retained or instituted is not dependent on the evidence as to its utilitarian effects, but on the strength of popular beliefs and sentiments not easily influenced by such evidence. These beliefs and sentiments have their roots in a people's culture. They are conditioned by a multitude of factors, such as the character of social institutions, social, economic and political ideas, etc. If at a given time such beliefs and sentiments become so oriented that they favour the abolition of the death penalty, facts like those presented in this paper will be acceptable as evidence, but are likely to be as quickly ignored if social changes provoke resurgence of the old sentiments. When a people no longer likes the death penalty for murderers it will be removed no matter what may happen to the homicide rate. This is what has happened in the past in connexion with crimes against property.

Sellin published *The Death Penalty* in 1959, from which these extracts are taken.

* * *

The controversy about the death penalty

Questions of the legitimacy or the propriety of this or that form of punishment of criminals have frequently been raised in the past, and the controversies have sooner or later ended with the abolition or modification of the punishment. The death penalty, one of the oldest of all punishments, has been under attack for centuries, especially since Beccaria published his influential essay *On Crimes and Punishments* in 1764. The movement for the abolition of capital punishment, the effect of which has already been described, can be said to date from that year. Since then the struggle about this punishment has been one between ancient and deeply rooted beliefs in retribution, atonement or vengeance on the one hand, and, on the other, beliefs in the personal value and dignity of the common man that were born of the democratic movement of the eighteenth century, as well as beliefs in the scientific approach to an understanding of the motive forces of human conduct, which are the result of the growth of the sciences of behaviour during the nineteenth and twentieth centuries. If these newer trends of our thinking continue undisturbed the death penalty will disappear in all the countries of Western culture sooner or later.

The arguments for or against the death penalty may be divided into two classes. One of them contains what might be called the dogmas. Among the dogmas that uphold the death penalty, one might mention, in particular, the following:

1. the death penalty is the only punishment by which the murderer can really expiate his crime;
2. the death penalty is the only just punishment for murder;
3. the death penalty is more humane than life imprisonment.

Against the death penalty we find arrayed dogmas such as these:

1.   man has no right to take away life, the gift of the Creator;
2.   retaliation is not a defensible basis for a penal system;
3.   the death penalty is unjust.

Variations on the above themes could be added. All dogmas have one thing in common. They rest on absolute or categorical principles. They must be accepted on faith. Those who embrace them most fully and earnestly would maintain that faith even if experience would demonstrate that the use of the death penalty is socially harmful or beneficial, or lacks or possesses this or that practical value.

In the other class fall the arguments which might be called empirical or utilitarian. It is characteristic of modern man, reared in an age of scientific orientation, that he wishes to use scientific thoughtways in the approach to his problems. He does not like to be considered irrational. When he formulates public policies he wants to think that such policies are based on scientific facts and not alone on sentiments and emotions, but the strength of the latter is often such that he is led to invent or pervert facts in order to justify actions that are basically prompted by his feelings. Therefore it is often difficult to determine whether or not those who advance utilitarian arguments for or against the death penalty base their position fully on them or merely use them to disguise irrational feelings which really motivate their behaviour but which they cannot or do not wish to expose.

Whether these utilitarian arguments are or are not basic to those who use them, they differ from dogmas in one fundamental way. They lay no claim to infallibility. They rest on evidence showing, or purporting to show, that the death penalty, as practised, produces certain demonstrable effects.

The main utilitarian arguments focus on the problem of deterrence. The supporters of the death penalty claim that it is a specific deterrent. They say that if there were no capital punishment more people would commit murders. Some say that the restraining influence of the death penalty is particularly strong on psychopaths, or that it stays the hand of the fleeing criminal who might otherwise turn on his pursuer and kill him, or a witness to the crime in order to escape capture. The argument is, of course, an offshoot of the more inclusive one which holds that the threat of punishment in general has deterrent power, and in its purest form it would hold that no other kind of punishment could possess the same preventive effect as the death penalty.

Another argument of the same class is that, were the death penalty removed, an outraged community would in certain cases resort to lynch justice and the victim's family to private vengeance or vendetta.

Occasionally one hears the arguments that the death penalty has eugenic value in that it prevents the procreation of dysgenic human strains, that it is more economical than imprisonment or that it affords society maximum protection by removing the offender permanently from society.

The opponents of the death penalty either challenge the validity of the above claims or maintain that in so far as they are valid the same effects could be produced by other and to them more acceptable means. They admit that the death penalty prevents an executed offender from causing future injury to society, but they say that this certainty is bought at the risk of possible miscarriages of justice, the irreparable nature of the punishment preventing the later rectification of judicial errors. They also claim that when juries or judges regard a death penalty as too severe, they may render verdicts contrary to facts and thus make a mockery of justice. They point to the fact that the existence of the death penalty sometimes incites to murder and they claim that no evidence exists to prove that it is a specific preventive of murder.

It is a curious fact that the chief arguments for or against the death penalty have remained remarkably unchanged since the beginning of the debate. In the meanwhile, however, there have been great changes in their meaning. If, as many people say, the death penalty is a moral necessity and the only just retribution for crime, or that the sense of justice of a people requires it, it is obvious that the last two centuries have seen great transformations in concepts of morality and justice. We have abolished torturing forms of punishment like breaking on the wheel and burning at the stake; we no longer see either justice or morality in hanging for theft. If, on the other hand, we say that the death penalty is a great preventive because the fear of such an ignominious death holds prospective criminals in check, history shows that we increasingly tend to substitute other punishments for it, that we have exerted ourselves in discovering ways and means to make executions as painless and rapid as possible, and that we have further reduced prevention by hiding executions from public view and giving them the least possible official publicity. These incontrovertible facts signify that while a sense of justice and high moral concepts are constant in man, because they are necessary to all social life, the ideas of what is just and moral change. The people of some nations that formerly regarded it as just, moral and proper to hang a thief, brand a rogue and burn a witch, now either consider it immoral to take life at all as a punishment or immoral to take it except in extremely abnormal circumstances such as in wartime. Therefore, it seems obvious that the existence of the death penalty does not depend on any immutable principle. Like all social policies it depends on changes in attitudes and beliefs which are influenced by the conditions and circumstances of social life.

Unlike the dogmas, the statements of fact contained in the utilitarian arguments can be subjected to a scientific examination. We shall dismiss some of these arguments briefly. As for the eugenic argument, for instance, even if one could show that murderers generally have more than a normal number of undesirable traits, neither their execution nor their sterilisation would have any measurable effect on the frequency of such traits in future generations, as any geneticist would be able to show. In any case sterilisation would effectively prevent the transmission of such traits. As for the economic argument, it obviously rests on the assumption that murderers in prison cannot be self-supporting as a group and that they must always remain a financial burden on the public unless they are executed. However, the death penalty can hardly be defended on this basis. In a well-organised penal system, murderers as a group can undoubtedly earn their keep. If the system is not well-organised the fault rests with the public or the administration. No one would seriously suggest that people should be executed, not because of their crimes but because the state has made it impossible for them to be self-supporting during imprisonment because it has taken no proper steps to achieve that end.

In this report we shall examine in greater detail a few of the utilitarian claims about the death penalty. No exhaustive treatment of any one of them is possible. It would seem desirable to find an answer to the following questions at least.

1. Is it true that the death penalty is a specific deterrent to murder? A subsidiary question in this connexion could be examined. Is it true that the death penalty effectively protects law enforcement officers in the exercise of their duties?
2. Is it true that innocent persons are, at times, executed?
3. Is it true that the availability of the death penalty at times acts as a stimulus to murder?
4. Is it true that imprisonment of murderers does not afford adequate protection of society, because they will remain a threat to fellow prisoners or the prison staff while incarcerated and may, if pardoned or paroled, again commit murder?
5. Is it true that the removal of the death penalty would result in a resort to lynch justice?

Deterrence

Among the utilitarian arguments there is no doubt that the most widely used is the argument that the death penalty is a social necessity because it effectively deters people from committing murder.[1]

When we think of deterrence, restraint or prevention—these terms are used interchangeably—we usually think of the effect which a punishment has (1) on the future conduct of the person punished and (2) on the future conduct of others. Some writers distinguish these two effects by calling the one individual and the other general prevention. In the case of the executed death penalty individual

---

1   The most extensive, recent, and well-documented discussion of deterrence is found in the *Report of the Royal Commission on Capital Punishment*, 1949–53 (506 pp. London; HMSO, 1953), Appendix 6, pp. 328–80, 'The Deterrent Value of Capital Punishment.' See also Karl F. Schuessler, *The Deterrent Influence of the Death Penalty*, The Annals of the American Academy of Political and Social Science, 284:54–62, November 1952.

prevention is, of course, completely effective. This is the one executed punishment in connexion with which general prevention alone can be studied.

The process of deterrence is obviously a psychological one. It presumes in this connexion that life is regarded by man as a precious possession which he wishes to preserve more eagerly, perhaps, than any other of his attributes. He would therefore defend it to the utmost against every threat, including the threat of capital execution. Every such threat, it is assumed, arouses his fear and as a rational being he would try to conduct himself in such a manner that the threat would be avoided or that, once materialised, it would be nullified. It is further assumed that the potential threat is made vivid to him by the fact that he knows that the death penalty exists.

If the death penalty carries a potential threat which has a restraining influence on human conduct, we may assume that the greater the threat the more effective it would be. Now, the term 'death penalty' as used in discussions concerning its deterrent power may mean many things. First, we have the death penalty defined by law as a mandatory or discretionary punishment for crime. Then we have the death penalty that looms as a possible threat to a person arrested for, or accused of a capital offense, and the death penalty pronounced but not yet executed. Finally, we have the death penalty actually applied to the offender. Presumably, the potential power of deterrence of the death penalty is not the same at all these levels of manifestation. Were it present in the law alone it would be completely robbed of its threat. Death is still the legal punishment for murder in Belgium, but it has, except for one 'accident' so to speak and after World War II against collaborators with the enemy, never been applied since 1863. Under such circumstances even the knowledge that persons are still arrested and prosecuted for murder and even sentenced to death in Belgium would contain no threat of death to potential murderers in that country. We arrive then at the conclusion that if the death penalty is to have any restraining effect there must be an adequate threat of execution, but no one has ventured to calculate how great the risk of possible execution must be in order to constitute an adequate threat. It seems reasonable to assume that if the death penalty exercises a deterrent or preventive effect on prospective murderers, the following propositions would be true:

1. Murders should be less frequent in states that have the death penalty than in those that have abolished it, other factors being equal. Comparisons of this nature must be made among states that are as alike as possible in all other respects — character of population, social and economic condition, etc. — in order not to introduce factors known to influence murder rates in a serious manner but present in only one of these states.
2. Murders should increase when the death penalty is abolished and should decline when it is restored.
3. The deterrent effect should be greatest and should therefore affect murder rates most powerfully in those communities where the crime occurred and its consequences are most strongly brought home to the population.
4. Law enforcement officers would be safer from murderous attacks in states that have the death penalty than in those without it.

We are compelled to make certain assumptions. First we must decide what element in the death penalty gives it a maximum of deterrent power. We can assume — those who debate the issue do it generally speaking — that it is the execution which by its finality is the strongest agency of deterrence. We should therefore examine the effect of executions on murder rates. This brings us to a second necessary assumption. We do not know with any great degree of accuracy how many murders punishable by death occur. In the United States, for instance, where only murders in the first degree or similar murders are subject to the death penalty, no accurate statistics of such offenses exist, yet this is the only type of murder which people are presumably to be deterred from committing. Most deaths are no doubt recorded, but among deaths regarded as accidental or due to natural causes or suicide there are no doubt some successful murders. Where the killer never becomes known it is often impossible to determine if the death was the result of a capital murder. This is, of course, a problem which exists in all countries. We are everywhere compelled to use other statistics than those of strictly capital homicides.

Most advanced countries today possess statistics of reported deaths classified by cause of death. One of these is homicide, i.e. deaths wilfully caused by others. Students of criminal statistics have examined these data with some care and have arrived at the conclusion that the homicide death rate is adequate for an estimate of the trend of murder. This conclusion is based on the assumption that the proportion of capital murders in the total of such deaths remains reasonably constant ... One may challenge the assumption, but the fact remains that there are no better statistical data on which to base arguments about deterrence. Other statistics, such as conviction statistics, have greater defects.

Capital punishment as cause for murder

Editor's note: Sir Ernest Gowers was deeply impressed by Sellin's argument that in some rare cases capital punishment may be a positive incentive to commit a capital crime. The assertion seems implausible to 'reasonable' people, but it deserves some attention. It is also worth noting the observation that of 167 prisoners hanged in Bristol in the nineteenth century, 164 had witnessed one or more public executions, and that in France a majority of prisoners guillotined before 1939 had observed other decapitations. The striking Victorian case of David Bennett in 1932 (see page 260) suggests that the traditional theory of deterrence was irrelevant in his case.

* * *

It is a curious fact that there are cases on record which show that the desire to be executed has caused persons to commit a capital crime. Such crimes are indirect forms of suicide as a rule, the individual involved being unable to take his own life. In other instances a pathological desire to die by execution has been noted.

These cases must have once been fairly frequent,[2] because Denmark, by an ordinance of 18 December 1767, deliberately abandoned the death penalty in cases where 'melancholy and other dismal persons (committed murder) for the exclusive purpose of losing their lives'. A leading Danish jurist of that period explained that this limitation was introduced because of,

the thinking that was then current among the unenlightened that by murdering another person and thereby being sentenced to death, one might still attain salvation whereas if one were to take one's own life, one would be plunged into eternal damnation.[3]

The ordinance was ineffective in one case, at least, that of Jens Nielsen, who was born in 1862 and spent a most unhappy and unfortunate childhood. In 1884 he was sentenced to sixteen years of hard labour for theft and arson. The following year he tried to kill a prison guard. He was tried, sentenced to death and received a commutation to life. He was then placed in solitary confinement. A year later he tried again to kill a guard, 'realising that he could not stand solitary confinement, did not have the nerve to commit suicide and wanted to force his execution'.

He was again tried, sentenced to death and the sentence commuted. In 1892, having remained in solitary confinement all that time, he tried again to kill a guard. This time he got his wish, was sentenced to death and executed, 8 November 1892.

It may well be that cases of this type no longer are common, but they have not disappeared completely. Less than three decades ago, one occurred in Lyons, France, described by Dr Edmond Locard, chief of the police science laboratory of that city.[4]

A couple attended the Celestine Theatre in Lyon. When the

---

2   A large number, from the middle of the seventeenth century to 1829, can be found in H. von Weber's 'Selbstmord als Mordmotiv', Monatsschrift f. Kriminalbiologie u. Strafrechtsreform, 28:161–81, April 1937.

3   Quoted by Johannes Andenaes, 'General prevention—illusion or reality'. *Jour. of Crim. Law, Crimin., and Police Science*, 43:176–98, July–August 1952.

4   Edmond Locard, 'Le crime sans cause.' *La Giuslizia Penale*, Rome, Pt. I, 45:411–22, November 1939.

curtain had risen, the hall being half dark, the husband saw his wife fall forward. He raised her and discovered that she had been struck in the back. The knife was in the wound. The show stopped. The wounded was removed to the foyer where she died. The killer made no resistance when he was arrested. He admitted his crime. His victim was a complete stranger to him, as was her husband. He did not know their names. He had no reason to wish them ill. Although the deed appeared that of one demented, judicial investigation was started. No reason that could explain the act was discovered. On the other hand, the criminal revealed no sign of insanity. He was an honourable worker, pious, honest, without vices; he could not be exculpated by insanity or furor, to use the terms of the law. After the sentence to death he gave the following strange explanation:

> I do not want to sin. For some time I have felt temptations against purity. I fear I cannot remain chaste. I could not think of suicide, which is a sin more serious than fornication. I therefore decided to commit a capital crime, for thus I would have time to repent before my execution and would arrive immaculate in Heaven!

Frederick Field, who in 1931 committed two murders in London, is described by Inspector Robert Fabian of Scotland Yard, as 'the only man in the records of the Yard who may be said to have committed suicide by judicial hanging' and Robert Irwin, who committed a triple murder in New York in 1937 was driven by a desire to commit a similarly devious suicide.[5]

To what extent the desire for punishment of such an extreme nature in order to fulfill an urge for self-immolation may be more subtly hidden in the motivation of murderers is a problem for psychiatrists. The cases where this motivation is brought clearly to light are no doubt rare and those involved would probably be found to be mentally deranged and placed in appropriate institutions. However, without the existence of the death penalty these rare murders might not have occurred.

---

5   *American Weekly*, 20 March 1955.

8

A life for a life?

Sir Ernest Gowers

Sir Ernest Gowers (1880–1966), educated at Rugby and Cambridge, rose steadily through the civil service, and chaired several royal commissions. He was regional commissioner for civil defence in London 1940–45.

Gowers was best known for his books *Plain Words: a guide to the use of English* (1948), *The Complete Plain Words* (1954) and a revision of H.W. Fowler's *A Dictionary of Modern English Usage* (1965).

Prime Minister Clement Attlee appointed him to chair the Royal Commission on Capital Punishment, 1949–53 and he became a convinced abolitionist. He wrote *A Life for a Life? The Problem of Capital Punishment* (1956), which enabled him to express his own opinion, excluded from the royal commission report because of its restricted mandate.[1]

Earlier he wrote:

Before serving on the Royal Commission I, like most other people, had given no great thought to this problem. If I had been asked for my opinion, I should probably have said that I was in favour of the death penalty and disposed to regard abolitionists as people whose hearts were bigger than their heads. Four years of close study of the subject gradually dispelled that feeling. In the end I became convinced that the abolitionists were right in their conclusions—though I could not agree with all their arguments—and that so far from the

---

1   The royal commission was limited to reporting on the introduction of degrees of murder, methods of execution, and application of the prerogative of mercy.

sentimental approach leading into their camp and the rational one into that of the supporters, it was the other way about.

The following extracts are taken from Chapters 4, 5, 7, and 8 of *A Life for a Life? The Problem of Capital Punishment.*

* * *

I should have expected that the abolitionists, when setting out the arguments against capital punishment, would give greater prominence to the objection that it demands the existence of an executioner. 'I do not put it as an important point at all,' said the representative of the Howard League. I am surprised at that. I am not suggesting that the hangman is necessarily a brutal person; I am sure the present one is not. But, as a witness remarked, 'A man who wants to be an executioner is in a class by himself'. We maintain a State institution which, we are told, inspires quite a considerable number of people with a desire to earn a little pocket-money by playing the leading part in a grim, barbaric ritual killing of a fellow-creature. Very few realise that ambition, but to some of the less fortunate may be given the partial satisfaction of hanging dummy criminals and sometimes even strapping the legs of real ones and seeing them fall when the lever is pulled. 'The ambition,' said the Royal Commission, 'that prompts an average of five applications a week for the post of hangman ... reveals qualities of a sort that no State would wish to foster in its citizens.'

So long as capital punishment remains, the State cannot help fostering them. Dr Hunkin [formerly Bishop of Truro] may have been right in saying that it should be made clear to the executioner that his final act is an 'act comparable to that of an artilleryman bombarding the enemy in battle'. But I cannot believe that candidates for the job look at it quite like that, or that the conception would be easy to put across to them.

Whether the interest that trials and executions for murder sometimes arouse is more accurately described as 'morbid sensationalism' or a 'quasi-religious sense of awe' is a question that everyone will answer for himself; it is outside the range of evidence and argument. But that it sometimes leads to imitative crime is a fact. Such cases have undoubtedly occurred. 'They do not seem to be extremely numerous,' said Professor Thorsten Sellin, 'but the record is quite impressive nevertheless.' The details of some bizarre examples may be found in his evidence before the Royal Commission. Some men, tired of life, seem to have adopted murder as a devious means of ending it, one at least because he had conscientious scruples against suicide.

> I cite them [said the Professor] merely as a counterbalance to the other type of case which probably also exists, but which we know very little about—namely those that one could actually prove had been deterred by the specific knowledge that the death penalty threatened.

The late Sir Norwood East also said that he had known cases in this country in which insane persons have committed murder as a way of suicide. But he did not think that it affected the general question of the justification of capital punishment. 'I do not think', he said, 'anybody has ever proposed doing away with railways because insane people sometimes throw themselves under railway trains.' Even those who would not accept the implication that our death chambers and our railway trains were of comparable usefulness to the community might still agree that these cases must be so rare, and the mentality of the persons concerned so unusual, that this odd occasional result of capital punishment cannot be allowed any very great weight in assessing the objections to it. A more serious objection of the same sort is that for that strange class of persons known as 'psychopaths' the death penalty certainly acts sometimes as a challenge, giving an additional spice to their crimes.

> I have known many people [said Sir David Henderson] who have told me that they thought their destiny was to the gallows ... and I have known of people who have been influenced by the crime of others and have regarded it as a form of self-glorification ... I do not say that occurs frequently, but it has occurred in my experience.

Such are some of the reasons commonly put forward by those who maintain that, since capital punishment is a thing inherently evil, it is for those who would keep it to prove their case. It is perhaps improbable that any or all of them would persuade to that opinion anyone who does not hold it already. The fact is that fundamentally each side takes its stand on dogma. On the one side is the dogma that it is 'right' that one who takes life should forfeit his own. On the other side is the dogma that it is 'wrong' that the State should take life. They might be called the Old Testament and the New Testament dogmas. Neither is absolute: one side admits that not every murderer need be executed; the other that there may be circumstances in which it is justifiable for the State to take life. But it is essentially on this difference of dogma that the burden of proof turns, and dogma is a matter of faith, not of reason. It may be reinforced—or perhaps sometimes shaken—by facts that play on the emotions, but is unlikely to be affected by rational argument.

One of these dogmas seems to lead us into a blind alley. If the onus of proof lies with the abolitionists—if, in the present Home Secretary's words, it is for them to establish clearly that there is an alternative to capital punishment which is as satisfactory both as a deterrent and to the public conscience—and if evidence from abolitionist countries is rejected because they are 'different', then there is an end of the matter. It can never be clearly established except by trying it. There is nothing more to be said.

As there is something more I want to say, I shall assume that the onus is on the supporters of capital punishment, and I do so the more readily because, for reasons I shall explain, that is what I myself think. We will therefore return to the question of what evidence there is for the proposition that the death penalty alone can adequately serve the purposes of punishment—retribution, deterrence and reformation—in relation to the crime of murder. Since its deterrent value is what is most commonly claimed as its justification, it will be well to begin with that …

There is no reason to have a 100 per cent deterrent if an 80 per cent deterrent is sufficient to deter.

So the question we have now to examine is what evidence there is to support the contention that the extra 20 per cent of deterrency that we may assume to be possessed by the death penalty over imprisonment is necessary to public security. Twenty-five years ago, the Select Committee reported:

> Our prolonged examination of the situation in foreign countries has increasingly confirmed us in the assurance that capital punishment may be abolished in this country without endangering life or property or impairing the security of society.

But this verdict has always been discounted because the split within the Committee left the Report to be signed only by members who probably started as abolitionists. The question was re-examined with great thoroughness by the Royal Commission. They took much evidence about the experiences of foreign countries, many of which they visited. They also had the advantage of evidence from Professor Thorsten Sellin of the University of Pennsylvania, Secretary-General of the International Penal and Penitentiary Commission, whose study of the subject qualifies him to speak with perhaps unrivalled authority. The evidence they took about the deterrent value of capital punishment will be found summarised in a fifty-page appendix (no. 6) to their Report.

A story told to the Royal Commission by Professor Cornil, Professor of Criminal Law at the University of Brussels, provides a striking warning against assuming a causal connexion between executions and the murder rate. Professor Cornil told how in 1918 the Belgian countryside was terrorised by armed gangs who broke into farmhouses and murdered the farmers if they resisted. The members of one of the gangs were arrested and tried, and the five leaders were sentenced to death. (Death is still the legal punishment for murder in Belgium, but the sentence has not been carried out since 1863.) Contrary to the usual custom, the Attorney-General pressed for the death sentence on the leader of this gang to be carried out. 'His presence in the community could only be, at whatever moment, a cause of danger and scandal.' The Minister of Justice refused, and followed the usual practice of reprieving the man. The series of robberies then suddenly came to an end for some reason that has never been explained.

Professor Cornil adds:

> Whenever I relate this incident, I cannot refrain from pointing out how narrowly we escaped a grave danger. Suppose for a moment that this man ... had been put to death, and then that special crime had disappeared almost immediately. What a victory for the advocates of capital punishment! They certainly would not have hesitated to conclude that this improvement was due to the deterrent effect of capital punishment and it is quite probable that the death penalty ... would have been reinstated and retained for a long time.

(The reprieved murderer is said to be now a good citizen, leading a useful life.)

The Royal Commission's comment on the deterrent effect of the death penalty on habitual criminals were:

> It is in the nature of the case that little could be adduced in the way of specific evidence that criminals had been deterred by the death penalty. What an offender says on his arrest, probably some time after the commission of the crime, is not necessarily a valid indication of what was in his mind when he committed it; nor is it certain that a man who tells the police that he refrained from committing a murder because he might have to swing' for it was in fact deterred wholly or mainly by that fear. Moreover we received no evidence that the abolition of capital punishment in other countries had in fact led to the consequences apprehended by our witnesses in this country; though it is fair to add that any comparison between Great Britain and those countries, with the exception of Belgium, is vitiated by the differences in social and industrial conditions and in density of population. But we cannot treat lightly the considered and unanimous views of these experienced witnesses, who have had many years of contact with criminals ... It seems inherently probable that, if capital punishment has any unique value as a deterrent, it is here that its effect would be chiefly felt, and here that its value to the community would be greatest.

Even Lord Buckmaster admitted the argument was a strong one. But he added:

> It is a hypothetical argument, and I should have thought that those who brought it forward should justify their opinion by pointing out whether in the countries where capital punishment has been abolished, burglary being universal, the burglars have taken to carrying pistols or not. It is a matter which should be tested by facts, and I have never seen a case quoted showing in any such place where capital punishment was abolished, from that date burglars went about armed ... Both in the State of Illinois and in the State of New York murder is a capital offence. Do you suggest that this stops people from carrying pistols in Chicago or New York?

There is, as the Commission said, no evidence from other countries to justify this assumption. There is indeed evidence that of recent years a tendency for young criminals to carry arms has been apparent in more than one country. But this cannot be linked with the abolition of the death penalty. We have it here: Lord Waverley, in his evidence, remarked on the difference in this respect between what he called the 'new gangster type of criminal' and 'the orthodox professional of the old type'. It has occurred in Belgium also. The Public Prosecutor of Brussels, in a statement made to the Select Committee, said:

> The younger generation of burglars are more frequently armed than the older. But this new tendency has got nothing to do with the abandonment of the death penalty, as this new fashion of being armed has only grown up half a century after the death sentence has been practically abolished. This new fashion ... seems to have come from France; it seems to be a copy of what the young French burglars do, and you must not forget that in France the death penalty is executed.

Still, of the utilitarian arguments in favour of capital punishment, this is the most impressive. It has moreover the singular property of working both ways. If burglars do not carry arms, it must be the fear of death that deters them. If an outbreak of armed burglary occurs, it must be the worst possible moment to remove this deterrent. And the argument gains force by lending itself easily to rhetoric. 'Would you gamble with the lives of our policemen? Would you like our police forces to have to go about armed?' No one would wish to be accused of giving an affirmative answer to these questions.

Whether the abolition of capital punishment would mean, as is often asserted, that the police would have to be armed, is a question on which little direct evidence is available, since in most of the places where it has been abolished the police were already armed. Exceptions are Norway, Denmark, Queensland and New Zealand. In none of these did abolition lead to arming the police. In Denmark the police, who were unarmed up to the outbreak of the last war, were given pistols after it; but that was fifteen years after abolition, and there can have been no connexion between the two events.

We must now turn to the other category of evidence — that drawn from statistics. This is usually presented by abolitionist witnesses with the object of showing that abolition in other countries has not led to an increase in the number of homicides. As we have seen, it was the evidence of this sort given to the Select Committee in 1930 that convinced them that capital punishment could safely be abolished in this country ...

As was pointed out to the Royal Commission by one of their witnesses, the countries that have found the death penalty unnecessary are very varied. They include countries large and small, industrial and agricultural, countries of Latin, English-speaking, and other races, and countries in Europe, North and South America, Asia and Australia. The witness said he was puzzled why it should be supposed that Englishmen are so peculiarly brutal by nature that they need some special deterrence from murder, unnecessary elsewhere. In Belgium, the European country most like ours, the results are said to have been so conclusive that further argument has been silenced, and the lesson seems to have been learned that the best way of inculcating respect for human life is to refrain from taking it in the name of the law. Such, at least, was the testimony given to the Select Committee by the Belgian Minister of Justice.

Others who hesitate to accept the evidence point to the fact that nine American States, as well as New Zealand, reimposed the death penalty after making the experiment of doing without it. But this does not seem to justify the inference that murders had increased in consequence of abolition. The reasons for reimposition, so far as they can be ascertained, are given in Appendix 6 of the Commission's Report, and 'it appears that statistics have seldom been the main reason for restoration'.

Professor Sellin thought that the main reason was always the same; something happened which aroused popular feeling, probably quite irrationally, and the Legislature rushed into imposing the death penalty. He added:

> If we look at some of the States that abolished the death penalty round about 1914, we find that they restored it during the demobilisation period. There were things happening then, and it was assumed that it had been a mistake to abolish the penalty and they reintroduced it; yet the homicide rates of later years indicate that there was no relationship between the two.

Others again argue that doubt is thrown on the validity of the inferences drawn from abolitionist countries by the increase in crime that took place in France some fifty years ago when for some years French Presidents commuted almost all death sentences. But this, too, seems fallacious. The reasons for the increase were the subject of a special investigation by the French Minister of Justice, and the conclusion was that since the increase in non-capital homicides had been much greater than in those punishable with death, no argument could be drawn from the figures regarding the death penalty. The Report attributed the increase in crimes of violence almost entirely to the great increase in drunkenness at that time.

Of the 91 reprieved murderers serving sentences in 1952, no fewer than 79 were in the 'star' class; that is to say, people who were considered as not likely to be a bad influence. Twenty-two of them were in 'open' prisons, where 'there is no wall round the prison, no bars on the windows, and no guards are posted'. It may be said that this is natural enough when the worst murderers have been executed and is no guide to what might happen if all murderers were punished with imprisonment. But the murderers for whom a reprieve was not justified are not always those most likely to behave badly in prison. In countries where capital punishment has been abolished, the story is always the same:

> Murderers are no more likely than any other prisoners to commit acts of violence against officers or fellow-prisoners or to attempt escape; on the contrary, it would appear that in all countries murderers are on the whole better behaved than most prisoners.

Conclusion

Such are the facts and arguments that led me to the conclusion that capital punishment ought to be abolished. Before I explain why it seems to me the right verdict on the evidence, I must make clear that it is limited in two respects.

First, I am speaking only of the use of capital punishment as a penalty for murder in Great Britain in peace-time at the present day. Some of those who advocate its continuance have done so on the ground that we should be most unwise to try to do without it in some of our colonies. Others have argued that it would be illogical and hypocritical to abolish it in this country after having recently participated in an orgy of judicial execution in Germany. But unless one believes that it is always in all circumstances wrong for a State to take life—and I am not one of those who do—one may hold that capital punishment ought to be abolished for murder in Great Britain without committing oneself to any opinion on such questions as whether it can safely be dispensed with in primitive communities, or whether it was right to eliminate a set of gangsters who got control of a great nation and brought untold suffering on countless people, or whether death is a proper punishment for rebels and traitors, or whether reasons of State justified the beheading of Lady Jane Grey or Mary Queen of Scots, or whether shooting Admiral Byng was a suitable way of encouraging our other admirals. Quite different considerations enter into those questions.

Secondly, when I say that I think capital punishment 'ought' to be abolished, I must not be thought to be expressing any opinion on the question whether it would be prudent or practicable to abolish it without some further education of public opinion. I do not know. That is a question of politics, and I am not a politician. But I have watched the political game from a ringside seat for long enough to know how profoundly true is the old saying that politics is the art of the possible. Some have expressed the fear that, in the present state of public opinion, if shocking murders occurred soon after abolition, there might be outbreaks of lynching. I cannot believe that is a real risk. But it does seem possible that such murders might provoke here, as they have done elsewhere, a popular demand, perhaps politically irresistible, for the reimposition of the death penalty. That would indeed be unfortunate. No one will question the truth of the Royal Commission's remark that though reform of the criminal law ought sometimes to give a lead to public opinion, it is dangerous to move too far in advance of it. How far in advance it can risk being is a practical question, not one of principle. Some very experienced politicians—Lord Templewood and Mr Chuter Ede for instance—think that the public are ready to follow a bold lead. I hope they are right.

I have previously suggested that the conclusion to which one will be led by the evidence depends essentially on where one thinks the burden of proof lies, and that the question of where the burden of proof lies depends on which of two opposite dogmas one accepts. Those dogmas are reached emotionally by faith rather than intellectually by reason, and it is idle to argue which is 'right'. All I can say is that to me what I have called the 'Old Testament' dogma of 'a life for a life' makes less appeal emotionally than does the 'New Testament' dogma, which forbids the taking of life by way of retribution. For me, therefore, the burden of proof lies with the supporters of capital punishment.

It would be difficult to say just what it was that converted me to this view; it was the cumulative effect of many things, including such considerations as the right approach for a professedly Christian people, the manifestly objectionable, not to say repulsive, features of capital punishment and the morbid interest they excite, the possibility, however small, of hanging an innocent man and the large part that the element of vengeance seems to play in the demand for capital punishment. Perhaps the turning-point was when I learned what a large number of applications there were for the post of hangman. Any State institution, I thought, that inspires ambitions of that sort in its citizens, and satisfies some of them, though it does not necessarily stand condemned, surely does need to justify itself on utilitarian grounds.

Even though the dogma of 'a life for a life' may settle the question for those who believe in it, and make utilitarian reasons superfluous, the rational arguments will no doubt continue to be much canvassed. As I have said, they are felt to be more respectable than the emotional ones. It is clear from the opinions cited earlier that the principal rational arguments used in favour of the death penalty are four. One is that public opinion demands it. A second is that to punish all murderers by imprisonment, some of them for a very long time, would present insuperable difficulties to the prison authorities. A third is that death is a more humane punishment than long imprisonment. A fourth is that if the deterrent effect of the death penalty were removed more murders would be committed.

The argument that popular opinion demands the death penalty is not really a rational argument; it takes us back into the realm of dogma. It may be a practical reason why the death penalty cannot be got rid of, but it is not a rational justification of it unless it is based on rational grounds. So far as it is possible to judge, popular opinion in favour of the death penalty is not in the main based on rational grounds; it rests in the main on acceptance of the dogma that death is the only fitting retribution for murder.

As to the argument that insuperable difficulties would be created for the prison authorities, all that need be said is that this does not happen in countries that have abolished capital punishment, and the Home Office, who ought to know, do not think it would happen here.

The argument that death is more humane than long imprisonment has been given unmerited prominence by what Sir Alexander Paterson said about it in the very different prison conditions of twenty-five years ago. It is a protean argument, which can be made to do all sorts of things. Beccaria used it in favour of abolition; for, he said, imprisonment would be a greater deterrent: the continued example of a man deprived of his liberty was a much more powerful preventive than the fear of death. On the other hand, a correspondent writing recently to a daily newspaper carried the argument to surprising lengths as a reason for retaining capital punishment: to abolish it, he said, would be very unfair to murderers; he understood that most of them would welcome death in expiation of their crimes, and they ought not to be denied the right to die. That long imprisonment is unquestionably a very dreadful thing may no doubt serve as a partial counter to anyone who bases the case for abolition on its excessive cruelty to the offender, but it cannot be made to do much more. As an argument for maintaining capital punishment it does not seem to deserve any higher place than Sir Winston Churchill gave it when he warned the House of Commons not to forget that, at any rate in some cases, the gulf between imprisonment and death was not nearly as wide as some people thought. The dreadfulness of long imprisonment has to be weighed against the fact that death takes away all opportunity of reformation, and I should not myself feel any doubt about the side to which the scales inclined.

There remains the argument that without the uniquely deterrent value of capital punishment more murders would be committed. This is the only serious utilitarian argument in favour of capital punishment, and the one on which thoughtful supporters of it almost wholly rely. It is also the argument that can be put most readily to the test of evidence in the proper sense of the word; and, as we have seen, such evidence as there is goes to show that the abolition of capital punishment does not in fact have this result.

But I have little doubt that, in the last resort, it is emotion rather than reason that will decide the issue. To quote Professor Sellin once more:

The question whether the death penalty is to be dropped, retained or instituted is not dependent on the evidence as to its utilitarian effects, but on the strength of popular beliefs and sentiments not easily influenced by such evidence. When a people no longer likes the death penalty for murderers it will be removed, no matter what may happen to the homicide rates.

9

The unique deterrent

Gerald Gardiner

Gerald Gardiner, Baron Gardiner of Kittisford (1900–1990), was educated at Harrow and Oxford. After serving in World War I, he was called to the Bar in 1925 and in 1958 became chairman of the General Council of the Bar. He served for eleven years on the Lord Chancellor's law reform committee, edited *Law Reform NOW* (1963), and was joint chairman of the National Campaign for the Abolition of Capital Punishment. Created a life peer in 1963, he became Lord Chancellor of Great Britain in the Wilson government of 1964–70.

The following extracts are from *Capital Punishment as a Deterrent: and the Alternative* (1956).

* * *

There is, of course, a distinction between murder and those offences from which capital punishment was removed in the last century. In the case of murder, death is less likely to operate as a unique deterrent. If capital punishment was not found in practice to have a greater deterrent effect than a long sentence of imprisonment to deter a man from stealing a sheep, it is less likely that it has such an effect to deter a man from committing murder. If capital punishment did not prove to have the exceptional quality as a deterrent which it was claimed to have in the case of those crimes which are generally premeditated, it is less likely to have such an effect in the case of that crime which is usually less premeditated than any other crime.

It is therefore clear from our own experience in England that,

85

whatever one might have thought in theory, the facts show that it is not true to say that capital punishment is in practice a greater deterrent than other forms of severe punishment, and that there is consequently no foundation for the assumption, so often made in the past, and on every occasion shown by experience to be unfounded, that its abolition would lead to an increase in the crime.

The movement against capital punishment in the last century was almost entirely due to Samuel Romilly. All through the great debates of 1808–18 he substantially confined himself to two arguments:

1. The chief deterrent to crime is not barbarity of punishment but certainty of conviction. The former only results in decreasing the latter and is therefore futile.
2. Brutal punishments accustom the people to brutality and themselves tend to increase crimes of violence: violence breeds violence.

Romilly must have been one of the first public men to appreciate the effect of State sadism, and it would perhaps be as well to remember that while the extreme disorder of sadism in the aggressive psychopath is plain enough, there is a little of this disorder in all of us, high and low. History records more than one example of a judge whom we now recognise as having suffered from this disorder. And as to the effect of the State's example, John Bright said long ago:

A deep reverence for human life is worth more than a thousand executions in the prevention of murder; it is, in fact, the great security of human life. The law of capital punishment, whilst pretending to support this reverence, does in fact tend to destroy it.

The movement against capital punishment in this century was almost entirely due to Roy Calvert, a Quaker, who largely confined himself to the same two arguments except that he was able to show, as Romilly could not, that what Romilly had said would be the consequence of abolishing capital punishment had in fact happened, not only here but wherever in the world capital punishment had been abolished.

It may be worthwhile considering at this point why the judges were wrong. Whatever we may think of their humanity, they were not to be blamed for the view which they took as to what the result of abolition would be, because at that time—unlike the present time—there was no evidence whatever as to what actually happened when capital punishment was abolished for any offence, because it had never been done: it was anyone's guess.

If a judge expresses the opinion, e.g. that the degree of violence in crimes of violence has increased, he is expressing an opinion on a matter which his office makes him peculiarly well qualified to judge: the judges go all over the country hearing the full facts as to the actual crimes committed. But for some reason the House of Lords, and the public generally, have always assumed that the judges are also experts on the question of deterrence.

When one is considering deterrence against crime, one is considering e.g. Snooks, who was thinking of doing a housebreaking 'job', but what with this, and what with that, he decided not to. The question is 'Why?' Snooks is the man the judge never sees. The judges never see those who are deterred, and it is respectfully suggested that there is nothing in the training or Court experience of judges, who are not required to make any study of penology, and some of whom have never visited a prison, which enables them, any better than the reader, to know what are those things in the hearts and minds of men and women which deter them from committing criminal offences. As a Select Committee appointed to consider these questions in 1819 said in their Report:

> Highly as the Committee esteem and respect the judges, it is not from them that the most accurate and satisfactory evidence of the effect of the penal law may reasonably be expected. They only see the exterior of criminal proceedings after they are brought into a Court of Justice. Of the cases which never appear there, and of the causes which prevent their appearance, they can know nothing … From any opportunity of observing the influence of punishment upon those classes of men among whom malefactors are most commonly found, the judges are, by their stations and duties, placed at a great distance.

The central conflict in the field of penal reform during the last 150 years has been whether, as the judges have always asserted, the chief deterrent to crime is severity of punishment, or whether, as Romilly and other students of penology have always asserted, the chief deterrent to crime is certainty of conviction. It is suggested that experience has increasingly shown that Romilly was right, and that if the conviction rate—that is to say the proportion of convictions to crimes known to the police goes up, crime goes down; if the conviction rate goes down, crime goes up. As a matter of ordinary common sense it should not be surprising to learn that what really decides Snooks, apart from his conscience and how he was brought up by his father and mother to know the difference between right and wrong, is whether, on the one hand, he thinks that if he does the 'job' he will 'get away with it'; or whether, on the other hand, he thinks that if he does it he will be caught and punished.

This does not, of course, mean that the degree of punishment has no deterrent effect. Of course it has. What it does mean is that the actual degree of punishment is of relatively little importance compared with the degree of certainty of conviction. A very strong committee from the Council of the British Medical Association said to the Royal Commission:

> With the present degree of development of scientific study of the mind and conduct, science has taught us that human motivation is so complex, so often deep and semiconscious or unconscious, that we would suggest to you that a really thorough scientific inquiry into the efficacy of the deterrent theory of punishment, which is so widely held today, might well bear good fruit, and possibly surprising results. The rather easy and facile assumption that the possibility of severe pains and penalties if a certain action is done is a powerful deterrent, may well be proved to be not as valid as is so widely thought.

It may be so. It is, however, sufficient to rely on the fact that wherever it can be tested by facts, experience has shown that in the field of crime the degree of prospect of conviction is of much more importance than the degree of punishment. Archbishop Temple, who understood human nature, put the point in this way:

> Recent experience has shown that in many cases public opinion revolts against the execution of condemned criminals, and indeed the proportion of reprieves tends steadily to increase. Moreover, observation seems to leave no doubt with regard to the chief quality of effectiveness in deterrent punishment. It is not the severity of the penalty inflicted, but the certainty both of detection and of the exaction of the penalty required by law, whatever this may be. If then, as seems unquestionable, we have reached a stage where the expectation of execution has been rendered definitely uncertain, so that there is always hope of reprieve, the death penalty will be less deterrent than a life sentence without the possibility of reprieve. No doubt it is logically absurd to be more deterred by certain imprisonment for life than by possible execution with life imprisonment as the alternative; but few men are governed by logic, and criminals less than most: and as a matter of psychology the introduction of uncertainty, even though it only be as between death and a life sentence, weakens the deterrent influence of the present law as compared with a life sentence certain to take effect.
>
> The fact that a man sentenced for life may gain his discharge after a long period does not have this effect of uncertainty, because his doing so is conditional upon something else altogether—namely, future good conduct. What is required for effective deterrence is that there shall be prescribed for the crime a penalty which will then and there be inflicted. Our modern sentiment has robbed the death penalty of its chief defence. This is of great importance when we remember that all punishment should contain the remedial or reformative element, for, as has been said, this element is at its minimum in the death penalty. Unless, therefore, it can be pleaded that that penalty is uniquely deterrent, which in modern conditions it is not, the case against it seems overwhelming.

History, it is suggested, shows that, as civilisation advances, in spite of many arrests and setbacks, a punishment which had seemed a proper one to an earlier generation begins to be felt by a gradually increasing number of good citizens to be out of accord with the standard of civilisation reached by their country. It is increasingly felt to be 'brutal', 'barbaric'. History shows, too, that at this point those who consider that severity of punishment is the chief deterrent to crime and wish to keep the punishment in question on that ground, find themselves in a dilemma which they have rarely been prepared to face. If, on the one hand, they insist on the punishment in question being widely used, the sooner the increasing dislike of it is likely to result in its complete abolition. If, on the other hand, they agree to its being used more sparingly, they gravely weaken their own argument, because the less it is used the less its deterrent effect will be. From this dilemma there is no escape.

It is, however, only right to say that some of the strongest supporters of capital punishment faced the dilemma boldly when before the Royal Commission, e.g. Mr Justice Humphreys saying:

> The mere retention on the Statute Book of the death sentence as the only one to be passed upon a conviction for murder, has in my opinion no deterrent effect at all. On the other hand, the practical certainty that if caught and convicted of murder, he will lose his life, would I think deter many criminals from carrying and using lethal weapons or from resorting to violence upon apprehension.

Romilly would have entirely agreed with this. When, however, Mr Justice Humphreys went on, 'the Prerogative of Mercy should be exercised only in very exceptional cases', and when the Lord Chief Justice also expressed the view that there were too many reprieves—that is to say that there ought to be more hanging and not less—they were following their view to its logical conclusion but to one which, it is respectfully suggested, is increasingly impractical in the existing climate of opinion.

The fact is that we are now in that unsatisfactory, and even dangerous, half-way stage in which the intelligent murderer knows that the long odds are that he will not be hanged—there being now about 12 executions a year in respect of about 145 murders. This is not merely because of an increase in the percentage of reprieves. It is primarily because, as has happened before, the increasing public dislike of a punishment increasingly regarded as barbaric makes juries reluctant to convict, which again decreases the conviction rate and consequently the deterrent effect of any punishment at all. We have not yet reached the point described before the Royal Commission of 1866 where criminals were said to prefer to be indicted capitally because the chance of getting off was so much greater. Nevertheless, the position in relation to murder charges is serious, and is yearly growing more serious. As the Home Office said in 1924:

> In consequence of the strong proofs of guilt necessary for conviction of crimes punishable by death, the proportion of acquittals for murder is higher than for most other crimes, and an acquittal in such cases does not necessarily imply failure to detect the perpetrator of the crime.

If this was true in 1924, it is even more true today with the increase in the dislike of the penalty. Among the first 10,000 cards and letters received by the National Campaign when it first started, a common enquiry was whether one who felt strongly about the use of death as a punishment ought to refuse to serve on a jury in such a case, or ought to serve and refuse in any circumstances to agree to a conviction. Naturally no prosecution for murder takes place unless the prosecuting authority is satisfied that the charge ought to be made. Yet, if given almost any opportunity, juries find verdicts of insanity, or manslaughter, or acquit. As the Lord Chief Justice said to the Royal Commission: 'You get verdicts of manslaughter sometimes in quite astonishing cases.' Apart from verdicts of insanity and manslaughter, the actual proportion of acquittals to convictions in murder trials in 1952–54 inclusive was as high as one to four.

No one suggests that there is any cause for all this except the increasing dislike of jurymen to bring in a verdict which may mean hanging. Even the compromise 'Guilty with a strong recommendation to mercy' might be less frequent if jurymen, who commonly think that the effect will be that the accused will not then be hanged, were aware of the fact that out of 75 men recommended to mercy by juries in 1940–49, 24 were nevertheless hanged. The only way to stop verdicts of manslaughter which should be murder, to stop juries sending sane men to Broadmoor, and to increase the conviction rate to the level which the facts justify, is to abolish capital punishment.

It is usually thought to be sensible to learn by one's own experience, and our own experience of what happened here when we abolished capital punishment here for other offences, in comparison with what we had been told the results would be, should be sufficient. It is an experience of exactly the same warnings, in exactly the same terms, by the same type of mind, as are made today of the consequences of abolition, followed by facts which proved that, when put to the test, those warnings were without foundation. It is said, however, that one or two freak countries have actually abolished capital punishment for murder, and that therefore we ought to look and see what has actually happened in those countries. One would have thought that our own experience at home would have been quite sufficient. However, let us look and see whether the experience of other countries has been the same as ours or different from ours.

Experience abroad

Capital punishment for murder has been abolished in Austria (1950), Belgium (1863), Denmark (1930), Finland (1949), Western Germany (1949), Holland (1870), Iceland (1944), Israel (1954), Italy (1948), Luxembourg (1822), Norway (1905), Portugal (1867), Sweden (1921), Switzerland (1942), and in 12 other countries; and in Nepal (1931); Travancore (1944); Queensland (1922); and in Maine (1887), Michigan (1847), Minnesota (1911), North Dakota (1895), Rhode Island (1852), and Wisconsin (1853) in the United States. Some countries in fact stopped executions long before formal abolition, e.g. Denmark has had no execution since 1892. There is no certainty as to what the position is in countries behind the Iron Curtain. In the United States there is no national policy; the question is one of State Law and the States mentioned above have abolished it while others have retained it. Apart from the British, therefore, France and Spain are the only Western civilised countries which retain capital punishment, France being the only other Western democracy.

There have now been two long and patient enquiries into the

consequences of abolishing capital punishment in the greater part of the civilised world—the Select Committee of 1929–30, and the Royal Commission of 1949–53. In their Report the Select Committee said:

> Our prolonged examination of the situation in foreign countries has increasingly confirmed us in the assurance that capital punishment may be abolished in this country without endangering life or property or impairing the security of Society.

Is there no alternative?

There are some who raise difficulties about the alternative punishment who would in any case support capital punishment on other grounds. There are others who know that the abolition of capital punishment for any offence, including murder, has never resulted in an increase in the crime, but are nevertheless genuinely hesitant about supporting its abolition for murder because they feel that men like Haigh and Heath could never safely be released, and that it would really be kinder to such men to despatch them as mercifully as we can rather than to leave them in prison in conditions in which they would tend to deteriorate after ten or twenty years.

To some it may be sufficient answer to point out that this is exactly what was said in the last century as an argument against the abolition of capital punishment for those crimes from which it was then abolished. Indeed, one of the principal reasons advanced in the last century for opposing the abolition of capital punishment for minor offences was that, in spite of both imprisonment and transportation, there was no satisfactory alternative punishment. Thus, in a debate on the Privately Stealing Bill in 1810, a Member asked:

> If the punishment in use were not to be retained, where would the learned and honourable gentleman [Sir Samuel Romilly] seek for others to be substituted for them?

In the debate on the 'Shoplifting' Bill in the same year, transportation was said by the then Chief Justice to be 'but a summer's airing by emigration to a warmer climate'. In an 1820 debate the Earl of Liverpool said:

> A great defect in our criminal legislation was one of a secondary punishment that might be substituted for the terror of death ... The terror of the pain of transportation for life just amounted to nothing at all.

Sir Robert Peel, in a debate in 1832, thought the secondary punishments of imprisonment and transportation quite insufficient. In the same year, Lord Eldon, a former Lord Chancellor, said:

> It was no easy task to find an appropriate secondary punishment; for that had employed his thoughts and attention for twenty-five years and he never could find what he considered a proper secondary punishment.

And in a debate in 1834 to abolish capital punishment for stealing a letter, the Duke of Richmond said:

> He thought that their Lordships ought not to abolish capital punishment for stealing letters until some good mode of secondary punishment had been adopted.

To others, who are not satisfied that the argument may not be sound now, even if it was proved not to be sound in the last century, it may be a sufficient answer that so large a majority of what are ordinarily regarded as the civilised countries of the world, which have abolished capital punishment, have not in practice found that the alternative punishment gives rise to any real difficulty.

The Norwegians, the Swiss, the Swedes and the Dutch are not unlike us. Of course they are foreigners, but are they not as civilised as we are? What is it that we fear? Is it supposed that these nations keep such men in solitary confinement, or in inhuman conditions, or for such periods that they deteriorate, when it is well known, for example, that the Scandinavian prison system is the best in the world? Is it feared that released men roam these countries committing further murders? No released murderer in any of these countries has ever committed a further murder.

Indeed, those who contend that a sentence of imprisonment for life is worse than death, ought logically to advocate that we ought to reprieve those we now hang, and hang those we now reprieve.

There are some, however, who always feel that what has proved practicable and beneficial in most civilised countries is likely to raise insuperable difficulties in England. This applies particularly in the field of law. That distinguished Judge, Mr Justice Frankfurter of the Supreme Court of the United States, when giving evidence before the Royal Commission, said:

> Nothing is more true of my profession than that the most eminent among them, for 100 years, have testified with complete confidence that something is impossible which, once it is introduced, is found to be very easy of administration.
>
> The history of legal procedure is the history of the rejection of reasonable and civilised standards in the administration of law by most eminent judges and leading practitioners. That is true of your country and mine. That is true of civil law and criminal law . . . Every effort to effect improving changes is resisted on the assumption that man's ultimate wisdom is to be found in the legal system as at the date on which you try to make a change.

To such people it may be a sufficient answer that the Select Committee obtained all the evidence on this point from the Home Office, prison governors, and others. They were of the opinion that the alternative would not be found in practice to give rise to any real problem.

To any who are not satisfied that similar fears raised in the last century, and then proved groundless, might not have substance now, and who feel unable to act on the experience of most of the civilised world, and who feel that the Report of the Select Committee was now some years ago, it may be a sufficient answer that the Royal Commission were expressly asked to report,

For how long and under what conditions persons who would otherwise have been liable to suffer capital punishment should be detained, and what changes in the existing law and the prison system would be required; and to enquire into and take account of the position in those countries whose experience and practice may throw light on these questions.

The Home Office evidence before the Commission was that:

Developments in prison administration in the last 20 years have materially altered the conditions of confinement for prisoners serving long sentences. While, therefore, the Commissioners remain of the opinion expressed (before the Select Committee) that a very long sentence of imprisonment is and must always be a dreadful thing, they do not consider that in present conditions its effect on prisoners would be such that it ought not to be contemplated.

The Royal Commission, having spent a long time enquiring into the whole position, confirmed the view of the Select Committee.

There may remain, however, some who are not prepared to accept either our own previous experience, or the experience of other countries, or the findings of any Committee or Commission, but want to form their own opinion on the facts.

A difficulty arises in that the relevant facts, which occupy 25 closely printed pages of the Royal Commission's Report, as well as three Appendices, are both voluminous and not at all easy to summarise. It might be thought that all that is necessary is to see what would in fact happen to those who are now hanged, and who must therefore be the 'worst' murderers. As, however, will be shown, many of those who are now hanged are in fact among those whom it would be easiest to reform. While, therefore, it is appreciated that those of the type of Haigh and Heath are the crux of the problem, it is necessary to begin by considering the position of reprieved murderers in general.

The following summary of the more material facts is primarily based on the Home Office evidence before the Royal Commission.

1. A sentence of imprisonment for life is never carried out literally.

Persons serving life sentences have died in prison before a definite term has been set to their sentences, but there is no case recorded in which it has been decided that a person shall be kept in prison until he dies. The actual periods are determined by the Secretary of State in accordance with the circumstances of the individual case. Each is reviewed at least every four years. The basic principle was thus stated by the Home Office.

> The punishment must be sufficient to deter others and to be accepted by public opinion as an adequate vindication of the law: it ought not to suggest that the crime of murder is regarded lightly by the State or can be put on the same level with other crimes. It is therefore desirable to grade the terms as far as possible according to the degree of culpability in each case. Account must also be taken of the length of sentences imposed by the Courts for other offences.

Subject to this, weight is given to the character and behaviour of the prisoner and to the likelihood of his committing further crimes of violence.

2. The Royal Commission say in their Report:

> There is a popular belief that prisoners serving a life sentence after conviction of murder form a specially troublesome and dangerous class. That is not so. Most find themselves in prison because they have yielded to temptation under the pressure of a combination of circumstances unlikely to recur. 'Taking murderers as a class,' said one witness, 'there are a considerable number who are first offenders and who are not people of criminal tendencies. The murder is in many cases their first offence against the law. Previous to that they were law-abiding citizens and their general tenor of life is still to be law-abiding.'
>
> Many other witnesses with experience of prison conditions said the same thing. It is true that they were speaking of the state of affairs today, when the crimes of murderers serving sentences of imprisonment have all been of a sort that justified the commutation of the death sentence. But the Home Office, giving evidence to the Select Committee of 1930,

expressed the opinion that, even if capital punishment were abolished, the greater number of prisoners serving sentences for murder would still be unlikely to 'give any exceptional trouble', though there would no doubt be some increase in that difficult class of prisoners 'who have not only committed murder but have been of criminal habits or tendencies, or are of a generally violent and insubordinate or sullen and morose temperament'.

This accords with the experience of countries where capital punishment has been abolished; the evidence given to us in the countries we visited, and the information we received from others, were uniformly to the effect that murderers are no more likely than any other prisoners to commit acts of violence against officers or fellow prisoners or to attempt to escape; on the contrary it would appear that in all countries murderers are, on the whole, better behaved than most prisoners. It must be remembered too that prisoners serving life sentences have a special incentive to good behaviour, since the time they have in fact to serve depends so largely on it.

An extreme form of this misconception is the belief that relaxation of the death penalty would mean the punishment by solitary confinement of some of those who would otherwise have been executed … It will be enough to say that in no countries we visited where capital punishment has been abolished or suspended did we find that solitary confinement was still employed as part of the sentence for the prisoner's crime. Neither in Britain nor in most other countries are persons convicted of murder subjected to prison conditions different in any way from those of other long term prisoners.

3. As the Home Office said to the Royal Commission, 'It is a rare thing to find that a reprieved murderer had been guilty of any previous crime of violence.'

The idea that those who are now hanged consist of a particularly dangerous class is equally unfounded. They do include a particularly dangerous class, but they also include many who fall into the general category described above, e.g. it was of Mrs Thompson, of R. v. Bywaters and Thompson (1922), that her prison governor said, 'I think if she had been spared she could have become a very good woman.' Ruth Ellis was one of the type whom the Royal Commission described as 'yielding to temptation under a combination of circumstances unlikely to recur'.

4. In the twenty years 1930 to 1949, 182 prisoners convicted of murder and reprieved were released, and the large majority of them are now good citizens.

A large proportion of reprieved murderers are in the Star class. In August 1952 these numbered 82 out of a total of 91. Many of them are today in open camp prisons without locks, bolts or bars. As the Royal Commission said: 'The great majority of reprieved murderers serve part of their sentence — often a large part — in open prisons.'

5. The evidence before the Royal Commission given by the Central After-Care Association was that in England and Wales 156 life sentence prisoners were discharged to their care during the years 1934 to 1948, of whom 127 had had no previous conviction, and that only 16 of these prisoners had to the knowledge of the Association been reconvicted since release, and only one of them had been convicted of a further crime of violence. This one exceptional case was so extraordinary as to require a separate paragraph.

This point is one of some importance because in the debate in the House of Lords in 1948 Lord Teviot said:

> With regard to the imposition of fifteen years' imprisonment, I understand that there are many cases where men have come out and have committed the same offence again. For that reason I feel that we should continue the present practice.

The fact is that in all our long history there is only one case in which a reprieved and released murderer has been convicted of a further murder. This was Walter Rowland (1947). This is also the one case of a subsequent conviction for violence, referred to above. It is, however, a matter of grave doubt whether Rowland did in fact commit this murder for which he was hanged. Such a statement should not be lightly made.

The facts are shortly as follows. A woman was killed by being struck on the head with a hammer. The question was one of identity. On his conviction Rowland protested his complete innocence from the dock, saying:

Somewhere there is a person who knows that I stand here today an innocent man. The killing of this woman was a terrible crime, but there is a worse crime being committed now, my Lord, because someone with the knowledge of this crime is seeing me sentenced today for a crime I did not commit. I have a firm belief that one day it will be proved in God's own time that I am totally innocent of this charge, and the day will come when this case will be quoted in the courts of this country to show what can happen to a man in a case of mistaken identity. I am going to face what lies before me with the fortitude and calm that only a clear conscience can give. That is all I have got to say, my Lord.

While he was in the condemned cell another man, David Ware, confessed that it was in fact he who had committed the murder, making three separate confessions, one of which was in considerable detail. The Court of Criminal Appeal, on Rowland's appeal, refused to allow Ware to be called as a witness. The Home Secretary ordered an enquiry to be held by a barrister in private. The barrister reported that Ware had withdrawn his confession. So Rowland was hanged.

This, however, was not quite the end of the story. Four years later Ware walked into a Police Station saying that he had killed a woman by hitting her over the head with a hammer. 'I do not know what is the matter with me. I keep on having an urge to hit women on the head.' He had in fact attempted so to murder a woman. He was charged with her attempted murder but found to be insane. It is on these facts that it is suggested that it is a matter of grave doubt whether Rowland did in fact commit the murder for which he was hanged. No other reprieved and released murderer in our history has ever even been convicted of a further such offence, nor has any reprieved murderer ever killed a prison warder.

For purposes of very rough classification murderers may be divided into the insane, others of abnormal mind (and particularly the aggressive psychopath), and the remainder. The 'remainder' formed the subject matter of the preceding paragraphs. Some of them are included among those now hanged. It will be seen from what has been said that, if not hanged, they would represent no special problem or difficulty.

The insane would be sent to Broadmoor, as now, because it has for centuries been part of the Common Law of England that no insane person should be hanged. Before, however, considering the last category—others of abnormal mind—it is essential to be quite clear in our minds whether we do or do not agree that the Common Law of England is right on this point. Before the Royal Commission the Lord Chief Justice was asked about the case of Ley (1947), who was found to be insane, and whom the Lord Chief Justice agreed was insane, 'I had no doubt that the prisoner was insane; his whole conduct, including his demeanour and evidence at the trial, showed a typical case of paranoia'. But when asked 'To revert to the case of Ley, I suppose you would not have wished that man to hang? You would not think it proper that he should hang?' the Lord Chief Justice said 'I should have thought it was very proper that he should have been hanged'.

The Royal Commission say in their Report:

We make one fundamental assumption, which we should hardly have thought it necessary to state explicitly if it had not lately been questioned in some quarters. It has for centuries been recognised that, if a person was, at the time of his unlawful act, mentally so disordered that it would be unreasonable to impute guilt to him, he ought not to be held liable to conviction and punishment under the criminal law. Views have changed and opinions have differed, as they differ now, about the standards to be applied in deciding whether an individual should be exempted from criminal responsibility for this reason; but the principle has been accepted without question. Recently, however, the suggestion has sometimes been made that the insane murderer should be punished equally with the sane, or that, although he ought not to be executed as a punishment, he should be painlessly exterminated as a measure of social hygiene. The argument is in each case the same—that his continued existence will be of no benefit to himself, and that he will be not only a useless burden, but also a potential danger to the community, since there is always a risk that he may escape and commit another crime. Such doctrines have been preached and practised in National-Socialist Germany, but they are repugnant to the moral traditions of Western civilisation and we are confident that they would be unhesitatingly rejected by the great majority of the population of this country. We assume the continuance of the ancient and humane principle that has long formed part of our common law.

This is not a matter for argument because it is an ethical question. But it is necessary for us to be clear whether we agree with the Common Law of England that insane men and women ought not to be hanged, or whether we agree with Fascist and Communist philosophy that it is right to 'liquidate' or 'destroy' men and women, not as a punishment for a crime for which they have responsibility, but as a measure of social hygiene if the government thinks fit.

When considering those of abnormal mind, the aggressive psychopath, like Haigh and Heath, is of course the crux of the problem. Such men are highly dangerous to the community. Sir David Henderson, a considerable authority on psychopaths, thus described them to the Royal Commission:

> They fail lo appreciate reality, they are fickle, changeable, lack persistence of effort and are unable to profit by experience or punishment. They are dangerous when frustrated. They are devoid of affection, are cold, heartless, callous, cynical, and show a lack of judgement and forethought which is almost beyond belief. They may be adult in years, but emotionally they remain as dangerous children whose conduct may revert to a primitive, sub-human level. Neville Heath and John George Haigh are extreme examples. We are dealing with conduct abnormality of such a degree and type as to constitute the greatest potential danger to the individual and his victim.

When Romilly was told that capital punishment ought not to be abolished because there was no satisfactory alternative, he always replied that if there was no satisfactory alternative it was about time we improved our prison system.

For many years the government has been urged by students of penology to provide an institution in effect a half-way house between a mental hospital and a prison—where those of abnormal mind, and particularly the aggressive psychopath, could be kept with safety, and which would be a research institute for such cases, and in which they could be kept in conditions in which they would not deteriorate as they might do if kept in prison. Such institutions already exist in several countries which have abolished capital punishment, and this advice was supported in 1949 by the Home Office Advisory Council on the Treatment of Offenders, who then recommended its adoption to the Home Secretary, and it was endorsed by the Select Committee on Estimates in 1952. At last this advice has been accepted by the government and such an institution is now to be built. It is to this institute that those of abnormal mind, and particularly the aggressive psychopath, ought to be sent. Until the building is ready, aggressive psychopaths should be placed in a separate wing at Broadmoor.

There are at least four good reasons why the aggressive psychopath and similar criminals ought not to be hanged.

1. While there is not as yet any known speedy psychiatric cure, they tend to lose their aggressive impulse in middle age and it cannot, therefore, be said of any of them that he would require to be detained, even in such an institution, for life.

2. We are living in days in which, as we ourselves know, a gibbering lunatic in an asylum, hearing voices and muttering away to himself, may with insulin treatment, electric shock treatment, leucotomy, drug therapy and other forms of medical treatment, be back with his family three years later, living a reasonably normal life. Apart, therefore, from his tendency to grow out of his aggressive impulses, it is quite impossible to say that the psychopath can never be cured.

3. It is true that at present we know little about the treatment of extreme aggressive psychopaths, but this is partly because we hang the worst of them, and as long as we go on hanging

them we shall not add sufficiently to our medical knowledge
about them. If we had hanged the insane, the same would have
been true about insanity.

4.   It is not their fault that they are psychopaths and such
      men have little responsibility for their crimes. As Sir David
      Henderson said to the Royal Commission:

> It is essentially constitutional, something which is inborn, something
> which is akin to the lack of intellectual development which characterises
> the mental defective … If our ethical code feels justified in sending
> them to the gallows then let it be so, but at the same time let us clearly
> understand that such persons are driven by what may be called their
> collective unconscious to deeds of violence which are as uncontrollable
> as a tidal wave.

If we are clear that it is wrong to hang the insane who may be
homicidal and highly dangerous, it is difficult to say that it is not
wrong to hang the aggressive psychopath. Who are we to kill men
and women on the ground that we have decided that they would be
happier dead?

The Home Secretary appears lately to have adopted a practice of
no longer hanging so many aggressive psychopaths, influenced no
doubt by the evidence about them before the Royal Commission. Yet
the supporters of capital punishment make no enquiry as to what is
being done with them.

It is suggested that even in the case of the aggressive psychopath
hanging ought to be abolished because the fact is that we just do
not know enough about any man or woman to be able to say with
certainty either that they can never be restored to mental health,
or that they are permanently incapable of reformation. It is very
respectfully suggested that the statement of the Lord Chief Justice
in the 1948 debate in the House of Lords: 'In the sort of cases
which I have instanced to your Lordships, I feel that no question
of reformation can in any possible circumstances arise', is to make
an assumption which does less than justice either to the medical
profession or to God.

The Royal Commission's finding was:

> Our conclusions, then, on this part of our terms of reference are that
> persons not mentally abnormal who would otherwise have been liable to
> suffer capital punishment could suitably be detained in the conditions now
> found in long-term prisons in England and Scotland, though we think
> that these admit of some improvements; that the principles now followed
> by the Secretaries of State in determining the actual length of detention
> in each case are in general appropriate for the purposes of punishment,
> deterrence and the protection of the public, without undue risk of causing
> moral and physical deterioration in the prisoner; and that if, in exceptional
> cases an exceptionally long period of detention is called for, the additional
> risk of such consequences ought not to be held to rule it out.

They further recommended that the mentally abnormal should
be sent to an institution of the kind referred to above, where the
conditions of life would be quite different to prison conditions—a
course justified by the small degree of responsibility which the
psychopath has for his actions.

If, therefore, capital punishment was abolished in England there
are many who are now hanged who would raise no problem at all;
the insane would be dealt with as they are at present; and those of
disordered mind, of whom the aggressive psychopath is the extreme
example, would be kept in tolerable conditions, leaving it, as it is
now, to the Prison Commissioners to say when they can safely be
released. There is no reason to suppose that the research institute for
these cases, which is now being built, will not result in the medical
profession finding a way of treating the disorder of psychopathy, as
they have in the case of nearly all disorders in the past.

If, therefore, the supposed difficulty of the alternative punishment
is the only ground on which capital punishment is to be justified,
the answer is that we are ourselves not justified in deliberately killing
men and women on an a priori assumption that those in question
are too ill ever to be cured by the doctors, or too depraved ever to be
capable of reformation. Who can say what can be done with a man
or a woman in ten years?

There is, therefore, no rational ground for supposing that the alternative punishment in England would create any special difficulty, which it does not in practice create in the majority of the civilised countries of the world.

An examination of the emotional case for capital punishment

Apart altogether from the rational case for capital punishment, there is an emotional case for capital punishment. Men and women have emotions as well as reason and the word 'emotional' is not intended to be used in any derogatory sense. There are noble emotions and ignoble emotions. Owing to the nature of the emotional case for capital punishment it has no connexion whatever with the rational case, although in argument the two are usually inextricably confused.

The emotional case for capital punishment is easily recognised when heard, but less easy to define. It is based on the emotions of fear and anger, neither of which, in the case of murder, can be said to be unnatural. Because murder is so largely a crime of the disordered mind, and therefore irrational, we are all in danger of being murdered, and fear of the murderer is natural enough. So, too, is anger, or hatred, or 'righteous indignation', whatever word one chooses to use. Any ordinary person, reading of some unfortunate girl, first raped and then strangled with a stocking, or of some poor child brutally done to death, naturally feels very angry. The emotional case for capital punishment is an instinctive reaction to these mingled feelings of fear and anger, and usually finds its expression in the following forms:

'A man like that deserves to be hanged.'

'An eye for an eye and a tooth for a tooth.'

'Pay him out in his own coin.'

'I know what I'd like to do with a man like that.'

'Hanging's too good for him.'

'Why all this sympathy with murderers? Why not a bit of sympathy with their unfortunate victims for a change?'

'A man who kills ought to be killed himself.'

'He may be mad, but what's the use of keeping a man like that?'

'I wouldn't mind stringing him up myself.'

For obvious reasons it is less easy to answer an emotional argument than a rational one. Some of the forms in which the emotional argument is expressed are, however, so common that they deserve separate consideration; and one general observation may perhaps properly be added.

An eye for an eye

Of all the emotional arguments this is the one most commonly advanced. Neither the Church nor the State give any support to the idea that vengeance should have any place in punishment. In the 1948 debate the Archbishop of Canterbury said:

> Within the Church itself always, and in the world so far as is practicable, the law of love, with its power to forgive, to convert, to reform and to refashion must permeate and shape the application of the law of punishment.

Before the Royal Commission the Home Office agreed that there was:

> no longer in our regard of the criminal law any recognition of such primitive conceptions as ... retribution ... I think that is a principle that is inherent in our modern conception of penology ... there is a school of thought in this country which would still regard vengeance and vindication of the law as a feature of our system. It is not a principle which animates any proposal which comes from the Home Office.

There appears, however, to be misunderstanding of the Christian position, judging from a letter from a constituent received by his Member of Parliament at the time of the 1948 debate:

> I am a Christian to all intents and purposes and it's our creed that it's an eye for an eye and a tooth for a tooth, and we are going against our

own religion by doing away with something that has been taught to us for donkey's years.

If a modern code of penal conduct ought to be based on an Old Testament text, it depends, as we all know, on the particular text chosen. One can choose 'An eye for an eye and a tooth for a tooth'; or, from a later period of Jewish history, one may take Ezekiel, 'As I live, saith the Lord God, I have no pleasure in the death of the wicked, but that the wicked turn from his way and live.'

'An eye for an eye'—the *lex talionis* of Moses—was one of the great advances in the moral development of mankind: replacing, as it did, a code which allowed a greater injury to be inflicted on the wrongdoer than that which he had himself inflicted on his victim. As the Archbishop of Canterbury said of 'an eye for an eye' in the 1948 debate:

> It is well to remember that in its origin it was a restraint upon vengeance. It does not require that equivalent punishment, but it says that no punishment should go beyond that limit: no more than one eye for one eye, and no more than one tooth for one tooth.

The years passed and the Rabbis in the course of the years began to deprecate the infliction of capital punishment. In the *Mishnah* it is stated that a Sanhedrin were themselves called murderers if the death penalty was inflicted more than once in seven years and some Rabbis affirmed that once in seventy years was far too frequent. Indeed,

> there is no doubt that the extreme rarity of Jewish judicial executions is to be explained by the almost insurmountable difficulties imposed by Rabbinic regulations as conditions precedent to a conviction leading to a capital sentence. At least two witnesses were required who should have seen the crime from the same place or have been visible to each other and who had actually warned the malefactor of the nature and consequences of the act he was about to commit.

Today, Israel has abolished capital punishment while British Christians defend it by repeating, parrotwise, a text of the history of which they are clearly unaware, and the original connotation of which they plainly do not understand and in apparent ignorance of the fact that it is a text which was expressly and in terms condemned in the New Testament.

For a hundred years before the rise of Hitler the standard of international morality required that governments, when they issued statements should tell the truth, and not lies, and when they made treaties should keep them and not break them. Not infrequently lies were told and treaties were broken, but, in view of the standard, they felt it necessary to explain that the lie was inadvertent or otherwise excusable, and that the breach of the treaty was in some way justified. What was completely new under Hitler was the avowal that a government naturally and rightly told a lie if it paid it to do so, and intentionally entered into international agreements which it never intended to carry out. The standard had been officially torn up. We are still suffering from this grave fall in the standard of international morality.

'Ye have heard that it hath been said an eye for an eye and a tooth for a tooth, but I say unto you that ye resist not evil.' It is not a precept which we find it easy to follow. We regard it as the true, if distant, standard of morality, but are conscious how far we are from achieving it. What, however, is completely new is to be told that the New Testament has now been officially torn up, and that we positively ought to base our present conduct on an Old Testament text which was expressly and in terms rejected by Christ. In turn we are to reject Him and return to the laws of the Jews in the time of Moses.

Nothing could more forcibly illustrate the weakness of a case which requires to be defended on such grounds. Yet it must be repeated that this Old Testament text is perhaps the commonest of all the emotional grounds used to support capital punishment. At a recent 'Brains Trust' on capital punishment in London, after questions which had elicited the facts as to deterrence and the alternative punishment, the simple question was asked 'What is the justification for capital punishment?', and the Chairman called on one of the 'Brains', a military Member of Parliament who supports capital punishment, to reply. After a long pause he said 'Well, in my opinion the real justification for capital punishment is "An eye for an eye and a tooth for a tooth".' Of such are our legislators who support capital punishment.

Why sympathy for murderers instead of their victims?

This gibe at those who believe that we shall be a cleaner and healthier country when we have abolished capital punishment has been equally commonly used in both centuries, e.g. on one of the Bills to abolish capital punishment for small larcenies in 1832 it was complained in the House of Lords that 'All the sympathy was for the villain, and none was displayed for the poor honest man'.

So far from this being true, many of those who support abolition do so because of their concern to reduce the murder rate. They believe that steps could be taken to that end, and that consideration should be given, for example, to the following steps:

1. In November 1955 our Police Force was 9,689 policemen and 250 women police short of establishment. 'Prevention is better than cure' applies to crime as well as to disease. The restoration of 10,000 police who are missing from their beats would probably do more to reduce crime in this country than any other single step.

2. It is because those who support abolition are deeply concerned about the girl on Dartford Common that they want to end those murders which are committed by the types of disordered mind on which hanging, with all the resulting press sensationalism and publicity surrounding murder trials, has the effect it undoubtedly has. Such murders can only be prevented by removing the cause—capital punishment.

3. In England any criminal seems to be able to get hold of a gun. Licences to hold firearms should be less readily granted, particularly for pistols and revolvers, and the provisions of the Firearms Act should be much more rigidly enforced.

4. The conviction rate in murder should be restored to its

true level—which can only be done by abolishing capital punishment.

5. The public obtain from the newspapers the impression that whenever a question of insanity arises in a murder case there is a great forensic battle between psychiatrists called for the prosecution and for the defence. This is not so. In most of such cases, in about a third of which the accused is found insane on arraignment, there is no dispute at all because the prison doctor and all concerned agree that the man is obviously insane and was obviously insane when he committed the murder. The diagnosis is obvious and admits of no doubt. Would it not have been very much better if this simple and obvious diagnosis had been made before he committed the murder instead of after? Medical evidence given before the Royal Commission suggests that there is no such inherent impracticability in this suggestion as should deter us from thinking on these lines.

But, whether or not any or all of these five proposals find acceptance, it is a travesty of the truth to suggest that those who are now opposed to capital punishment are not as concerned for the victims of the crime as those who support it. On the contrary, their belief that on the whole its abolition would be likely to lead to some decrease in murder is one of the reasons why they would like to see the end of the use of death as a punishment. It is not a question of sympathy with murderers, but of our own self-respect. We did not abolish drawing and quartering out of sympathy with traitors, but because its continuance would not have been consistent with the self-respect of a civilised country.

He deserves to be hanged

Hitler started his killings by killing off the insane in the asylums. His view was that they did not deserve to live because they consumed food and performed no function useful to the community, besides which some of them were homicidal and highly dangerous. Having killed them, he then turned his attention to the Jews and other groups whom he decided did not deserve to live. It may be a matter of doubt whether there is any man or group of men who are themselves fit to decide that some other man or group of men do not 'deserve' to live.

The conception that in murder cases capital punishment is what a man 'deserves' is untenable. In the first place, as the Royal Commission state as the first of their 'Summary of Conclusions and Recommendations':

> The outstanding defect of the law of murder is that it provides a single punishment for a crime widely varying in culpability.

As they say:

> There is perhaps no single class of offences that varies so widely both in character and in culpability as the class comprising those which may fall within the comprehensive common law definition of murder.

The conception that death 'deserves' death is the unconscious echo of 'an eye for an eye'. Yet we do not in fact take an eye for an eye. Why not?

When it is realised that the 'worst' murders are those by men like Haigh and Heath, who, because of their degree of mental disorder, have little real moral responsibility for what they do ('driven ... to deeds of violence which are as uncontrollable as a tidal wave'), and the genesis and history of 'an eye for an eye' are understood, it will be appreciated that to say that a man 'deserves' to be hanged is little more than an expression of emotion devoid of any real meaning. There are murder charges where the sympathies of all those connected with the case are rather with the accused than with the man who was killed. They are cases in which the victim has behaved so outrageously to the accused and given him such provocation in fact (as opposed to provocation in law), sometimes over a period of years, that finally the accused, pent with anger (which he would no doubt call 'righteous indignation') and a desire for revenge, kills the victim. If, or to the extent that, we support capital punishment on the emotional argument, are we not in grave danger of doing no more than repeating the act of the murderer, and with as much or as little excuse?

Capital punishment still means that from time to time we take some man, woman or youth out of a cell and deliberately kill them on a gallows. In truth the emotional 'argument' for such killings is no more than the expression of those feelings of anger and revenge that are the common murderer's excuse.

And so, to the end of history, murder shall breed murder, always in the name of right and honour and peace, until the Gods are tired of blood and create a race that can understand.

10

Reflections on the guillotine

Albert Camus

Albert Camus (1913–1960), a French novelist and dramatist, was born in Algeria. His novels include *The Outsider* (1942), *The Plague* (1947), and *The Fall* (1957). In 1957 he won the Nobel Prize for Literature. He died in 1960 in a motor accident. This translation of the following article by Richard Howard was first published in 1957.

Camus' work was dominated by his search for moral standards and individual responsibility in a shifting, featureless, and apathetic modern society. He turned away from the political 'line pushing' of his youth and applied his unsparing analysis to human problems, not to provide a platform for a party or pressure group but to erect signposts for individual wayfarers.

He was not a moral relativist:

> I stand as far as possible from that position of spineless pity in which our humanitarians take such pride, in which values and responsibilities change places, all crimes become equal, and innocence ultimately forfeits all rights.

Most abolitionist material is statistical and cautious. Camus' writing has a powerful emotional appeal—but the emotion springs from the evidence.

* * *

Shortly before World War I, a murderer whose crime was particularly shocking (he had killed a family of farmers, children and all) was condemned to death in Algiers. He was an agricultural worker who had slaughtered in a bloody delirium, and had rendered his offence still more serious by robbing his victims. The case was widely publicised, and it was generally agreed that decapitation was altogether too mild a punishment for such a monster. I have been told this was the opinion of my father, who was particularly outraged by the murder of the children. One of the few things I know about him is that this was the first time in his life he wanted to attend an execution. He got up while it was still dark, for the place where the guillotine was set up was at the other end of the city, and once there, found himself among a great crowd of spectators. He never told what he saw that morning. My mother could only report that he rushed wildly into the house, refused to speak, threw himself on the bed, and suddenly began to vomit. He had just discovered the reality concealed beneath the great formulas that ordinarily serve to mask it. Instead of thinking of the murdered children, he could recall only the trembling body he had seen thrown on a board to have its head chopped off.

This ritual act must indeed be horrible if it can subvert the indignation of a simple, upright man; if the punishment which he regarded as deserved a hundred times over had no other effect on him than to turn his stomach. When the supreme act of justice merely nauseates the honest citizen it is supposed to protect, it seems difficult to maintain that this act is intended—as its proper functioning should intend it—to confer a greater degree of peace and order upon the city. Justice of this kind is obviously no less shocking than the crime itself, and the new 'official' murder, far from offering redress for the offense committed against society, adds instead a second defilement to the first. This is so apparent that no one dares speak openly of the ritual act itself. The officials and the journalists whose responsibility it is to speak of it, as if conscious of the simultaneously provocative and shameful aspects of such justice, have devised a kind of ceremonial language for dealing with it, a language reduced to the most stereotyped formulas. Over breakfast we may read, on some back page of our newspaper, that the condemned man 'paid his debt to society', that he 'expiated his crime', or that 'at five o'clock this morning justice was done'. Officials deal with this man as 'the accused', 'the patient', or merely refer to him as the CAM (*Condamné à mort*). Capital punishment, one might say, is written about only in whispers. In a highly organised society such as ours we acknowledge a disease is serious by the fact that we do not dare speak of it openly. In middle-class families, it was long the rule to say that the oldest daughter had a 'weak chest', or that Papa suffered from a 'growth': to have tuberculosis or cancer was regarded as something of a disgrace. This is even more certainly true in the case of capital punishment: everyone does his best to speak of it only in euphemisms. The death penalty is to the body politic what cancer is to the individual body, with perhaps the single difference that no one has ever spoken of the necessity of cancer. Yet we do not usually hesitate to describe the death penalty as a regrettable necessity, justifying the fact that we are killing someone because it is 'necessary', and then not speaking of what we are doing because it is 'regrettable'.

My intention, on the contrary, is to speak of it crudely. Not out of a taste for scandal, and not, I think, because I am morbidly inclined. As a writer I have always abhorred a certain eagerness to please, and as a man I believe that the repulsive aspects of our condition, if they are inevitable, must be confronted in silence. But since silence, or the casuistry of speech, is now contributing to the support of an abuse that must be reformed, or of a misery that can be relieved, there is no other solution than to speak out, to expose the obscenity hiding beneath our cloak of words. France shares with Spain and England the splendid distinction of being among the last countries on this side of the Iron Curtain to retain the death penalty in its arsenal of repression. This primitive rite survives in our country only because an ignorant and unconcerned public opinion has no other way to express itself than by using the same ceremonial phrases with which it has been indoctrinated: when the imagination is not functioning, words lack the resonance of their meanings and a deaf public scarcely registers a man's condemnation to death. But expose the machinery, make people touch the wood and the iron, let them hear the thud of heads falling, and a suddenly aroused public imagination will repudiate both vocabulary and punishment alike.

When the Nazis staged public executions of hostages in Poland, they first gagged their prisoners with rags soaked in plaster so they could not cry out some final word of liberty or rebellion. It may seem an effrontery to compare the fate of these innocent victims with that of our condemned criminals, but apart from the fact that it is not only criminals who are guillotined in France, the method is the same: we gag our guilty with a stuffing of words, though we cannot justly affirm the legitimacy of their punishment unless we have first considered its reality. Instead of saying, as we always have, that the death penalty is first of all a necessity, and afterwards that it is advisable not to talk about it, we should first speak of what the death penalty really is, and only then decide if, being what it is, it is necessary.

Speaking for myself, I believe the death penalty is not only useless but profoundly harmful, and I must record this conviction here before proceeding to the subject itself. It would not be honest to allow it to appear as if I had arrived at this conclusion solely as a result of the weeks of inquiry and investigation I have just devoted to the question. But it would be equally dishonest to attribute my conviction to sentimentality alone. I stand as far as possible from that position of spineless pity in which our humanitarians take such pride, in which values and responsibilities change places, all crimes become equal, and innocence ultimately forfeits all rights. I do not believe, contrary to many of my illustrious contemporaries, that man is by nature a social animal; the opposite, I think, is probably nearer the truth. I believe only that man cannot now live outside a society whose laws are necessary to his physical survival, which is a very different thing. I believe that responsibility must be established according to a reasonable and effective scale of values by society itself. But the law finds its final justification in the benefit it provides, or does not provide, the society of a given place and time. For years I have not been able to regard the death penalty as anything but a punishment intolerable to the imagination: a public sin of sloth which my reason utterly condemns. I was nevertheless prepared to believe that my imagination influenced my judgement. But during these weeks of research, I have found nothing which has modified my reasoning, nothing which has not, in all honesty, reinforced my original conviction. On the contrary. I have found new arguments to add to those I already possessed; today I share Arthur Koestler's conclusion without qualification: capital punishment is a disgrace to our society which its partisans cannot reasonably justify …

Instead of vaguely evoking a debt that someone has paid to society this morning, would it not be more politic—if we are interested in setting an example—to profit by this excellent opportunity to remind each taxpayer in detail just what sort of punishment he can expect? Instead of saying, 'If you kill someone you will pay for it on the scaffold,' would it not be more politic—if we are interested in setting an example—to say instead:

> If you kill someone, you will be thrown into prison for months or even years, torn between an impossible despair and a constantly renewed fear, until one morning we will sneak into your cell, having taken off our shoes in order to surprise you in your sleep, which has at last overcome you after the night's anguish. We will throw ourselves upon you, tie your wrists behind your back, and with a pair of scissors cut away your shirt collar and your hair, if it should be in the way. Because we are perfectionists we will lash your arms together with a strap so that your body will be arched to offer unhampered access to the back of your neck. Then we will carry you, one man holding you up under each arm, your feet dragging behind you, down the long corridors, until, under the night sky, one of the executioners will at last take hold of the back of your trousers and throw you down on a board, another will make sure your head is in the lunette, and a third one will drop, from a height of two metres twenty centimetres, a blade weighing sixty kilograms that will slice through your neck like a razor.

For the example to be even better, for the terror it breeds to become in each of us a force blind enough and powerful enough to balance, at the right moment, our irresistible desire to kill, we must go still further. Instead of bragging, with our characteristic pretentious ignorance, that we have invented a swift and humane means of killing those condemned to death, we should publish in millions of copies, read out in every school and college, the eyewitness accounts and medical reports that describe the state of the body after execution. We should particularly recommend the printing and circulation of a recent communication made to the Academy of Medicine by Doctors Piedelièvre and Fournier. These courageous physicians, having examined, in the interests of science, the bodies of the condemned after execution, have considered it their duty to sum up their terrible observations thus:

> If we may be permitted to present our opinion on this subject, such spectacles are horribly painful. The blood rushes from the vessels according to the rhythm of the severed carotids, then coagulates. The muscles contract and their fibrillation is stupefying. The intestine undulates and the heart produces a series of irregular, incomplete, and convulsive movements. The mouth tightens, at certain moments, into a dreadful grimace. It is true that the eyes of a decapitated head are immobile, the pupils dilated; fortunately, they cannot see, and if they exhibit no signs of disturbance, none of the characteristic opalescence of a cadaver, they at least have no capacity for movement: their transparency is that of life, but their fixity is mortal. All this may last minutes, even hours, in a healthy subject: death is not immediate … Thus each vital element survives decapitation to some extent. There remains, for the physician, the impression of a hideous experiment, a murderous vivisection followed by a premature burial.

I could cite many eyewitness accounts. But as for myself, I hardly need or know how to go further. After all, I make no claim that the death penalty is exemplary: indeed, this torture affects me only as what it is—a crude surgery practiced in conditions that deprive it of any edifying character whatsoever. Society, on the other hand, and the State (which has seen other tortures) can easily bear such details; and since they favour preaching examples, they might as well make them universally known so that a perpetually terrorised populace can become Franciscan to a man. For who is it we think we are frightening by this example constantly screened from view; by the threat of a punishment described as painless, expedient, and on the whole less disagreeable than cancer; by a torture crowned with all the flowers of rhetoric? Certainly not those who pass for honest (and some are) because they are asleep at such an hour, to whom the great example has not been revealed, and who drink their morning coffee at the hour of the premature burial, informed of the operation of justice, if they happen to read the newspapers, by a mealy-mouthed bulletin that dissolves like sugar in their memory. Yet these same peaceful creatures furnish society with the largest percentage of its homicides. Many of these honest men are criminals without knowing it. According to one magistrate, the overwhelming majority of the murderers he had tried did not know, when they shaved themselves that morning, that they were going to kill someone that night. For the sake of example and security alike, we should brandish rather than disguise the agonised face of our victim before the eyes of every man as he shaves himself in the morning.

We must either kill publicly, or admit we do not feel authorised to kill. If society justifies the death penalty as a necessary example, then it must justify itself by providing the publicity necessary to make an example. Society must display the executioner's hands on each occasion, and require the most squeamish citizens to look at them, as well as those who, directly or remotely, have supported the work of those hands from the first. Otherwise society confesses that it kills without consciousness of what it does or what it says; or that it kills yet knows, too, that far from intimidating belief, these disgusting ceremonies can only awaken a sense of criminality, and thoroughly undermine public morale. Who could be more explicit than a judge at the end of his career? Counselor Falco's courageous confession deserves careful attention:

> On only one occasion during my years on the bench I recommended
> a verdict in favour of execution of the accused and against the
> commutation of his punishment; I decided that despite my position I
> would attend the ceremony — with complete objectivity, of course. The
> man in question was not at all sympathetic, not even interesting: he had
> brutally murdered his little daughter and then thrown her body down a
> well. Nevertheless, after his execution, for weeks, and even for months,

my nights were haunted by this memory ... I served in the War like everyone else, and I saw an innocent generation killed before my eyes; yet confronted with the memory of that dreadful spectacle, I still can say I never once experienced the same kind of bad conscience I felt as I watched the kind of administrative assassination known as capital punishment.

Bacon was right: no passion is so weak that it cannot confront and master the fear of death. Vengeance, love, honour, grief, even fear of something else—all are victorious over the fear of death in one circumstance or another. And shall cupidity, hatred, or jealously not accomplish all that love or patriotism or the human passion for liberty are able to achieve? For centuries the death penalty, often accompanied by various barbarous refinements, has tried to restrain the incidence of crime; yet crime persists. Why? Because the instincts which confront and war against each other within man are not, as the law would have them, constant forces in a state of equilibrium. They are variable forces that die and triumph one after another, whose successive imbalances nourish the life of the mind in the same way that electrical oscillations, occurring with sufficient frequency, establish a current. Consider the series of oscillations passing from desire to satiation, from decision to renunciation, which all of us experience in a single day and then multiply these variations to infinity and we may form an idea of the extent of our psychological proliferation. These imbalances, these disequilibriums are generally too fugitive to permit any one force to gain control of the entire self. Yet it sometimes happens that a single element of the soul's resources can break free and occupy the entire field of consciousness; no instinct, even that of self-preservation, can then oppose the tyranny of this irresistible force. In order that the death penalty be really intimidating, human nature itself would have to be different from what it is, would have to be as stable and serene as the law itself. It would no longer be life, but still-life.

But life is not still-life, is not stable, not serene. Which is why, surprising as it may seem to those who have not observed or experienced in themselves the complexity of the human situation, the murderer for the most part considers himself innocent when he commits his crime. Before being judged, the criminal acquits himself He feels he is — if not entirely within his rights — at least extenuated by circumstances. He does not reflect; he does not foresee; or if he does, it is only to foresee that he will be pardoned — altogether or in part. Why should he fear what he regards as highly unlikely? He will fear death after being judged, not before his crime. Therefore, in order to intimidate effectively, the law must permit the murderer no escape, must be implacable in advance, must admit no possibility of an extenuating circumstance. Who among us would dare to demand this?

And even if we did, there is still another paradox of human nature to consider. The instinct of self-preservation, if it is a fundamental one, is no more so than that other instinct less often discussed by academic psychologists: the death instinct which at certain times demands the destruction of the self or of others. It is probable that the desire to kill frequently coincides with the desire to die or to kill oneself. The instinct of self-preservation thus finds itself confronted in variable proportions by the instinct for self-destruction. The latter is the only means by which we can altogether explain the numerous perversions which — from alcoholism to drug addiction — lead the self to a destruction of which it cannot long remain ignorant. Man desires to live, but it is vain to hope that this desire can control all his actions. He desires to be annihilated as well — he wills the irreparable, death for its own sake. It so happens that the criminal desires not only his crime, but the misery that accompanies it, especially if this misery is unbounded and inordinate. When this perverse desire grows until it gains control of the self, the prospect of being put to death is not only impotent to restrain the criminal, but probably deepens even further the abyss into which he plunges; there are situations in which one kills in order to die. Such singularities suffice to explain how a punishment that seems calculated to intimidate the normal mind has in reality nothing whatever to do with ordinary psychological processes. All statistics show, without exception — in the countries which have abolished it, as well as in the others — that there is no connexion between the death penalty and the incidence of crime.

This incidence, in fact, neither rises nor falls. The guillotine exists; crime exists: between them there is no other apparent connexion than that of the law. All we are entitled to conclude from the figures provided by statisticians is this: for centuries crimes other than murder were punished by death, and this supreme punishment, deliberately repeated, caused none of these crimes to disappear. For several centuries these crimes have no longer been punished by death, yet they have not increased in number, and the incidence of some has even diminished. Similarly, murder has been punished by capital punishment for centuries, yet the race of Cain has not disappeared from the earth. In the thirty-three nations that have abolished the death penalty or no longer impose it, the number of murders has not increased. How can we therefore conclude that the death penalty is really intimidating?

Its partisans can deny neither these facts nor these figures. Their only and ultimate reply is significant; it explains the paradoxical attitude of a society which so carefully conceals the executions it claims as exemplary:

> It is true that nothing proves that the death penalty is exemplary; it is even certain that thousands of murderers have not been intimidated by it. But we cannot know who has been intimidated by such a penalty; consequently, nothing proves that it does not serve as an example.

Thus the greatest of all punishments, the penalty that involves the ultimate forfeiture of the condemned man and concedes the supreme privilege to society, rests on nothing more than an unverifiable possibility. Death, however, does not admit of degrees of likelihood; it fixes all things — blame and body alike — in its definitive rigidity. Yet it is administered in our country in the name of a possibility, a calculation of likelihood. And even if this possibility should be reasonable, would it not have to be certitude itself to authorise certain and absolute extinction? Yet the man we condemn to die is cut in two not so much for the crime he has committed as for the sake of all the crimes that might have happened, but which have not happened — which could occur, but somehow will not occur.

Hence, the greatest possible uncertainty appears to authorise the most implacable certitude of all.

Punishment, penalising rather than preventing, is a form of revenge: society's semi-arithmetical answer to violation of its primordial law. This answer is as old as man himself, and usually goes by the name of retaliation. He who hurts me must be hurt; who blinds me in one eye must himself lose an eye; who takes a life must die. It is a feeling, and a particularly violent one, which is involved here, not a principle. Retaliation belongs to the order of nature, of instinct, not to the order of law. The law by definition cannot abide by the same rules as nature. If murder is part of man's nature, the law is not made to imitate or reproduce such nature. We have all known the impulse to retaliate, often to our shame, and we know its power: the power of the primeval forests. In this regard, we live — as Frenchmen who grow justifiably indignant at seeing the oil king of Saudi Arabia preach international democracy while entrusting his butcher with the task of cutting off a thief's hand — in a kind of middle ages ourselves, without even the consolations of faith. Yet if we still define our justice according to the calculations of a crude arithmetic, can we at least affirm that this arithmetic is correct, and that even such elementary justice, limited as it is to a form of legal revenge, is *safeguarded* by the death penalty? The answer must again be: No.

We scarcely need to point out how inapplicable the law of retaliation has become in our society: it is as excessive to punish the pyromaniac by setting his house on fire as it is insufficient to punish the thief by deducting from his bank account a sum equivalent to the amount he has stolen. Let us admit instead that it is just and even necessary to compensate the murder of the victim by the death of the murderer. But capital punishment is not merely death. It is as different, in its essence, from the suppression of life as a concentration camp from a prison. It is undeniably a murder which arithmetically cancels out the murder already committed; but it also adds a regularisation of death, a public premeditation of which its future victims are informed, an *organisation* which in itself is a source of moral suffering more terrible than death. There is thus no real compensation, no equivalence. Many systems of law regard a premeditated crime as more serious than a crime of pure violence. But what is capital punishment if not the most premeditated of murders, to which no criminal act, no matter how calculated, can be compared? If there were to be a real equivalence, the death penalty would have to be pronounced upon a criminal who had forewarned his victim of the very moment he would put him to a horrible death, and who, from that time on, had kept him confined at his own discretion for a period of months. It is not in private life that one meets such monsters.

Here again, when our official jurists speak of death without suffering, they do not know what they are talking about, and furthermore they betray a remarkable lack of imagination. The devastating, degrading fear imposed on the condemned man for months or even years is a punishment more terrible than death itself, and one that has not been imposed on his victim. A murdered man is generally rushed to his death, even at the height of his terror of the mortal violence being done to him, without knowing what is happening: the period of his horror is only that of his life itself, and his hope of escaping whatever madness has pounced upon him probably never deserts him. For the man condemned to death, on the other hand, the horror of his situation is served up to him at every moment for months on end. Torture by hope alternates only with the pangs of animal despair. His lawyer and his confessor, out of simple humanity, and his guards, to keep him docile, unanimously assure him that he will be reprieved. He believes them with all his heart, yet he cannot believe them at all. He hopes by day, despairs by night. And as the weeks pass his hope and despair increase proportionately, until they become equally insupportable. According to all accounts, the colour of his skin changes: fear acts like an acid. 'It's nothing to know you're going to die,' one such man in the Fresnes prison said, 'but not to know if you're going to live is the real torture.' At the moment of his execution Cartouche remarked, 'Bah! a nasty quarter of an hour and it's all over.' But it takes months, not minutes. The condemned man knows long in advance that he is going to be killed and that all that can save him is a reprieve which operates, so far as he is concerned, like the will of heaven itself. In any case he cannot intervene, plead for himself: he is no longer a man, but a thing waiting to be manipulated by the executioners. He is kept in a state of absolute necessity, the condition of inert matter, yet within him is the consciousness that is his principal enemy.

When the officials whose trade is to kill such a man refer to him as 'luggage', they know what they are saying: to be unable to react to the hand that moves you, holds you, or lets you drop—is that not the condition of some package, some *thing*, or better still, some trapped animal? Yet an animal in a trap can starve itself to death; the man condemned to death cannot. He is provided with a special diet (at Fresnes, diet no. 4 with *extras* of milk, wine, sugar, preserves, and butter); he is encouraged to eat well—if necessary he is forced to eat. The animal must be in good condition for the kill. The thing—the animal—has a right only to those corrupted privileges known as caprices. 'You'd be surprised how sensitive they are!' declared one sergeant at Fresnes without a trace of irony. Sensitive? Unquestionably—how else recover the freedom and dignity of will that man cannot live without? Sensitive or not, from the moment the death sentence is pronounced, the condemned man becomes part of an imperturbable mechanism. He spends several weeks within the cogs and gears of a machine that controls his every gesture, ultimately delivering him to the hands that will lay him out on the last device of all. The luggage is no longer subjected to the operations of chance, the hazards that dominate the existence of a living being, but to mechanical laws that permit him to foresee in the minutest perspective the day of his decapitation.

His condition as an object comes to an end on this day. During the three-quarters of an hour that separates him from his extinction, the certainty of his futile death overcomes everything: the fettered, utterly submissive creature experiences a hell that makes a mockery of the one with which he is threatened. For all their hemlock, the Greeks were humane: they provided their criminals a relative liberty at least, the possibility of postponing or advancing the hour of their own death; and of choosing between suicide and execution. For reasons of security, we carry out our justice by ourselves. Yet there could not be real justice in such cases unless the murderer, having made known his decision months in advance, had entered his victim's house, tied him up securely, informed him he would be put to death in the next hour, and then used this hour to set up the apparatus by which his victim would be despatched. What criminal has ever reduced his victim to a condition so desperate, so hopeless, and so powerless?

This doubtless explains the strange quality of submission that is so often observed in the condemned man at the moment of his execution. After all, those who have nothing to lose by it might make a last desperate effort, preferring to die by a stray bullet or to be guillotined in a violent struggle that would numb every sense: it would be a kind of freedom in dying. And yet, with very few exceptions, the condemned man walks quite docilely to his death in dismal impassivity. Which must be what our journalists mean when they tell us the condemned man died courageously. What they really mean, of course, is that the condemned man made no trouble, no attempt to abandon his status as luggage, and that we are all grateful to him for his good behaviour. In so disgraceful a business the accused has shown a commendable sense of propriety in allowing the disgrace to be disposed of as soon as possible. But the compliments and character references are just another part of the general mystification that surrounds the death penalty. For the condemned man often behaves 'properly' only to the degree that he is afraid, and deserves the eulogies of our press only if his fear or his despair are sufficiently great to sterilise him altogether. Let me not be misunderstood: some men—political prisoners or not—die heroically, and we must speak of them with the admiration and respect they deserve. But the majority of those condemned to death know no other silence than that of fear, no other impassivity than that of horror, and it seems to me that the silence of fear and horror deserves still more respect than the other. When the priest Bela Just offered to write to the relatives of one young criminal only a few minutes before he was to be hanged, and received these words in answer: 'I don't have the courage, not even for that,' one wonders how a priest, at such a confession of weakness, could keep from falling on his knees before what is most miserable and most sacred in man. As for those who do not talk, those who show us what they have gone through only by the puddle they leave in the place they are dragged from, who would dare say they died as cowards? And by what name shall we call those who have brought these men to their 'cowardice'? After all, each murderer, at the moment of his crime, runs the risk of the most terrible death, while those who execute him risk nothing, except perhaps a promotion.

No—what the condemned man experiences at this moment is beyond all morality. Neither virtue, nor courage, nor intelligence, not even innocence has a share in his condition at that moment. Society is reduced at one blow to that condition of primitive terror in which nothing can be judged and all equity, all dignity, have vanished.

As for the law of retaliation, it must be admitted that even in its primitive form it is legitimate only between two individuals of whom one is absolutely innocent and the other absolutely guilty. Certainly the victim is innocent. But can society, which is supposed to represent the victim, claim a comparable innocence? Is it not responsible at least in part, for the crime which it represses with such severity? This theme has been frequently developed elsewhere, and I need not continue a line of argument which the most varied minds have elaborated since the eighteenth century. Its principal features can be summed up, in any case, by observing that every society has the criminals it deserves.

The determined responsibility of alcohol for crimes of blood is still astounding. One lawyer (Guillon) has estimated that it is a factor in 60 per cent of all such cases. Dr Lagriffe sets the rate somewhere between 41.7 and 72 per cent. An investigation conducted in 1951 at the distribution centre of the Fresnes prison, among inmates guilty of breaches of common law, revealed 29 per cent were chronic alcoholics and 24 per cent had alcoholic backgrounds. Finally, 95 per cent of all murderers of children have been alcoholics.

Does this come down to saying that every alcoholic must be declared non-responsible by a State which will strike its breast in horror until the entire populace drinks nothing but fruit juice? Certainly not. No more than it comes down to saying that the facts of heredity eliminate responsibility and guilt. A criminal's real responsibility cannot be determined exactly. All calculation is powerless to take into account the total number of our ancestors, alcoholic or not. At the other end of time, such a number would be ten times greater than the number of inhabitants of the earth at present. The total of diseased or morbid tendencies which could be transmitted is thus incalculable. We enter the world burdened with the weight of an infinite necessity, and according to logic must agree on a situation of a general non-responsibility. Logically, neither punishment nor reward can be distributed accurately, and therefore all society becomes impossible. Yet the instinct of self-preservation, in societies and individuals alike, requires, on the contrary, the postulate of individual responsibility; a responsibility that must be accepted, without day-dreaming of an absolute indulgence which would coincide with the death and disappearance of any society whatsoever. But the same line of reasoning that compels us to abandon a general non-responsibility must also lead us to conclude that there is never, on the other hand, a situation of total responsibility, and consequently no such thing as absolute punishment or absolute reward. No one can be rewarded absolutely, not even by the Nobel prize. But no one must be punished absolutely if he is found guilty, and with all the more reason if there is a chance he might be innocent. The death penalty, which neither serves as an example nor satisfies the conditions of retaliative justice, usurps in addition an exorbitant privilege by claiming the right to punish a necessarily relative guilt by an absolute and irreparable penalty.

One unpunished crime according to the Greeks, infects the whole city. Innocence condemned to death, or crime excessively punished, leaves a stain no less hideous in the long run.

Such is the nature of human justice, it will be said, and despite its imperfections, after all, even human justice is better than the operation of despotism or chance. But this rueful preference is tolerable only in relation to moderate punishment. Confronted by death sentences, it is a scandal. A classic work on French law excuses the death penalty from being subject to degree in the following words: 'Human justice has not the slightest ambition to insure proportion of this nature. Why? Because it knows itself to be imperfect.'

Must we therefore conclude that this imperfection authorises us to pronounce an absolute judgement, and that society, uncertain of realising justice in its pure state, must rush headlong with every likelihood of error, upon the supreme injustice? If human justice knows itself to be imperfect, might not that knowledge be more suitably and modestly demonstrated by leaving a sufficient margin around our condemnations for the eventual reparation of error? This very weakness in which human justice finds extenuating circumstances for itself in every case and on every occasion—is it not to be accorded to the criminal himself as well? Can the jury in all decency say,

> If we condemn you to death by mistake, you will surely forgive us in consideration of the weaknesses of the human nature we all share. But we nevertheless condemn you to death without the slightest consideration of these weaknesses or of this common nature?

All men have a community in error and in aberration. Yet must this community operate on behalf of the tribunal and be denied to the accused? No, for if justice has any meaning in this world, it is none other than the recognition of this very community: it cannot, in its very essence, be separated from compassion. Let it be understood that by compassion I mean only the consciousness of a common suffering, not a frivolous indulgence that takes no account of the sufferings and rights of the victim. Compassion does not exclude punishment, but it withholds an ultimate condemnation. It is revolted by the definitive, irreparable measure that does injustice to man in general since it does not recognise his share in the misery of the common condition.

As a matter of fact, certain juries know this well enough, and often admit the extenuating circumstances of a crime which nothing can extenuate. This is because they regard the death penalty as too extreme and prefer to punish insufficiently rather than to excess. In such cases, the extreme severity of the punishment tends to sanction crime instead of penalising it. There is scarcely one session of the assize courts of which one cannot read in our press that a verdict is incoherent, that in the face of the facts it appears either insufficient or excessive. The jurors are not unaware of this. They simply prefer, as we should do ourselves, when confronted with the enormity of capital punishment, to appear confused, rather than compromise their sleep for nights to come. Knowing themselves imperfect, at least they draw the appropriate consequences. And true justice is on their side, precisely to the degree that logic is not.

How can European society in the twentieth century survive if it does not defend the individual by every means within its power against the oppression of the State? To forbid putting a man to death is one means of publicly proclaiming that society and the State are not absolute values, one means of demonstrating that nothing authorises them to legislate definitively, to bring to pass the irreparable. Without the death penalty, Gabriel Péri and Brasillach would perhaps be among us still; we could then judge them, according to our lights, and proudly speak out our judgement, instead of which they now judge us, and it is we who must remain silent. Without the death penalty, the corpse of Rajk would not still be poisoning Hungary, a less guilty Germany would be received with better grace by the nations of Europe, the Russian Revolution would not still be writhing in its shame, and the blood of Algeria would weigh less heavily upon us here in France. Without the death penalty, Europe itself would not be infected by the corpses accumulated in its exhausted earth for the last twenty years. Upon our continent all values have been overturned by fear and hatred among individuals as among nations. The war of ideas is waged by rope and knife. It is no longer the natural human society that exercises its rights of repression, but a ruling ideology that demands its human sacrifices. 'The lesson the scaffold always provides,' Francart wrote, 'is that human life ceases to be sacred when it is considered useful to suppress it.' Apparently it has been considered increasingly useful, the lesson has found apt pupils, and the contagion is spreading everywhere.

From the humanitarian idylls of the eighteenth century to its bloody scaffolds the road runs straight and is easily followed; we all know today's executioners are humanists. And therefore we cannot be too suspicious of humanitarian ideologies applied to a problem like that of capital punishment. I should like to repeat, by way of conclusion, that my opposition to the death penalty derives from no illusions as to the natural goodness of the human creature, and from no faith in a golden age to come. On the contrary, the abolition of capital punishment seems necessary to me for reasons of qualified pessimism, reasons I have attempted to explain in terms of logic and the most realistic considerations. Not that the heart has not made its contribution to what I have been saying: for anyone who has spent several weeks among these texts, these memories, and these men—all, intimately or remotely, connected with the scaffold—there can be no question of leaving their dreadful ranks unaffected by what one has seen and heard. Nevertheless, I do not believe there is no responsibility in this world for what I have found, or that one should submit to our modern propensity for absolving victim and killer in the same moral confusion. This purely sentimental confusion involves more cowardice than generosity, and ends up by justifying whatever is worst in this world: if everything is blessed, then slave camps are blessed, and organised murder, and the cynicism of the great political bosses—and ultimately, blessing everything alike, one betrays one's own brothers. We can see this happening all around us. But indeed, with the world in its present condition the man of the twentieth century asks for laws and institutions of convalescence that will check without crushing, lead without hampering. Hurled into the unregulated dynamism of history, man needs a new physics, new laws of equilibrium. He needs, most of all, a reasonable society, not the anarchy into which his own pride and the State's inordinate powers have plunged him.

It is my conviction that the abolition of the death penalty will help us advance toward that society. In taking this initiative, France could propose its extension on either side of the Iron Curtain; in any case she could set an example. Capital punishment would be replaced by a sentence of perpetual forced labour for criminals judged incorrigible, and by shorter terms for others. As for those who believe that such punishment is still more cruel than capital punishment itself, I wonder why, in that case, they do not reserve it for Landru and his like and relegate capital punishment to secondary offenders. One might also add that such forced labour leaves the condemned man the possibility of choosing his death, whereas the guillotine is a point of no return. On the other hand, I would answer those who believe that a sentence of perpetual forced labour is too mild a punishment by remarking first on their lack of imagination and then by pointing out that the privation of liberty could seem to them a mild punishment only to the degree that contemporary society has taught them to despise what liberty they have.

That Cain was not killed, but bore in the sight of all men a mark of reprobation is, in any case, the lesson we should draw from the Old Testament, not to mention the Gospels, rather than taking our inspiration from the cruel examples of the Mosaic law. There is no reason why at least a limited version of such an experiment should not be attempted in France (say for a ten-year period), if our government is still capable of redeeming its vote for alcohol by the great measure in behalf of civilisation which total abolition would represent. And if public opinion and its representatives cannot renounce our slothful law which confines itself to eliminating what it cannot amend, at least, while waiting for a day of regeneration and of truth, let us not preserve as it is this 'solemn shambles' (in Tarde's expression) which continues to disgrace our society. The death penalty, as it is imposed, even as rarely as it is imposed, is a disgusting butchery, an outrage inflicted on the spirit and body of man. This truncation, this living severed head, these long gouts of blood, belong to a barbarous epoch that believed it could subdue the people by offering them degrading spectacles.

Today, when this ignoble death is secretly administered, what meaning can such torture have? The truth is that in an atomic age we kill as we did in the age of steelyards: where is the man of normal sensibility whose stomach is not turned at the mere idea of such clumsy surgery? If the French state is incapable of overcoming its worst impulses to this degree and of furnishing Europe with one of the remedies it needs most, let it at least reform its means of administering capital punishment. Science, which has taught us so much about killing, could at least teach us to kill decently. An anesthetic which would permit the accused to pass from a state of sleep to death, which would remain within his reach for at least a day so that he could make free use of it, and which in cases of refusal or failure of nerve could then be administered to him, would assure the elimination of the criminal, if that is what we require, but would also provide a little decency where today there is nothing but a sordid and obscene exhibition.

I indicate these compromises only to the degree that one must sometimes despair of seeing wisdom and the principles of civilisation impose themselves upon those responsible for our future. For certain men, more numerous than is supposed, knowing what the death penalty really is and being unable to prevent its application is physically insupportable. In their own way, they suffer this penalty too, and without any justification. If we at least lighten the weight of the hideous images that burden these men, society will lose nothing by our actions. But ultimately even such measures will be insufficient. Neither in the hearts of men nor in the manners of society will there be a lasting peace until we outlaw death.

11

The unexamined death

Hans W. Mattick

Hans W. Mattick (1920–1978), born in Dresden, became a great authority on crime delinquency and correction. A sociologist in the Illinois prison service 1950–55, he was assistant warden at Cook County Jail in Illinois 1955–58. Recruited by Professor Norval Morris, an expatriate Australian, he was lecturer in sociology and criminology at Chicago University 1960–66, associate director of the Centre for Studies in Criminal Justice at Chicago University Law School 1966–72, and a full professor 1972–78.

His article 'The Unexamined Death', from which the following extracts are taken, was first published in 1963 and reprinted in 1966.

*   *   *

A paradox in our modern world lies in the ambivalence we exhibit toward scientific methods when they are applied to human affairs. We have applied them to the material world and have achieved a remarkable degree of control over nature. Our accomplishments in these respects tend to beguile us into the conceit that man is a rational animal. When we view the relations between men and the social order, however, we are confronted with the cold war, contemporary race relations and a host of continuing social problems that must make us qualify the degree of rationality that men have achieved. In the social sphere, instead of the application of scientific methods, we see the results of emotionalism, irrationality, ethnocentrism and tradition. It is not that the general methods of science do not have

135

some application to the affairs of men. On the contrary, the social sciences have made considerable progress over the last one hundred years. Yet social institutions and the relations between men in society still reflect, for the most part, the traditions of a pre-scientific age. This is particularly the case in that area of social problems related to crime and punishment.

The general methods of science are based upon an enumeration of facts ordered into some rational scheme that enables one to make comparisons and draw logical inferences. There is no reason why such methods cannot be applied to the field of crime and punishment, but too often they are not. Instead, men out of fear, pride, anger, and other emotional qualities, simply react in traditional ways and never stop to examine just what it is that they are doing. The more serious the offense the stronger the emotional reaction and the less the inclination to examine, in some systematic way, whether this emotional response is achieving any purpose. Since murder is the most serious offense one man can perpetrate against another, it calls out in us the strongest emotional response and we react in kind by inflicting the death penalty upon the offender. Whether this traditional pattern of behaviour ever accomplishes anything other than to increase the absolute number of killings among us is seldom examined by rational methods. Presumably we put murderers to death in order to decrease the number of killings among us, but whether there is a cause and effect relationship between inflicting the death penalty and the number of homicides is not inquired into. It is taken for granted as being self-evident. Even the self-evident, however, is sometimes called into question as we well know from the fact that today we agree the world is round, though for many ages men took it for granted that the world was flat. In the same way then, we will call into question the self-evident qualities of the death penalty.

Public policy

We propose to examine here a form of death about which many persons have an opinion, but few have any facts or knowledge.

The question before us is an evaluation of capital punishment as an instrument of public policy. Questions of public policy, especially when they are a matter of life and death, should be resolved on the basis of a rational consideration of means and ends. The means should be appropriate to the end and the end should represent the objective we actually want to achieve. Expressions of sentiment and appeals to the emotions have their place in life, but should not be the basis for a decision about the deliberate imposition of the death penalty by the State upon an individual. The ultimate decisions that men make on behalf of the organised community should rest firmly on facts, evidence and knowledge. It is in this spirit that we propose to examine the evidence of what is known about the death penalty. Then, having examined the evidence with an open mind, we may reach conclusions that accord with our knowledge.

J. Edgar Hoover, Director of the FBI, recently remarked, 'Certainly, penetrative and searching thought must be given before considering any blanket cessation of capital punishment.' If we take this injunction seriously, we must leave aside theories or assertions based on sentiment and convictions grounded on faith. Appeals to humanity, justice, right and equality are usually in the nature of conclusions and must come after the facts. In advance of an examination of the evidence, such appeals are peculiarly difficult to reduce to a form in which agreement is possible. Whether, and in what sense, the punishment fits the crime is a question that cannot be prejudged on the basis of a strong conviction, for the strength with which convictions are held often bears little relationship to the truth of the conviction. Instead, we must resort to an examination of testable propositions. Once the testable propositions have been submitted to an examination in the light of evidence, there will be a basis for forming a judgement.

Deterrent

Probably the most common, and apparently the most speciously convincing, argument made in favour of capital punishment is that it is alleged to be a deterrent to murder. The theory is that the would-be murderer, mindful of the threat to his own life allegedly posed by the existence of capital punishment, would refrain from taking the life of another. A more complex form of this theory focuses its attention not on any specific murderer, but generalises to all would-be murderers of the future and maintains that the execution of any particular murderer will, allegedly, serve to deter future would-be murderers in general. Such propositions lend themselves to a variety of tests and must, therefore, be taken seriously. They also contain some implicit assumptions about the mental functions of potential murderers, for they are formulated in the style of a stimulus response psychology. The notion is that the presence (and awareness) of capital punishment as a stimulus will lead to the response, avoidance of murder. We will not take the time to address the question of the adequacy of this psychological model of human behaviour at this time, but will allow it to stand or fall with the test of the behaviour it imputes to would-be murderers.[1]

One way to test this deterrent theory of capital punishment is to compare homicide rates in States with and without the death penalty. If the restraint of that penalty were the decisive factor in controlling the number of homicides, the logic of the argument would lead us to expect low homicide rates in capital punishment States and high homicide rates in States that have abolished the death penalty. Instead of adopting such an over-simplified procedure, however, proper distinctions have to be made. There are marked regional differences in homicide rates, e.g. the south-east quadrant of the U.S. has had the highest homicide rates for many years and all the States in that quadrant make frequent use of capital punishment. A comparison between Illinois and Georgia (homicide rates of 5.5 and 11.7 per 100,000 population, respectively, in 1964) would not be fair because

---

1   The reader will recognise this form of stimulus-response psychology as a survival from Jeremy Bentham's so-called utilitarian philosophy (c. 1820), with its simple-minded 'hedonistic calculus' of balancing pleasures and pains, which, in turn, is a hoary descendant of a similar psychology originally elaborated in considerable detail in Plato's *Republic* (c. 387 B.C.). The passage of 2,300 years, the faithful believers in this theory of deterrence should be told, has seen some progress in psychology, notably in the twentieth-century works of Freud, Dewey, Mead, Adler, Jung, and Lewin. The image of man as a wholly rational 'calculator' of pleasures and pains has come to be recognised as an over-simplified, inadequate model of the well-springs of human behaviour.

of social, economic and cultural differences between populations and areas in the northern and southern part of the country. Rural and urban, white and non-white, industrial and agricultural differences must be taken into account in making comparisons between States. A southern State with a past tradition of slavery, with a more recent tradition of vigilante 'justice', with the correlates of a declining landed aristocracy with concepts of 'family honour', the 'purity of womanhood', feuding and duelling, all of which put a high premium on a resort to personal violence and tend to devalue the life of the dissenter and the alleged 'inferior', would also tend to have high homicide rates as a cultural product of this complex of factors. A test of the deterrent theory of capital punishment should not be biased by the intrusion of such extraneous considerations.

A better test of the deterrent function imputed to the death penalty is to make a comparison of geographical entities that are truly comparable. Therefore, the comparison to be made will be of States comparable as to rural-urban distribution of population, contiguous in space, similar in their level of industrial-agricultural development, and in their heterogeneity of ethnic and racial stocks. If we choose Michigan, an abolition State with one large dominant city (Detroit), and compare its homicide rate with that of Illinois, the comparison will not suffer from too many limitations. On the basis of the evidence in Table 1, it would appear that the deterrent effect of capital punishment on homicide rates cannot be established. The case is not stated any stronger than it is because the issue may well be more complex than this simple comparison.

A more limited and more specific test of the deterrent function of capital punishment on homicide rates was made in 1935 in the city of Philadelphia. The investigator counted the number of homicides that occurred sixty days before an execution and sixty days after an execution. He chose five different executions, each of which had received adequate publicity so that knowledge of their having taken place was reasonably widespread in the community. The specific theory to be tested was whether the deterrent effect of the death penalty would be reflected in the sixty-day periods after each execution when, it would appear, deterrence would be most active.

The results of this investigation revealed that in the five sixty-day periods before an execution, when the deterrent effect was supposedly weakest, there was a total of ninety-one homicides in Philadelphia. By way of contrast, in the five sixty-day periods following an execution, when the deterrent effect should have been strongest, there was a total of 113 homicides. Although, again, the results of this special study

Table 1

Homicide Rates (HR) per 100,000 Population in the U.S., Illinois and Michigan; and Executions in the U.S. and Illinois for the Years 1950 through 1964: a Comparison of a Capital Punishment State and an Abolitionist State.

Year	United States		Illinois		Michigan		Diff. in H.R. for Mich.
	H.R.	Exec.	H.R.	Exec.	H.R.	Exec.	
1950	5.1	82	5.3	3	4.1	0	– 1.2
1951	4.9	105	5.0	0	4.5	0	– 0.5
1952	5.0	83	5.8	4	3.9	0	– 1.9
1953	4.8	62	5.6	1	4.5	0	– 1.1
1954	4.8	81	5.4	0	4.3	0	– 1.1
1955	4.7	76	5.7	0	4.6	0	– 1.1
1956	5.0	65	5.9	0	3.9	0	– 2.0
1957	5.1	65	6.0	0	4.1	0	– 1.9
1958	4.7	48	4.5	1	3.1	0	– 1.4
1959	4.8	49	4.0	0	4.2	0	0.2
1960	5.0	57	4.9	0	4.3	0	– 0.6
1961	4.7	42	4.8	0	3.9	0	– 0.9
1962	4.5	47	5.3	2	3.3	0	– 2.0
1963	4.5	21	5.1	0	3.3	0	– 1.8
1964	4.8	15	5.5	0	3.3	0	– 2.2
Averages	4.8	60	5.3	0.73	4.0	0	–1.3

Homicide rates for 1950 to 1958 derived from a table in Commonwealth of Mass., *Report and Recommendations*, Special Commission Established for the Purpose of Investigating and Studying the Abolition of the Death Penalty in Capital Cases, 30 December 1958, p. 15. Homicide rates for 1959 to 1964 derived from FBI, Uniform Crime Reports, 1959–64. Note that in every year except 1959, Michigan, the state without capital punishment, has a lower homicide rate than Illinois. Executions derived from FBP, *National Prisoner Statistics*, 'Executions 1930–64,' April 1965.

cannot be considered conclusive, the evidence in this case does not substantiate the deterrent effect of the death penalty on the homicide rate.

Somewhat similar conclusions may be inferred, in the case of Chicago. We note that the number of homicides fluctuates quite independently of the number of executions during the years 1952–64 ...

Why should student after student of capital punishment arrive at the conclusion that its deterrent effect cannot be demonstrated from the evidence available? We have already adverted to the kinds of assumptions about human psychology that are made by the proponents of capital punishment. Their notion is that the stimulus or awareness of capital punishment will elicit the response of non-murder in the mind of a would-be murderer, or in the minds of the general public. The primitive sense in which the reflex action of stimulus-response can be said to 'work', however, is in the sense of conditioning at the sub-rational level as in the case of Pavlov's dogs whose mouths watered when a bell was rung. Such conditioning is brought about in men or dogs *only if the stimulus and response are closely and invariably related.* When we contemplate the time-span between a murder that is successfully prosecuted and the execution that follows upon it, we see an enormous elapse of time between the stimulus and the response. The Chessman case, in which about twelve years elapsed between crime and punishment (stimulus and response), was simply a striking example of this inordinate time-span. If we average out the elapsed time between the death sentence and execution of the fifteen men who were executed in 1964, or the same period between sentence and December 1964 for the 315 persons awaiting execution in the United States at that time, we find that, on the average, twenty-seven months have elapsed between stimulus and response. A period of twenty-seven months is an impossible time-span over which to expect the stimulus response pattern to be effective, either in the mind of a particular murderer or in the mind of the public at large.

Emotional crime

The kind of rationality assumed by the deterrent theory of capital punishment may be present in the minds of legislators at the time of their deliberations about crime and punishment and may even be present in the minds of most persons in their reflective moments. To attribute the qualitative thinking of a deliberative body to the participants in an emotional situation that leads to murder, however, is a gross oversimplification of the psychological forces involved in homicide. Deliberative bodies and persons detached in reflection are not likely to get into situations that lead to murder. Homicide is, by and large, an affair of the emotions which involves relatives, friends and associates. Homicides where the offender and the victim are strangers are relatively less frequent and fall into two distinct classes: homicides that are an outgrowth of a property offense, and the physical assault by a stranger on a stranger. The latter type of homicide is extremely rare but usually dramatic, and thus attracts widespread attention by the mass media. An analysis of the victims of homicide will tend to demonstrate the emotional nature of murder and the relationship between the offender and the victim. The data are given in Table 2.

Table 2 reveals that in at least 72.4 per cent of the cases of homicide it includes, the victim and the offender were related by blood or marriage or knew each other sufficiently well to get involved in an emotional relationship. In the 27.6 per cent balance of the cases, the relationship between the victim and the offender cannot be determined from the data. From what is known in general about the relationship between victims and offenders, however, a conservative estimate of acquaintanceship between them can be assumed in an additional third of the present indeterminate cases. Such an assumption would bring about 80 per cent of all the homicide cases into the personal-emotional relationship that is characteristic of murder. At the same time, this is not to deny a large emotional component to the remaining indeterminate cases. It is well known that most of the homicides that accompany robbery are the result of fear, panic or mutual assault. Similarly, sexual assaults, by their very nature, are seldom the result of cold calculation and deliberate planning. It should not be surprising that more than half of the 100 homicides perpetrated by females on children in Table 2 are cases of infanticide and, as such, represent the actions of a most emotionally distraught mind.

Considering the emotional nature of the overwhelming proportion of homicides, *it should be clear that the rationality and calculation assumed by the deterrent theory of the proponents of capital punishment is directed*

Table 2

Victims of Convicted Murderers in England and Wales 1900–49

Type of Victim	Convicted Offenders			
	Male	Female	Total	%
Parent	19	1	20	1.7
Wife or Husband	211	13	224	18.5
Children	93	100	193	16.0
Sweetheart	120	–	120	9.9
Mistress or lover	180	4	184	15.2
Quarrel victim (but none of the above)	103	–	103	8.5
Woman, jealousy or revenge (but none of the above)	30	2	32	2.6
Sub-Total: Victim known to offender	756	120	876	72.4
Robbery victim	154	7	161	13.3
Woman, in sexual assault (but none of above)	44	–	44	3.6
Police or prison officer	19	–	19	1.6
Miscellaneous	107	3	110	9.1
Sub-Total: Relationship underterminable	324	10	334	27.6
GRAND TOTAL	1080	130	1,210	100
Per Cent	89.3	10.7	100	100

Derived from Table 2, UK Royal Commission, p. 330.

precisely to those persons least capable, or likely to exhibit it. A further corollary of this theory would lead us to expect higher homicide rates in abolition States than capital punishment States. For, were would-be murderers to some degree rational and calculating, it would be a matter of 'common sense' for offenders to lure their victims into abolition States so that, if they were apprehended, they would escape the death penalty. As shown in Table 1, however, as well as in many other studies on this subject, the evidence for such 'rational actions' on the part of homicidal offenders is not reflected in the homicide rates of abolition States.

The economic argument

Another testable proposition that is sometimes put forward by the proponents of capital punishment is the economic argument in favour of the death penalty. It is asserted that it is 'cheaper' to execute a man than to maintain him in prison for life, or for a long term of years. Unfortunately no studies on the economics of capital punishment have been published. We do, however, know something about the costs of maintaining prisoners in idleness, in inadequate prisons. Such penal institutions are, by and large, pure consumption units which make great demands on public funds.

There are two ways of addressing the assertion that it is 'cheaper' to execute a man than to maintain him in prison under a long sentence. The first is to make explicit the meaning of this assertion, for it implies a great deal more than it says.

Professor Sellin has summarised the counter-argument as follows:

As for the economic argument, it obviously rests on the assumption that murderers in prison cannot be self-supporting as a group and that they must always remain a financial burden on the public unless they are executed. However, the death penalty can hardly be defended on this basis. In a well organised penal system murderers as a group can undoubtedly earn their keep. If the system is not well organised, the fault rests with the public or the administration. No one would seriously suggest *that people should be executed, not because of their crimes, but because the State has not made it possible for them to be self-supporting during imprisonment* because it has taken no proper steps to achieve that end.

Despite the many assertions made about the deterrent effect of capital punishment by its proponents, there is a good deal of indirect evidence to indicate that most of them do not take their own arguments seriously. If the object of the death penalty is to serve as a deterrent to all would-be murderers of the future, then certainly the logical thing to do would be to bring home its lesson most forcefully to the greatest possible number of persons, as was done through unusual circumstances in Chicago in the year 1962. Yet no one has proposed that executions should be held in great stadiums and be televised in order to bring the full deterrent effect into the living rooms of every family in the community. Such a suggestion shocks our sensibilities. The State legislator in a capital punishment State who would sponsor a bill to bring this about would not only have his bill defeated, but he would not long enjoy the support of the voters or his colleagues. Such publicity, designed to achieve the deterrent function, is considered inhuman and unthinkable. Still, it is a logical extension of the capital punishment argument.

Instead we conduct our executions behind prison walls. They take place, mostly, at night.[2] A highly restricted number of persons actually witness them, mainly because it is part of their occupations. When news of the event is broadcast or printed, the many intervening persons and processes between the execution and the public have managed to depersonalise the penalty and it soon seems remote. The recapitulations of the crime, which took place long ago, stir vague and indefinite memories. In two days the whole thing is, for the most part, forgotten. The guilty and the innocent, the condemned and the reprieved, the criminal and the victim, recede in the memory and are lost to the public mind.

There are a number of other aspects of capital punishment that lend themselves to investigation. The partisans of abolition point to

---

2   In America, that is.

the irrevocability of the death penalty if an error in justice is made. The James Foster case of 1956 in Georgia and the John Rexinger case of 1957 in San Francisco are only the most recent examples of persons positively identified as capital offenders, convicted and sentenced to death, only to be saved by the confessions of the actual offender some time later. Had either of these men been executed, not only would it have been a drastic miscarriage of justice, *but all motive to either further investigation of their cases or to obtain confession on the part of the actual murderers would have been dissipated.* Convictions and executions of the innocent were the direct cause of abolition in Maine and Rhode Island.

Just as we have avoided sentimental arguments about capital punishment based on blood lust and cynicism, so have we avoided sentimental arguments based on humanitarianism and an optimistic view of human nature. Nothing that has been said here should be construed as an argument against society's right to protect itself against homicidal offenders. We are not against self-defense in an emergency situation. Faced with the possibility of becoming a victim, or of witnessing the possibility of one's loved ones becoming a victim, any man is entitled to take any measures required to deal with the situation at hand, including the killing of the offender. This is, however, *quite different from the cold-blooded, deliberate infliction of the death penalty by the State months or years after the original offense occurred.* When we act in our corporate capacities, through our laws, which are supposed to be the product of rational processes, our means should be suited to our ends. If the object of capital punishment laws is to reduce the number of homicides in our society, there should be evidence to indicate that this objective is being achieved. If this objective is not being achieved, then we are, in our corporate capacity, *no better than the murderers whom we would murder.* If the object of our laws relating to murder is to protect society from future murder, then life sentences or a term of years in prison will effect the same end without our having to resort to murder in our corporate capacity.

On the basis of the evidence presented above, and in many other studies, there is no reason to believe that capital punishment serves any rational purpose for society. On the contrary, the evidence indicates that those who favour capital punishment are sentimentalists, pure and simple. The hardheaded and practical people who say, 'let us examine the evidence', find that the evidence cannot support the arguments asserted with strong conviction, and embellished by special-pleading anecdotes, by the proponents of capital punishment. The means and ends of this public policy are not related and, therefore, the death penalty does not deal with the homicide problem.

The reader may well wonder why, under these circumstances, capital punishment continues to remain on the statute books. Others may take an uneasy 'comfort' in the notion that historical trends in capital punishment indicate that the death penalty is being applied with less and less frequency over time. Such well-meaning, but naïve, persons believe that the death penalty will disappear through disuse and that, for practical purposes, this is tantamount to abolition. Persons who reason this way betray their ignorance about some of *the real functions that capital punishment serves*, for far more than the death of 'a few' persons convicted of murder is involved. For one thing, the lazy prosecutor whose main interest lies in increasing his conviction rate in the furtherance of his political career finds the mere existence of the death penalty on the statute books to be *an exceedingly useful, coercive, device for obtaining easy convictions.* In the bargaining system of justice that too frequently exists, the lazy prosecutor can always offer not to invoke the death penalty in exchange for a plea of guilty from a defendant who may be difficult to prosecute on the basis of the evidence. Such a coercive use of the death penalty disproportionately exposes the innocent to the possibility of execution for they have no motive to plead guilty. The bargaining power that the mere existence of capital punishment gives to the lazy, but ruthlessly ambitious, prosecutor is the most immoral of reasons for retaining it, but it may help to explain why prosecutors tend to favour the death penalty, and why capital punishment will not disappear through disuse, but must be abolished by affirmative action.

More generally, of even greater importance is the baneful negative effect that the mere existence of the death penalty has on the whole system of the administration of criminal justice. As long as the ultimate sanction in our system of administering criminal justice is a *negative* one, it is that much more difficult to make the criminal law and all its instrumentalities perform a *positive* function on behalf of society. Where the foundation stone of the system of criminal justice is wholly negative, as the death penalty is, then the negative symbolic effect of the mere existence of capital punishment pervades the whole system, for the dead can be neither corrected nor rehabilitated—they are negated. Over against the positive measures attempted by the law, by probation, by the prison system with its rehabilitation programs, by half-way houses and by parole, stands this ultimate negative contradiction that says, in the last analysis the system of criminal justice is negative. It is for reasons of this kind that the death penalty, even if it is *never* applied, should be abolished from the statute books. There can be little comfort in the increasing reluctance on the part of society to exercise capital punishment if its mere existence has such undesirable uses and pervasive negative effects.

Finally, it should be pointed out that as long as people place their faith in the death penalty as an effective remedy for dealing with the serious problem of homicide, they are also effectively barring the way to an investigation of alternative ways of coming to grips with the prevention of murder. A primitive society that is convinced that illness is caused by possession by evil spirits would simply consider modern medicine and social science as dangerous and irrelevant nonsense. Every study that has been made of capital punishment, however, tends to indicate that it is the death penalty that is the dangerous and irrelevant nonsense, because all of the effects that it can be demonstrated to have are negative and its positive functions, if any, continue to elude us. The venerable Socrates, who was executed in 399 BC, maintained to the bitter end that 'the unexamined life is not worth living'. Our examination of capital punishment has led to the conclusion that the unexamined death is not worth dying. Jesus Christ, who was executed at the beginning of our era, said, at the end, 'Father, forgive them, for they know not what they do.' We are still executing people today, and there is still no evidence that we know what we are doing when we inflict the death penalty. Every rational inquiry into the relation between the death penalty and murder has demonstrated that *capital punishment is irrelevant to the homicide rate*. It is, however, a cruel, expensive and demoralising irrelevancy to maintain. Since capital punishment is indefensible on any rational grounds, and since the only purpose it can serve is that of an irrational vengeance that is no better than the original homicide to which it answers in kind, it is high time that the death penalty be abolished.

12

Views on the alternative to capital punishment and the commutation of sentences

Sir John Vincent Barry, QC

Sir John Vincent Barry (1903–1969), a leading Australian jurist, was a Justice of the Supreme Court of Victoria 1947–69. He chaired the Criminology Department of the University of Melbourne 1951–69 and the Parole Board of Victoria 1957–69. In 1955 and 1960 he led Australian delegations to United Nations congresses on crime prevention and the treatment of offenders. As a barrister he had been active in the ALP, and was a federal candidate in 1943. He was awarded an LLD for *Alexander Maconochie of Norfolk Island* (1958), a study of an important penal reformer. His *The Courts and Criminal Punishments* (1969) was published posthumously.[1]

In 1966 he answered questions posed by the United Nations Bureau of Social Affairs, and his reply to one of them appears below.

* * *

On the basis of your professional experience and of informed opinion in your country, what 'alternative sanctions' should be applied?

A judicial sentence of imprisonment for life. The case should be examined at the expiration of seven years by an expert and

---

1   *Australian Dictionary of Biography*, vol. 13, 1993 by Bernard Teague.

independent Board, unless the responsible Minister requests the tribunal to examine it earlier. Unless there were exceptional circumstances, the first review at the expiration of seven years would not result in a recommendation for release. The function of the Board should be to report and recommend to the Executive Government, and the decision to act upon or reject the recommendation should remain with the government.

In Victoria, the Parole Board consisting (where males are involved) of a Supreme Court Judge, the Director-General of Social Welfare (of whose department the penal system is a division), and three men, who are at present a former chief stipendiary magistrate, a former chairman of the Indeterminate Sentences Board, now replaced by the Parole Board, and the president of the Prisoners' Aid Society, and (where females are involved) of the Supreme Court Judge and the Director-General and three women experienced in social problems, has the obligation of making a written report and recommendation each year to the responsible Minister with respect to all prisoners who were convicted of murder committed while under eighteen. If the Minister requests the Parole Board to do so, it must make a written report and recommendation to him with respect to any person who was sentenced to death but whose sentence was commuted to imprisonment. If the Minister accepts a recommendation for release, he must bring it before Cabinet in order to obtain a decision for release That can be made effective by resolution of the Executive Council, which is the constitutional body which gives legal effect to Cabinet decisions. The recommendation invariably requires the person released to be subject to parole supervision for a period of five or seven years, and to observe appropriate conditions of parole.

If a sentence of death upon a prisoner over eighteen years of age is commuted to imprisonment by Executive decision, the Executive is empowered by statute to fix a period of imprisonment, and within that period, a minimum term during which the prisoner shall not be eligible for release. Formerly the general practice was to commute a sentence of death to life imprisonment. During recent years, however, the practice of Cabinet when commuting a sentence of death has been to fix a long period of imprisonment with a substantial minimum term; e.g. forty years imprisonment, with a minimum term of thirty years. The reason for this current practice is largely political and to satisfy public feeling. I consider it is an undesirable practice, and that the former practice of commuting the death sentence to life imprisonment, which enabled the Minister to ask for a report from the Parole Board after, say, eight or ten or twelve or fifteen years had been served, is preferable.

In those cases where imprisonment is part of the alternative sanction:

1. *Should the sentence be indeterminate, indefinite, or to a prescribed term?* Indefinite, i.e., life.
2. *Who should determine the actual date of release of an offender?* The Executive Government, in the light of a report and recommendation from an independent Board.
3. *If a special agency, board or committee should advise upon or determine the date of release, what should be its powers and composition?* I consider the system in Victoria whereby the Parole Board makes a report and recommendation to the responsible Minister is satisfactory.
4. *Should there be a maximum time for which such offenders may be held in prison?* Not as a matter of legally unalterable stipulation.
5. *Should the conditions of imprisonment of offenders subject to an 'alternative sanction' differ from those applied to other types of offenders? (For example, should they never be held in open institutions?)* For practical reasons, such offenders should normally be held in security institutions, but if a prisoner is not an escape risk or dangerous, confinement in a medium security institution would not be inappropriate. When release is contemplated, a prisoner should spend six months or a year before release in a minimum security institution.
6. *Should the arrangements for supervision of such offenders differ from those provided for other prisoners when released from prison?* Experience in this State has shown that the officers of the Parole Service can exercise adequate supervision.

13

The victims of a hanging are you and me

Sir Eugene Gorman, QC

Sir Eugene Gorman, QC (1891–1973) was a Melbourne barrister with an exceptional range of interests and expertise from criminal to commercial law, and a consummate networker and fixer who served in the army in both world wars.[1]

This article, from the Melbourne *Herald*, 22 December 1966, and the one following, were published in Melbourne newspapers at the time of the Victorian government's decision to hang Ronald Ryan.

* * *

Once more our community is involved in the controversy which inevitably arises when government determines that a man's neck shall be broken by a hangman.

The facts of the present case are public property. A hardened criminal escaping from custody, seized a rifle with which, the court has found, he killed an unfortunate warder.

Had the criminal been shot dead on the spot his death would have been readily acceptable to most of us.

His record excludes him from sympathy and his ultimate crime should result in life imprisonment. His detention for life would be costly to the State.

He falls within the class of those who, in George Bernard Shaw's

---

1   *Australian Dictionary of Biography*, vol. 14, 1996 by Barry Jones.

words, 'give more trouble to the community than they are worth'.

The argument for his official slaughter is that Ryan should be put away as we would a mad dog.

'Why should we worry about Ryan?' people are asking.

My plea is not for Ryan, but for ourselves. From the moment a decision to hang a man is announced and up to the time it is put into effect and long afterwards, many thinking members of the community are affected.

They regard the official neck-breaking as intolerable to the imagination and discreditable to the State, and for this they must not be branded as mere sentimentalists.

As early as 1841, a Select Committee of the State Assembly of New York reported to the Assembly 'that the pronouncement of death, by law, ought to be forthwith and forever abolished'. Under Governor Rockefeller, a century and a quarter later, it was abolished.

Executions are no longer public, but furtive. This, of course, is quite illogical if the performance is designed as a deterrent. The last public execution in France was in 1939 when Weidmann, a murderer several times over, was guillotined.

Paris Soir published full-page pictures of the gruesome operation, but the officials connected with it, and the government itself, surprisingly enough, derived no satisfaction from this excellent publicity. Why, if it was a desirable happening?

For, as French writer Albert Camus urged, 'if capital punishment is to be exemplary, then the number of newspaper photographs should be multiplied, the entire populace invited and the ceremony televised for those unable to attend.

'How,' he asked, 'can a furtive murder committed in a prison yard serve as an example?'

We are at least entitled to eye-witness accounts and medical reports describing the state of the body after the hanging. I have heard a famous surgeon, now dead, give a gruesome description of cases when the hangman lacked the necessary expertness. Hanging is, at best, a very crude operation practised in conditions that make its duration uncertain and its performance horrible.

Few men have ever witnessed an execution without becoming

instantaneous converts to the abolition of the death penalty.

The supreme act of justice nauseates the citizen it is supposed to protect. The official murder, so far from offering a redress for the offence committed against society, adds instead a second defilement to the first.

Most men fear death but the fact is that the fear of death, no matter how great it may be, has never sufficed to harness human passions effectively. If the death penalty was to be really intimidating, human nature itself would have to be raised far above what it is. In the murderer, the fear of death comes after, not before, the commission of the crime. All statistics show and are supported by the report of the English Select Committee of 1930, that in the countries which have abolished the death penalty, as well as in others, there is no connexion between the death penalty and the incidence of crime.

In the thirty-three nations that have abolished the death penalty, or no longer impose it, the number of murders has not increased. The murder rate is no higher in Queensland and New South Wales where capital punishment for murder has been abolished, than it is in the four States that retain it.

Let us recognise an execution for what it ultimately is — a revenge which goes by the name of 'retaliation'.

And when the State kills, the way in which it is done, and what goes before, has features more appalling than any murder.

There is the devastating and degrading fear inflicted on the condemned man for weeks and sometimes for months, a punishment more terrible than death itself.

When the condemned creature is finally brought to the gallows he is no longer a man and a child of God but a thing waiting to be strangled by the hangman, kept alive to that moment for the performance of a disgusting and debasing ritual.

The chairman of the UK Royal Commission on Capital Punishment, 1949–63, Sir Ernest Gowers, wrote:

Before serving on the Royal Commission I, like most other people, had given no great thought to the problem. If I had been asked for my opinion, I should probably have said that I was in favour of the death penalty, and disposed to regard abolitionists as people whose hearts were bigger than their heads.

Four years of close study gradually dispelled that feeling. In the end I became convinced that abolitionists were right in their conclusions—though I could not agree with all their arguments—and that so far from the sentimental approach leading into their camp and the rational one into that of the supporters, it was the other way about.

Does this opinion, which can be matched from innumerable responsible sources, mean nothing to the Bolte government?

It is saddening and perturbing that the government should be impervious to rational discussion and impatiently obdurate in adhering to a decision that should never have been taken.

For eleven years the Bolte government has consistently reprieved murderers, some of whom were guilty of killings far more shocking than Ryan's.

The abrupt departure from what seemed to have become a settled practice requires that the people of Victoria should be told the reasons which make it necessary to hang Ryan.

14

Why can't we be reasonable about hanging?

Stanley Johnson

Stanley Johnson (1932–2018) studied law at the University of Melbourne, was chair of its Criminology Department 1958–78, and then practised as a barrister. His published works include *Criminal Homicide Rates in Australia* (1962). This extract is from *The Australian*, 17 December 1966.

* * *

I hope the minority of four in the Victorian Cabinet will yet oblige the majority of eleven to a statement of reasons for differentiating between the three death sentences the Cabinet considered last Monday.

Reasons may not be everything and it does an academic no harm to admit that truth is something greater than reason. But I have yet to discover that truth is inconsistent with reason.

If, in fact, there was no reasonable basis for Cabinet's decision it is hard to see how any defence of Ronald Ryan can take hold now. However, since in this case reason seems to come out against the hanging, I shall ignore the obviously bad advice of Charles I—'Never make a defence or apology before you be accused'—and will rush in with answers to arguments which might have affected the government.

157

Some answers

In the first place, Ryan's death can give no real compensation to the victim's family.

Secondly, Ryan, aged forty-two, is not getting equal justice with other murderers, nor with his younger accomplice in the escape, Peter Walker, who lives on because of the vagaries of juries.

Is it imperative that people should be given their just deserts, or does justice merely permit retributive brutality when brutes cannot be restrained? If the former, Ryan suffers justly and other murderers unjustly.

If the latter, and if mercy has any part in justice, why has Ryan not attracted the mercy extended to others? He dies, presumably because he was the older criminal—perhaps simply because he has an unattractive face.

There may be some exceptions to Abraham Lincoln's quip that every man is responsible for his own face after forty. Perhaps Dr Allan Bartholomew's research on cosmetic surgery for prisoners has come too late. Even though Ryan would not have been a candidate for it, the research itself may make community reactions to a pugnacious front more remedial.

Thirdly, the proposition that hanging might be more humane than life imprisonment is just cynical.

We could test it by leaving the choice to the condemned man. Like anyone else, he could contract out by suicide at any time. My guess is that, since life, and potentially vigorous community life, still goes on even in prison, a prisoner would normally adopt the normal attitude that while there is life there is hope.

A fourth possible reason is that Ryan is as good a scapegoat as any to be sacrificed as a general deterrent. The government might be aiming to deter other crimes of violence and also to provide a general social discipline, intended currently (judging by a remark from Sir Henry Bolte) to remind political demonstrators that civil disobedience should not cross over into criminal obstruction of the police.

Deterrent?

It is not difficult to concede that the death penalty operates as a deterrent, at least with the 42 per cent of Victorians, who, according to the latest Gallup Poll, favour the retention of capital punishment. That is a matter for introspection before statistical analysis.

Capital punishment must produce a long-term effect on society's attitude to killing, an influence that will operate—if only unconsciously—in even the most impulsive killing. What that effect is, however, one cannot be sure: it might add to, or it might lessen, the horror of killing.

The question therefore becomes: Does capital punishment operate *effectively* to deter murders? This one is a matter for statistics, and excellent statistical studies are available to those who are concerned with the truth.

Professor Thorsten Sellin, of Pennsylvania, has demonstrated convincingly that 'executions have no discernible effect on homicide death rates'.

Sellin was accepted by the Ceylon Commission of Inquiry on Capital Punishment in 1959 as 'the world's leading authority on statistical material relating to homicide and capital punishment', as he had been accepted before by similar commissions in Europe and America.

The figures of murders reported by the Victorian police since Tait was threatened with execution in 1962 are neither here nor there. The figures fluctuate widely, but even so the deviations from the growth line which is to be expected with increasing population are only just outside the statistical range of chance predictable from the 1945–61 reports.

The fluctuations are less a reflection of public violence than of the difficulty of recording that violence meaningfully. For instance, were the Ryan-Walker slayings one, two or four 'murders'? The Supreme Court found that they amounted to one murder and two manslaughters—which, of course, are arbitrary tags enabling action *about* violence. How do you measure violence as such? The behaviour to be deterred, and measured, will include also both attempts at murder and such non-negligent violence as might accidentally lead to death. For it was the latter for which Ryan is to be hanged.

When future historians look back on this era, they will possibly observe that murders and the attendant decisions to hang were not significantly influenced by each other, but were both products of a more diffuse, over-reactive boorishness in the community.

Certainly, nobody studying the operative causes or conditions of individual murderers seriously proceeds on the basis that they were any different in retentionist Victoria from abolitionist New South Wales. And if the hanging is not relevant to such a study, it is surely unjustifiable.

Potection of police and warders

The fifth possible explanation, and the only one that takes this decision on Ryan out of the class of a lottery, is that when a prisoner murders a guard he should be hanged as an example to other prisoners.

Is this just a nervous twitching, an attitude that we ought to 'do something', or is the case for hanging really stronger when no other sanction is left?

In New South Wales when Simmons and Newcombe, after breaking out of Long Bay, broke into the Emu Plains prison and murdered an officer, the death penalty was not restored. Ryan was not a life prisoner, of course, and other sanctions ARE available: longer imprisonment (which his accomplice will suffer), postponement of parole, Pentridge's H Division and solitary confinement, and the ordinary discipline of adjusting earnings, good-time remissions and other privileges.

But to the general issue. Australia has no great fund of experience or study of this threat to law-enforcement officers. We have to adapt lessons learnt in Britain and North America.

In England the Criminal Justice Bill of 1948 at first proposed that murder while escaping from lawful custody should remain as capital murder. That principle was enacted in the Homicide Act of 1957, remaining until total abolition of capital punishment in 1965.

The American State of Maine abolished capital punishment for murder in 1876, restored it in 1883 following an attack on a guard by an insane convict, and reabolished it finally in 1887.

In the US today North Dakota retains capital punishment only for treason and for murder in the first degree committed by a prisoner already serving a sentence for murder in the first degree. Rhode Island keeps it only for murder committed by a life prisoner.

Thus it is generally accepted that the prison officer has a stronger case than the police officer. The most telling dialogue on the issue, however, the Mulligan-Sellin exchange, concerns the police.

In 1954 Walter Mulligan, president of the Chief Constables Association of Canada, told the Canadian parliamentary committee enquiring into capital punishment:

> Our main objection is that abolition would adversely affect the personal safety of police officers in the daily discharge of their duties. It would be interesting to know, and if time had permitted I would have tried to obtain this vital information as to the number of policemen murdered in the execution of their duty in those parts of the world where capital punishment has been abolished.
>
> I submit that it will be found the number is much higher than in those countries where the death penalty is still in effect, and this point is the main one in our submission that our government should retain capital punishment as a form of security.

'This vital informaion' was thereupon acquired by Sellin and Father Donald R. Campion, S.J. In an extensive empirical study they found that, though the difference was not significant, the risks of police being killed by criminals are slightly less in cities in the states not having capital punishment. 'It is impossible to conclude that the states which had no death penalty had thereby made the policeman's lot more hazardous.' The figures for Chicago were so exceptional that they were omitted from the calculation, the mild point being taken that 'it would be indiscreet for anyone to claim that the death penalty in Chicago discouraged the killing of policemen in that city'.[1]

---

1   American Law Institute's Report on Capital Punishment, 1959.

The authoritative U.K. Commission on Capital Punishment 1953 was unimpressed by police and prison witnesses who 'were convinced of the uniquely deterrent value of capital punishment in its effect on professional criminals' and on life prisoners.

The report warned against basing a penal policy 'on exaggerated estimates of the uniquely deterrent force of the death penalty.'

In 1958 the Massachusetts Commission Investigating the Death Penalty adopted the findings of Prof. Albert Morris in a study of assaults with intent to kill committed over a decade by prisoners in 26 states. The data were supplied by wardens, and showed 'that such assaults occur more frequently in prisons in states which have the death penalty than they do in those which do not.'

If anything, Ryan's death will drive a wedge between officers and inmates, making it harder to win a discipline based on any co-operative focus on the insistent personal problems that really confront prisoners.

If this death penalty is not executed, should we fear that a prison officer will relax his efforts to enforce the law when the full discharge of his duties might place his own life in jeopardy?

That is always possible anyway. But it might be no loss to ease up on purely repressive measures if in their place we develop a constructive co-operative discipline.

I think that if the beast who sleeps in man could be held down by threats—any kind of threat, whether of gaol or retribution after death—then the highest emblem of humanity would be the lion tamer in the circus with his whip, not the prophet who sacrificed himself.

But don't you see, this is just the point: 'What has for centuries raised man above the beast is not the cudgel but an inward music; the irresistible power of warmest truth, the powerful attraction of its example.'[2]

In reason and in truth, this hanging is indefensible. It will not prevent another killing, nor will it reduce other violence. It is an unjust act of vengeance.

---

2   *Doctor Zhivago*, Boris Pasternak.

15

A creed for abolitionists

Arthur Koestler & C.H. Rolph

This brief summary of the main arguments and beliefs of the Abolitionists is taken from *Hanged by the Neck* by Arthur Koestler and C.H. Rolph (1961).

Arthur Koestler (1905–1983), born in Budapest, trained as a scientist at Vienna University, but became a journalist. Active in the Communist Party 1931–38, he became disillusioned with communist theory in practice while fighting for the Republic in the Spanish Civil War. His experiences as a prisoner of war under sentence of death are recorded in *Dialogue with Death* (1937). His masterpiece was *Darkness at Noon* (1941), a study of an old Bolshevik executed during the Moscow trials. He became a patron of the Anti-Hanging Committee, Victoria.

C.H. Rolph was the pen-name of Cecil Rolph Hewitt (1901–1994). He served in the City of London Police from 1921–46, rising to Chief Inspector. He was on the editorial staff of the *New Statesman* 1947–70. He became an exceptionally powerful advocate of police reform, abolition of the death penalty, and censorship.

* * *

One should not deride what is sometimes called the 'emotional' condemnation of the death penalty, for the emotions or inherent feelings can sometimes be a sure guide to what is right. But the abolitionist case is complete on other grounds; and it may be convenient to have, in summarised form, a 'creed' which crystallises one's thoughts:

1. Every kind of punishment deters; but the experience of abolitionist countries shows that the death penalty is neither a necessary nor a unique deterrent.
2. The death penalty is irremediable. When a mistake has been made—and it is known now that there have been mistakes—nothing can put it right.
3. The hangman is a disgrace to any civilised country. Doctors (through the B.M.A.) have made it clear that they would never take over the executioner's job by administering lethal injections. We depend, for our professional killers, on the type of person who voluntarily applies for the job of operating a rope and trapdoor.
4. Murder is largely committed by insane or psychopathic people, to whom the death penalty has little or no meaning.
5. Reliance on the death penalty discourages the reduction of crime which would follow an all-out attack on its social causes.
6. The death penalty foregoes all hope of reforming the offender.
7. Executions magnify the unwholesome news value of murder reports, leading to imitative crime.
8. This is the one public problem, above all, in which governments should lead the governed. 'The voice of the people' can be sane and rational, or irrationally impassioned when under the influence of demagogy or sensationalism.
9. There are worse crimes than direct murder, yet we punish them with prison sentences of a few years' duration—and often we do not punish them at all: fraudulent conspiracies, for example, which often result in ruin and even premature death for many victims.
10. The few murderers who would have to be imprisoned for life—perhaps one a year—are certain to be the mentally dangerous types who would have to be placed in lifelong confinement sooner or later, whether they murdered or not.
11. The Old Testament doctrine 'an eye for an eye', etc., totally rejected by the New Testament, was in any event no more than a relic of a Babylonian law which *prohibited the exaction of more than an eye for an eye.* Even so, we do not commit indecent

assaults on men convicted of indecent assault, or burn down the house of a person convicted of arson; and whereas the murderer's victim meets his death in minutes or seconds, we take an average of five months to kill the murderer, playing with him all the time.

12. Abolition of the death penalty has never made any difference to the number of murders in any country.

16

What about the victims?

Arthur Koestler & C.H. Rolph

To some extent, the cry 'What about the Victims?' might be regarded as a red herring when considering the death penalty, but as Koestler and Rolph point out in the extract below, every time the controversy about the death penalty arises, one of the most commonly used cries of the retentionists is this demand that we think of the victim and forget our sympathy for the murderer. As Koestler and Rolph point out, it has very often been abolitionists who have so far publicly urged the adoption of schemes to compensate victims of crime. In Victoria, the Anti-Hanging Council has as one of its three major objectives 'the securing of compensation for the victims of criminal attack and/or their families', and has sought deputations to present the case for legislation before state cabinet ministers. The council seeks to secure compassion for both criminal and victim, to replace the primitive paying back of violence by more violence by supporters of capital punishment.

The Koestler and Rolph extract below from *Hanged by the Neck*, states the United Kingdom position in 1961. In June 1964, a Criminal Injuries Compensation Board was set up in England to provide for *ex gratia* payments to victims and their families.

* * *

Every fresh public eruption of the death-penalty controversy produces its crop of 'Letters to the Editor' expressing angry astonishment that the abolitionists 'reserve all their sympathy for the murderer and

166

haven't a thought for his victim'. It is a monstrous untruth, which has nevertheless survived every exposure and will endure until the death penalty is finally abolished; but we must here expose its falsity yet again, since it must never be allowed to go by default.

The only people who have so far publicly urged the adoption of a scheme to compensate victims of crime are people who wish to see the death penalty abolished. Those who say that the abolitionist always forgets the victim are likely to be those who would resist the small addition to the National Insurance contribution that would enable victims to be compensated (2d a year would probably be enough, as we explain later). The ludicrous position at present is that, if you are disabled or hurt by falling downstairs at your place of employment, you will be compensated by the State under the National Health (Industrial Injuries) Act; whereas if someone pushes you downstairs at home with the intention of killing or maiming you, you will get nothing. The relatives of a murdered man get nothing. They are not the State's concern. What the State does is to catch the murderer (if he can be caught) and kill him. Or it will catch the violent robber or the rapist who has done injury to one of its proteges (if he can be caught) and send him to prison.

The victim (if he lives) and his dependants have to be satisfied with this. Eight hundred years ago a victim could lawfully take certain kinds of personal vengeance upon the man who had wronged him, but the law has gradually withdrawn this privilege from the victims and taken upon itself the duty of punishing. When a 'tort', a civil wrong, is found to be occurring on a sufficiently large scale to merit the interference of the State, that tort is made into a crime; and thereupon the victim loses virtually all rights except that of seeing his enemy go to prison — or to the gallows. Two hundred years ago, for example, a man who obtained goods or money by 'false pretences' could be brought into Court and sued for the return of the goods or money. He could not be prosecuted as a criminal because the law regarded his victim as a fool who probably needed the lesson in safeguarding his own property and interests. The expansion of commerce and the beginning of the credit system encouraged 'false pretences' until it became what in these days we should call a racket.

So in 1757 it was made a crime. Ever since, a steady proportion of the prison population has consisted of 'false pretence' experts, who now serve a prison sentence and come out to enjoy the salted-away proceeds of their crimes.

That, if you have not thought of it before, may seem daft enough. But consider another typical consequence of the law's concern for victims. About twenty years ago an American soldier and a teenage Welsh girl were together convicted of the murder of a London taxi-driver. The soldier had shot the cabby and robbed him of a few pounds. The soldier was executed, and the girl, being under eighteen, was imprisoned 'during His Majesty's pleasure'. She was released after eight years, and was then asked by two of our Sunday newspapers, bidding against each other in mounting thousands, to 'write' her reminiscences. They were 'ghosted' for her, and the fee she received was £4,500. Now for the true touch of irony. The widow and orphans of the murdered man received absolutely nothing—the State had discharged its obligation to them by killing the soldier and imprisoning the girl.

This is the state of affairs that has been accepted for centuries, without question, by the 'punishers', by those who demand 'an eye for an eye', by those who taunt the abolitionists with 'what about the victim?'

It was Miss Margery Fry who, at the age of 74, began in the last years of her life the campaign that is now at last engaging the leisurely attention of the government, a campaign to secure some compensation for victims and their dependants. She had found cases in which victims of robbery were disabled for life; she got to know a girl who was violently raped, partially lost her reason, and spent all her days in a wheeled-chair. None of them had ever had a penny by way of compensation—their assailants were either unknown or penniless, and there was no public fund from which the money could have come. Margery Fry needed facts and figures for her campaign. None of the well-known trusts and foundations was then interested in financing such a research: the criminal law dealt with all that— murderers were killed and assailants were imprisoned. If they were put on probation (but not otherwise) they could be ordered to pay some compensation; but since they were usually quite unable to do so, the order would merely mean a sentence of imprisonment, after all, for failing to comply. What more could be done?

Miss Fry found a young law student who had the time and enthusiasm to sit in the Old Bailey courts for three months and take notes about the financial resources of violent criminals and their victims. To pay him a modest fee (for even a law student has to eat) she 'sold a few securities'. His report sent her off to the Home Office, the Ministry of National Insurance, and the Treasury, with tentative proposals for the compensation of victims as National Health beneficiaries. The Home Office was sufficiently impressed to ask a number of provincial chief constables to give her facilities for a larger inquiry at provincial Assize Courts on similar lines to the 'pilot' study at the Old Bailey. Her facts and figures mounted, and she bombarded the government with them. In due course Mr R. A. Butler, the Home Secretary, referred the 'problem' to the Home Office Research Unit, which is staffed by some of the ablest social statisticians in the world.

They found difficulties, inevitably, and as Margery Fry had expected. What about the victim whose assailant was acquitted? What about husband-and-wife cases, the 'drunken Saturday night'? If the criminal is to be made to pay, how do you know whether his money was honestly come by? If he is to pay out of prison earnings, what good is the present derisory maximum of about five shillings a week? Even if the maximum could be £5 a week, how can a prisoner repay bank-robbery proceeds amounting to £20,000? If an ex-prisoner, or a convicted man on probation, is to pay by instalments some huge sum to a crippled victim, are you not keeping a man in lifelong servitude, as the evil-minded creditors in Dickens's day kept their enemies in the Fleet Prison? Won't some people let themselves be injured in order to share the compensation secretly with those who injured them?

There were dozens of questions like this, but perhaps the choicest of all was put forward by the political correspondent of *The Times* on 27 January 1961:

> The question arises whether public opinion is ripe for the introduction
> of a scheme which would involve 23 million workers accepting an

increase in their weekly stamp contributions to provide a general or limited insurance for victims of crime.

If those 23 million workers paid one penny a week each, the product would be nearly £5 million a year. Margery Fry's final estimate of the sum needed to meet all cases was £200,000 a year, and the government have more than once intimated that for a scheme confined to violent crimes 'against the person', this might possibly be enough—one twenty-fifth of the sum produced by a penny on the weekly stamp contribution. Yet *The Times* can solemnly say that there are 'doubts whether the Treasury would back a general scheme which could be said to amount to as big a change as the original introduction of the Industrial Injuries Act.' Do you not hear again the voices of Ellenborough, Paley, and Coke, with a muttering background supplied by Gradgrind, Scrooge, and the man who first ejaculated, 'I'm all right, Jack!'?

Two or three Members of Parliament, in 1958 and 1959, prepared private member's Bills in the hope of getting something done. (Each of them was an abolitionist.) One of these would have provided compensation only when a conviction was obtained, thus excluding a large class of deserving cases. Another would have depended entirely on the criminal's cash resources—thus, as we have said, turning a blind eye to the origin of those resources, but at least acknowledging the important principle of 'punitive restitution', which at present the criminal law treats as something mildly eccentric—the idea has been buried for centuries.

'What about the victim?' has long been more than an emotive catch-phrase among those who would see the death penalty abolished in this country. It is a vital and human part of an intelligent plan of action. It recognises, or should recognise, that there are other victims than the person murdered. There are his wife and family, his dependants and relatives, his close friends—an outspreading circle of people with a poignant claim upon our sympathy, to say nothing of a few self-evident but largely unrecognised claims upon the State. But there are also those who stand in the same relationship with the executed prisoner ... Have you ever known the widow or children of a man executed for murder, his fiancée, his parents? This is the experience of many social workers, particularly Probation Officers and those concerned in child welfare. And to know such victims of the death penalty, however casually or slightly, is to acquire a mental burden that is never to be shaken off, never to be lightened by sighing to oneself: 'Such things must be.'

An eye for an eye

This 'eye for an eye' doctrine is worth considering again. It appears after the Ten Commandments in the Book of Exodus, where the Lord speaks from Mount Sinai to his people. Having told them that a loyal servant's ear should be 'bored through with an awl' to indicate perpetual servitude he ordains that 'He that curseth his father or his mother shall surely be put to death,' while,

> if men strive, and hurl a woman with child, so that her fruit depart from her, and yet no mischief follow, he shall be surely punished, according as the woman's husband will lay upon him; and he shall pay as the judges determine. And if any mischief follow, then thou shalt give life for life, eye for eye, tooth for tooth, hand for hand, foot for foot, burning for burning, wound for wound, stripe for stripe.

And among the injunctions with which this code then concludes are the words which, over the centuries, have sent legions of innocent old ladies to their deaths: 'Thou shalt not suffer a witch to live'.

We have permission to relate here the sequel to a murder case which in November 1960 filled the newspapers in California, a State where juries can decide the sentences at homicide trials. Here, first, is the Associated Press report:

LOS ANGELES, 17 November. Superior Judge William E. Fox yesterday told the seven women of a jury that had just voted 'life imprisonment' for a sex-killer: 'I can't understand how you can allow this man to be set free after twelve years, as your verdict will permit. I can only hope

that he will not meet any of you ladies some night in a dark place.'
Several of the women left the jury box weeping. The verdict was against
RAYMOND w. CLEMMONS, 36, convicted of strangling the 19-year
old daughter of a Hollywood screen writer.

We have a letter from the girl's mother dated 30 November 1960.
This is what it says:

> I cannot believe that capital punishment is a solution—to abolish
> murder by murdering, an endless chain of murdering. When I heard
> that my daughter's murderer was not to be executed, my first reaction
> was immense relief from an additional torment: the usual catastrophe,
> breeding more catastrophe, was to be stopped—it might be possible
> to turn the bad into good. I felt that this man, the victim of a terrible
> sickness, of a demon over which he had no control, might even help
> to establish the reasons that caused his insanity and to find a cure for it.
> Maybe he became what he is because of unnamable humiliations and
> rejection. To become useful would be a way to cure him. Neither those
> seven brave women of the jury nor any other women would have cause
> to fear him after twelve years.
>
> My daughter was against capital punishment. When she was eight
> years old she came home from school one day and told me a little boy
> had thrown a glass of water over her. 'And what did you do?' I asked
> her. 'At first,' she said, 'I wanted to do the same to him, but I suddenly
> *saw* myself doing what *he* did. He would have won.' As she grew up, this
> idea grew into a desire to *help* the destroyer.
>
> If it is to be 'an eye for an eye and a tooth for a tooth', this will soon
> be a blind and toothless world.

At the mother's request we refrain from publishing her name. But
here are two other instances in which, to judge from the results of an
inquiry conducted by *Picture Post* in February 1956, the desire for an
expiatory killing has not been shared by the victim's relatives.

First, the case of Thomas Bancroft, sentenced to death and then
reprieved at Manchester in December 1955 for the murder of a
five-month-old baby, Roy Alan Hancock. The baby had been left

in Bancroft's care while the parents were at work. It was crying incessantly, and to 'try to soothe him and stop him crying' Bancroft took hold of the child and then (he said) his temper 'got the better of him'. His defence was manslaughter; he intended neither to kill the child nor to hurt it. When Mr William Hancock, the child's father, was told that Bancroft had been reprieved, he said: 'We are delighted. I know we have suffered, but hanging him would not bring our baby back to life.' And Mrs Hancock said: 'Nobody gains anything by hanging. I too, have been dreading 9 am today.'

Second, the case of Janet Marshall, a Nottingham schoolteacher, who was murdered in Northern France in August 1955. Here are extracts from letters written to the Editor of *Picture Post* by her brother and her sister-in-law — before anyone had been arrested for the murder.

We have for some time been in favour of the abolition of capital punishment. The murder of our dearly beloved sister, Janet Marshall, has only served to increase our conviction that this evil should be abolished.

In a further letter the brother wrote:

I now feel more convinced than ever that capital punishment is an evil and unnecessary thing. It might be thought strange that I have no bitterness whatever towards her murderer in spite of the dreadful hole it has made in my life, and this leads me to think that revenge is not a natural human emotion and that Christ's teaching on this matter was fundamentally sound. I never discussed this matter with my sister, although at times we ventured pretty close to it, but knowing how she and I so often agreed on issues of this kind I should not be surprised if her views on it were the same as mine.

Part III

The Case for Retention

17

An editor's dilemma

It would be difficult to exaggerate the editorial difficulty in assembling a publishable collection of strongly retentionist material for the first edition of *The Penalty is Death* in 1968. Until abolition in the United Kingdom, Canada, Australia, Ireland, and New Zealand, the retentionist philosophy was rarely propounded as such. Most retentionist speeches used to be of the admonitory, finger-wagging, 'but what if' variety, objecting to the time, form, and extent of abolition rather than the principle itself, and expressing fears of a future crime wave.

In 1968 the book had been concerned primarily with death as a punishment for civil crime in the modern secular state, terrorism, and treason; the religious (or pseudo-religious) arguments for and against executions were largely avoided, if not evaded. These arguments have a depressing circularity, consisting of an endless exchange of texts.

The emphasis on 'modern' was important. In antiquity, and with populations on the move, there were limited means to accommodate in their midst persons who were dangerous.

'Fundamentalist' retentionists regard the Noahic and Mosaic codes as the basis of modern law, still morally binding on believers ('Whoever sheds the blood of man, by man shall his blood be shed; for God made man in his own image', Genesis ix. 6), having been endorsed by St Paul. (The civil authority … 'is God's servant for your good. But if you do wrong, be afraid, for he does not bear the sword in vain; he is the servant of God to execute his wrath upon the wrongdoer', Romans xiv. 4).

Abolitionists claim almost universal support by Christian and Jewish leaders, stressing that retentionists are highly selective in their use of texts, forgetting that the Mosaic Law also prescribed death for disobedient servants, Sabbath breakers who kindled fire, witches, for cursing one's parents and working on the day of Atonement. Also the words of Christ (Matthew v. 38–42), St Paul (Romans xii. 17–21), and the experience of the early Church (denounced for its opposition to the death penalty by Julian the Apostate, c. A.D. 350) are hard to reconcile with the retentionist stance.

In his collection entitled *The Death Penalty in America*, Professor Hugo Adam Bedau obviously faced the same problems as the present editor. Indeed two essays printed under the general heading 'The Argument for the Death Penalty' can be of little assistance in advancing the retentionist argument. Professor Sidney Hook (who has publicly debated as an abolitionist on several occasions) writes, 'I conclude … that no valid case has so far been made for the retention of capital punishment, that the argument from deterrence is inconclusive and inconsistent.' He would permit the death sentence to be carried out only if the prisoner requested it and in the case of the hypothetical uncontrollable murderer who killed again in prison. Professor Jacques Barzun's highly subjective argument is based on the premise, 'Whereas the objector to capital punishment feels that death is the greatest of evils, *I feel* that imprisonment is worse than death', and that long prison terms are more dehumanising than execution. He does not, however, argue that the death penalty should be extended to all crimes involving heavy penalties.

The English writer C.S. Lewis (1898–1963) was not so much a supporter of retention as an opponent of the glib humanism or liberalism that he saw behind abolitionists. He reserved his sharpest barbs for advocates of 'moral relativity' who saw crime as a species of disease and would 'treat' the criminal, denying him his natural right to be punished so that, in accord with the Christian doctrine of 'desert', he might 'atone' for his crime as 'expiation'. Lewis did not leave his study at Magdalen College, Oxford, to examine the raw material of criminology and sociology. He may have had some difficulty in finding convicts who would conform to his assessment of their psychological and moral needs.

Lewis was intensely contemptuous of the 'deterrent' theory,

pointing out the extreme immorality of punishing A in order to induce B to change his behaviour—that is, ignoring A's personal needs in order to satisfy B's. Also he was quick to point out (as had Shaw) that hanging an innocent man was probably a greater deterrent in the community at large than executing the guilty.

18

A retentionist's view

Joseph de Maistre

Joseph de Maistre (1753–1821), a French (Savoyard) writer and diplomat, was one of the earliest and most articulate spokesmen for retention. He was employed by the King of Sardinia-Piedmont, and ambassador to Russia (1803–17). In his *St Petersburg Dialogues*, left incomplete at his death and published posthumously, he argued that Europe should be united under the Pope's rule, and that the executioner was the best bulwark society had against disorder. The importance of de Maistre lies in his enthusiastic advocacy of capital punishment, and profound seriousness and philosophical approach to the subject. The extract below is somewhat abstract, but repays close study.

* * *

The general law, visible and visibly just, is that *the greatest amount of happiness, even temporal, belongs, not to the virtuous man, but to virtue.* If it were otherwise, there would be neither vice nor virtue, merit nor demerit, and in consequence no moral order. Supposing that each virtuous action was repaid by some temporal advantage, the act, no longer having any higher purpose, could not merit a reward of this kind. Supposing on the other hand that, by virtue of a divine law, a thief's hand was to drop off when he committed a theft, men would refrain from stealing as they refrain from putting their hands under a butcher's chopper; and moral order would disappear completely. To reconcile this order (the only one possible for rational beings, as is shown by experience) with the laws of justice, it is necessary for virtue to be rewarded and vice punished, even in this world, but not always or immediately. It is necessary that much the greater share of temporal happiness should be allotted to virtue and that a proportional share of unhappiness should fall to vice, but that the individual should never be sure of anything, as is in fact the case. Any other hypothesis will lead you directly to the destruction of the moral order or to the creation of another world.

To come now to detail, let us start with human justice. Wishing men to be governed by men at least in their external actions, God has given sovereigns the supreme prerogative of punishing crimes, in which above all they are his representatives ...

This formidable prerogative of which I have just spoken results in the necessary existence of a man destined to inflict on criminals the punishments awarded by human justice; and this man is in fact found everywhere, without there being any means of explaining how; for reason cannot discern in human nature any motive which could lead men to this calling. I am sure, gentlemen, that you are too accustomed to reflection not to have pondered often on the executioner. Who is then this inexplicable being who has preferred to all the pleasant, lucrative, honest, and even honorable jobs that present themselves in hundreds to human power and dexterity, that of torturing and putting to death his fellow creatures? Are this head and this heart made like ours? Do they not hold something peculiar and foreign to our nature? For my own part, I do not doubt this. He is made like us externally; he is born like us but he is an extraordinary being, and for him to exist in the human family a particular decree, a fiat of the creative power is necessary. He is a species to himself. Look at the place he holds in public opinion and see if you can understand how he can ignore or affront this opinion! Scarcely have the authorities fixed his dwelling-place, scarcely has he taken possession of it, than the other houses seem to shrink back until they no longer overlook his. In the midst of this solitude and this kind of vacuum that forms around him, he lives alone with his woman and his offspring who make the human voice known to him, for without them he would know only groans. A dismal signal is given; a minor judicial official comes to his house to warn him that he is needed;

he leaves; he arrives at some public place packed with a dense and throbbing crowd. A poisoner, a parricide, or a blasphemer is thrown to him; he seizes him, he stretches him on the ground, he ties him to a horizontal cross, he raises it up: then a dreadful silence falls, and nothing can be heard except the crack of bones breaking under the crossbar and the howls of the victim. He unfastens him; he carries him to a wheel: the shattered limbs interweave with the spokes; the head falls; the hair stands on end, and the mouth, open like a furnace, gives out spasmodically only a few blood-splattered words calling for death to come. He is finished: his heart flutters, but it is with joy; he congratulates himself, he says sincerely, *No one can break men on the wheel better than I.* He steps down; he stretches out his blood-stained hand, and justice throws into it from a distance a few pieces of gold which he carries through a double row of men drawing back with horror. He sits down to a meal and eats; then to bed, where he sleeps. And next day, on waking, he thinks of anything other than what he did the day before. Is this a man? Yes: God receives him in his temples and permits him to pray. He is not a criminal, yet it is impossible to say, for example, that *he is virtuous, that he is an honest man, that he is estimable,* and so on. No moral praise can be appropriate for him, since this assumes relationships with men, and he has none.

And yet all grandeur, all power, all subordination rests on the executioner: he is the horror and the bond of human association. Remove this incomprehensible agent from the world, and at that very moment order gives way to chaos, thrones topple, and society disappears. God, who is the author of sovereignty, is the author also of chastisement: he has built our world on these two poles; *for Jehovah is the master of the two poles, and on these he makes the world turn.*[1]

Thus there is in the temporal sphere a visible and divine law for the punishment of crime, and this law, as stable as the society it upholds, has been carried out invariably from the beginning of time. Evil exists on the earth and acts constantly, and by a necessary consequence it must be continually repressed by punishment; indeed, we see over the whole globe constant action by every government to prevent

---

1   1 Samuel ii.8.

or punish criminal outrages. The sword of justice has no scabbard; it must always threaten or strike. What then do these complaints about the *impunity of crime* mean? For whom are the knout, the gallows, the wheels, and the stakes? Obviously for the criminal. The mistakes of courts are exceptions that do not shake the rule: I have, besides, several reflections to offer to you on this point. In the first place, these fatal errors are much less frequent than is imagined. If it is allowed to doubt, opinion is always contrary to authority, and the public ear listens avidly to the slightest suggestions of a judicial murder; a thousand individual passions can fortify this general inclination ...

That an innocent dies is a misfortune like any other; that is to say, it is common to all mankind. That a guilty man escapes is another exception of the same kind. But it always remains true, generally speaking, that *there is on the earth a universal and visible order for the temporal punishment of crimes*; and I must again draw your attention to the fact that criminals do not by any means cheat justice so often as might be ingenuously supposed in view of the infinite precautions they take to avoid it. There is often in the circumstances that betray the most cunning scoundrels something so unexpected, so surprising, so unforeseeable, that men who are called by their position or reflections to follow this kind of affair tend to believe that human justice is not entirely without a certain supernatural assistance in seeking out the guilty.

Allow me to add one more consideration to bring to an end this chronicle of punishments. Just as it is very possible for us to be wrong when we accuse human justice of sparing the guilty, since those we regard as being such are not really guilty, so it is equally possible on the other side that a man punished for a crime he has not committed has actually merited it by another completely unknown crime. Fortunately and unfortunately, there are several examples of this kind of thing shown by the confessions of criminals, and there are many more, I believe, of which we are ignorant. This last supposition deserves especially close attention, for, although in such a case the judges are extremely blameworthy or unfortunate, Providence, for whom everything, even an obstacle, is a means, makes full use of dishonesty or mistakes to execute the temporal justice we demand;

and it is certain that these two suppositions restrict considerably the number of exceptions. You can see, then, how far this assumed equality that I supposed at the beginning is already disrupted by the consideration of human justice alone.

I have often imagined a scene in which I want you to participate. I suppose that for some good reason a stranger to our planet comes here and talks to one of us about the condition of this world. Among the strange things that are recounted to him, he is told that corruption and vices, of which he has been fully informed, in certain circumstances necessitate men dying by the hand of men, and that we restrict the right of killing within the law to the executioner and the soldier. He will also be told:

> The one brings death to convicted and condemned criminals, and fortunately his executions are so rare that one of these ministers of death is sufficient for each province. As far as soldiers are concerned, there are never enough of them, because they kill without restraint and their victims are always honest men. Of these two professional killers, the soldier and the executioner, one is highly honoured and always has been by all the nations who have inhabited up to now this planet to which you have come; but the other has just as generally been regarded as vile. Try to guess on which the obloquy falls.

Surely this spirit from afar would not hesitate a moment; he would heap on the executioner all the praise which you did not feel able the other day to refuse him, in spite of all our prejudices, when you talked of this gentleman, to use Voltaire's phrase. 'He is a sublime being,' he would say to us,

> the cornerstone of society. Since crime is part of this world's order and since it can be checked only by punishment, once deprive the world of the executioner and all order will disappear with him. Moreover, what grandeur of soul, what noble disinterestedness must necessarily be assumed to exist in a man who devotes himself to services which are no doubt worthy of respect but which are so distressing and so contrary to human nature! For, since I have lived among you, I have

noticed that it hurts you to kill a chicken in cold blood. I am therefore convinced that opinion must cover him with all the honour necessary and so rightly owing to him. As for the soldier, he is on the whole an agent of cruelty and injustice. How many obviously just wars have there been? How many obviously unjust! How many individual injustices, horrors, and useless atrocities! I imagine therefore that opinion among you has very properly poured as much shame on the head of the soldier as it has thrown glory over the impartial executor of the judgements of sovereign justice.

You know the truth, gentlemen, and the extent of the spirit's mistake. In fact, the soldier and the executioner stand at the two extremes of the social scale, but in quite the opposite extremes put forward by this splendid theory. Nothing is so noble as the first, nothing so abject as the second ... The soldier is so noble that he ennobles what public opinion regards as most ignoble, since he can act as an executioner without debasing himself, provided however that he kills only his fellow soldiers and that he uses only his weapons to kill them.

19

Statements in favour of
the death penalty

J. Edgar Hoover

J. Edgar Hoover (1895–1972) was director of the Federal Bureau of Investigation (FBI) 1924–72. As a young man he pioneered the use of scientific methods in investigation and prosecution. The following material is taken from the *Annual FBI Law Enforcement Bulletin* in 1959, 1960, and 1961. He was a powerful political figure, and successive presidents were wary of offending hm.

*　*　*

The question of capital punishment has sent a storm of controversy thundering across our nation—millions of spoken and written words seek to examine the question so that decisions may be reached which befit our civilisation.

The struggle for answers concerning the taking of men's lives is one to which every American should lend his voice, for the problem in a democracy such as ours is not one for a handful of men to solve alone.

As a representative of law enforcement, it is my belief that a great many of the most vociferous cries for abolition of capital punishment emanate from those areas of our society which have been insulated against the horrors man can and does perpetrate against his fellow beings. Certainly, penetrative and searching thought must be given before considering any blanket cessation of capital punishment in a time when unspeakable crimes are being committed. The savagely mutilated bodies and mentally ravaged victims of murderers, rapists and other criminal beasts beg consideration when the evidence is weighed on both sides of the scales of Justice.

At the same time, nothing is so precious in our country as the life of a human being, whether he is a criminal or not, and on the other side of the scales must be placed all of the legal safeguards which our society demands.

Experience has clearly demonstrated, however, that the time-proven deterrents to crime are sure detection, swift apprehension, and proper punishment. Each is a necessary ingredient. Law-abiding citizens have a right to expect that the efforts of law enforcement officers in detecting and apprehending criminals will be followed by realistic punishment.

It is my opinion that when no shadow of a doubt remains relative to the guilt of a defendant, the public interest demands capital punishment be invoked where the law so provides. Who, in all good conscience, can say that Julius and Ethel Rosenberg, the spies who delivered the secret of the atomic bomb into the hands of the Soviets should have been spared when their treachery caused the shadow of annihilation to fall upon all of the world's peoples?[1] What place would there have been in civilisation for these two who went to their deaths unrepentant, unwilling to the last to help their own country and their own fellow men? What would have been the chances of rehabilitating Jack Gilbert Graham, who placed a bomb in his own mother's luggage and blasted her and 43 other innocent victims into oblivion as they rode an airliner across a peaceful sky?[2]

A judge once said,

> The death penalty is a warning, just like a lighthouse throwing its beams out to sea. We hear about shipwrecks, but we do not hear about the ships the lighthouse guides safely on their way. We do not have proof of the number of ships it saves, but we do not tear the lighthouse down.

---

1   Editor's note: In the light of Soviet technological achievements since 1957, the significance of the Rosenbergs' treachery seems much less apparent.

2   Editor's note: For a detailed report on the Graham case, see James Galvin and John MacDonald, 'Psychiatric Study of a Mass Murderer', *American Journal of Psychiatry*, May 1959.

Despicable crimes must be dealt with realistically. To abolish the death penalty would absolve other Rosenbergs and Grahams from fear of the consequences for committing atrocious crimes. Where the death penalty is provided, a criminal's punishment may be meted out commensurate with his deeds. While a Power transcending man is the final Judge, this same Power gave man reason so that he might protect himself. Capital punishment is an instrument with which he may guard the righteous against the predators among men.

We must never allow misguided compassion to erase our concern for the hundreds of unfortunate, innocent victims of bestial criminals.

*   *   *

The capital punishment question, in which law enforcement officers have a basic interest, has been confused recently by self-styled agitators 'against the evil of capital punishment'. A brochure released not long ago, pleading for 'rehabilitation' of murderers while passing lightly over the plight of the killers' innocent victims and families, charges that law enforcement officers 'become so insensitised by their dealings with vicious criminals that they go to the extreme of feeling that the death penalty is absolutely necessary'.

To add to the burden of conscience borne by peace officers, prosecutors, and jurists and to brand law enforcement officers as callous, unfeeling men 'insensitised' to the sanctity of human life are gross acts of injustice to these servants of the public. This ridiculous allegation is mutely refuted by the compassion which wells up in quiet tears flowing down the cheeks of hardened, veteran officers who too often see the ravaged bodies of victims of child molesters. There can be no doubt of the sincerity of many of those who deplore capital punishment. A realistic approach to the problem, however, demands that they weigh the right of innocent persons to live their lives free from fear of bestial killers against statistical arguments which boast of how few murderers kill again after 'rehabilitation' and release. No one, unless he can probe the mind of every potential killer, can say with any authority whatsoever that capital punishment is not a deterrent. As one police officer has asked, how can these 'authorities' possibly know how many people are not on death row because of the deterrent effect of executions?

Maudlin viewers of the death penalty call the most wanton slayer a 'child of God' who should not be executed regardless of how heinous his crime may be because 'God created man in his own image, in the image of God created He him' (Genesis i. 27). Was not this small, blonde six-year-old girl a child of God? She was choked, beaten, and raped by a sex fiend whose pregnant wife reportedly helped him lure the innocent child into his car and who sat and watched the assault on the screaming youngster. And when he completed his inhuman deed, the wife, herself bringing a life into the world, allegedly killed the child with several savage blows with a tire iron. The husband has been sentenced to death. Words and words and words may be written, but no plea in favour of the death penalty can be more horribly eloquent than the sight of the battered, sexually assaulted body of this child, truly a 'child of God'.

The proponents of 'rehabilitation' for all murderers quote those portions of the Bible which they believe support their lavender-and-old-lace world where evil is neither recognised nor allowed. But the Bible clearly reveals that enforcement of moral justice is nothing new to our age. In fact, in referring to man as the 'image of God', the Old Testament, so freely quoted by opponents of the death penalty, also states, 'Whoso sheddeth man's blood, by man shall his blood be shed: for in the image of God made He man' (Genesis ix. 6). There are many passages in the Old Testament which refer to capital punishment being necessary to enforce the laws of society. Since the Old Testament was written about and to a nation while the New Testament was written to individuals and to a nonpolitical body known as the Church, there is a difference in emphasis and approach. Certainly, however, the moral laws of the Old Testament remain with us today.

Misguided do-gooders frequently quote the Sixth Commandment, 'Thou shalt not kill', to prove that capital punishment is wrong. This Commandment in the twentieth chapter, verse 13, of Exodus has also been interpreted to mean: 'Thou shalt do no murder'. Then the twenty-first chapter, verse 12, says, 'He that smiteth a man, so

that he die, shall be surely put to death.' We can no more change
the application to our society of this basic moral law in the Old
Testament than we can change the meaning of Leviticus xix. 18:
'thou shalt love thy neighbour as thyself,' which Jesus quoted in the
New Testament.

To 'love thy neighbour' is to protect him; capital punishment acts
as at least one wall to afford 'God's children' protection.

* * *

Most states have capital punishment; a few do not. For the most part,
capital punishment is associated with the crime of murder. Some
states have high murder rates; some do not. Of those states with
low murder rates, some have capital punishment; some do not. The
number of murders that occur within a state as indicated by rates is
due to a wide range of social, human and material factors.

It would be convenient for a study of the effects of capital
punishment as a deterrent if states fell neatly into two groups: (1)
those with low murder rates and capital punishment; and (2) those
with high murder rates and no capital punishment. Or, if the user
of these statistics is making a case against capital punishment, he
would prefer to demonstrate that the states with low murder rates
are those that do not have capital punishment. But to expect such an
oversimplification of a highly complex subject is to engage in wishful
thinking or a futile groping for proof that is not there.

Some who propose the abolishment of capital punishment select
statistics that 'prove' their point and ignore those that point the
other way. Comparisons of murder rates between the nine states
which abolished the death penalty or qualified its use and the forty-
one states which have retained it either individually, before or after
abolition, or by group are completely inconclusive.

The professional law enforcement officer is convinced from
experience that the hardened criminal has been and is deterred from
killing based on the prospect of the death penalty. It is possible that the
deterrent effect of capital punishment is greater in states with a high
murder rate if the conditions which contribute to the act of murder

develop more frequently in those states. For the law enforcement officer the time-proven deterrents to crime are sure detection, swift apprehension, and proper punishment. Each is a necessary ingredient.

20

Capital punishment: your protection and mine

Edward J. Allen

Edward John Allen (1907–1990) was chief of police in Santa Ana, California. This essay, written in 1960, concentrates heavily on the Californian position. E.G. ('Pat') Brown, a Democrat, was governor of California 1959–67, and made several attempts to pass abolitionist legislation. All failed. Brown tried to extend his own power of commutation, but this was rejected. In 1966 Brown was defeated for re-election as governor by Ronald Reagan, an actor, an avowed retentionist, and later president of the United States 1981–89. In 1985 Allen was imprisoned for briefly defying a court order not to trespass at an abortion clinic.

*　*　*

In our own times the people of California have repeatedly (sixteen times from 1933 to 1960) turned back the constantly recurring repeal attempts of a militant minority and their malinformed minions. Yet, the present governor, with a seeming fixation, has vowed that he will foist the matter upon the California Legislature at succeeding sessions … and the same old tired arguments will be trotted out again: Capital punishment does not deter crime.

1. It 'brutalises' human nature.
2. The rich and powerful often escape the death penalty.
3. Swift and certain punishment is more effective.

4. Society is to blame for the criminal's way of life, so we ought to be more considerate of him.

Let us, then, apart from the demands of pure justice, which should be the only determining factor, examine the above claims for validity and provability.

Capital punishment does not deter crime

If this be true, then why do criminals, even the braggadocian Chessman type, fear it most? Why does every criminal sentenced to death seek commutation to life imprisonment? Common sense alone, without the benefit of knowledge, wisdom, and experience, convinces that we are influenced to the greatest degree by that which we love, respect or fear to the greatest degree—and that we cling most tenaciously to our most valued possessions. Life is indisputably our greatest possession. Additionally, there is no definitive proof anywhere that the death penalty is not a deterrent. There are merely the gratuitous statements of wishful thinkers, some of whom, because of the responsible duties of their positions, ought not to be making unprovable or misleading statements.

Parole and probation people, an occasional governor, prison wardens (some prefer to be called penologists), criminal defense attorneys, and often time prison chaplains advance this 'no deterrent' point of view. None doubts their sincerity, but they are hardly qualified to speak on the matter authoritatively or with pure objectivity. How can they possibly know how many people are not on death row because of the deterrent effect of the death penalty? Neither do they see the vicious, often sadistic despoiler or the cold-blooded professional killer plying their murderous trades. They encounter these predatory creatures after their fangs have been pulled; after they have been rendered harmless, deprived of the weapons and the opportunities to commit additional crimes. Naturally, in their cages they behave more like sheep than ravenous wolves.

Prison wardens are housekeepers, custodians of criminals after they have been convicted under our system of justice; hence, they see them when they are docile by compulsion, but certainly cunning enough to know that to 'spring' themselves they must 'make friends and influence people' of power and authority inside the prison walls, since their own criminal lives on the outside have deservedly brought upon them the judgement of society. It is neither the duty nor the prerogative of wardens or chaplains to decide matters of criminal justice. This has already been accomplished by the people, and their jobs, respectively, are to keep the gate locked, to feed, to clothe, and to guard—and to counsel, console, and convert. True, it is altogether human to develop sympathy for even a depraved and chronic criminal. I suppose a zoo keeper develops a fondness for the wild animals which the taxpayers pay him to feed and guard. Yet, what kind of a zoo keeper would he be if he opened the cage doors and released the voracious beasts to prey upon the public? This very act would throw a community into terror and alarm. Even so, if a wild beast attacked a human being, there would be less guilt attached, since such an animal acts from instinct and not malice aforethought. Not so, a rational human being who deliberately murders or defiles his fellow man. It might serve a good purpose if these 'bleeding hearts' could accompany those whose duty it is to examine first-hand; at the scenes of their crimes, the gruesome handiwork of those for whom they intercede. This might give them pause to properly weigh the public interest in their private scales of justice.

It is also put forth by those who would weaken our laws and, perforce, our ability to protect the innocent, that many murderers on death row claim they did not think of the death penalty when they committed their crimes. This is undoubtedly true. That is precisely the point. If they had thought of it, they would not have committed their crimes. Here we have the spectacle of a minute minority of convicted murderers convincing intelligent people that capital punishment is wrong because of their own failure to realise the consequences of their murderous conduct. Are we then to base our laws on this reasoning? What of the countless others who were deterred from murder through fear of the penalty? The implication is clear: even those murderers who didn't think of the death penalty would have been deterred had they given it consideration. Our laws are made for reasonable creatures, not to satisfy an abnormal handful. It is hardly the part of wisdom to be guided by the counsel and advice of an infinitesimally small band of bestial criminals. Further, the cunning individual and conspiratorial group who plot murder always imagine themselves too clever to get caught, or if caught, convicted.

It brutalises human nature

But the opposite is true. Wanton murder brutalises human nature and cheapens human life, not the penalty for its perpetration. Capital punishment is the guarantee against murder and the brutalisation of human nature. It places an inestimable value on human life—the forfeiture of the life of the despoiler. To allow heinous criminals to commit their crimes without the commensurate reparation of the death penalty would surely brutalise and degrade human nature and reduce society to a state of barbarism. True Christian charity is based upon justice, the proper concern for the weak and innocent, not upon a soft-headed regard for despicable and conspiratorial killers. Let us resort to right reason and view retribution and reparation in proper perspective.

The rich and powerful generally escape

There is truth in this statement and it is equally applicable to other penalties, not the death penalty alone. No one decries this discrimination more than law enforcement. The deals which allow criminals to escape justice are consummated by courts and attorneys. Attorneys present evidence to the courts and judges hand down sentences. Responsibility also devolves upon citizen jurors to return proper verdicts. If some citizens, courts, and lawyers fail in their duty, is the law itself to blame? Rather it is their administration of it. Surely, bribery, social position, or political pull ought not to influence the administration of justice, but admittedly they often do. Since this is so, it would be as logical to advocate the repeal of the entire criminal code. If one person escapes justice, it is unjust that another does not? Since justice does not always prevail, ought we abandon our striving for its attainment? Who would advocate the abolition of the Ten Commandments because they are honoured more in their breach than in their observance? Justice is still justice if no man is just! The defect, in this instance, lies in men, not in the law! Law enforcement firmly believes that all men should be treated equally at the bar of justice. There are attorneys, judges, governors, parole boards and that peculiar phenomena called 'Adult and Juvenile Authorities' who decree otherwise.

Jurors, governors and judges

Let us take the matter of justice, including capital punishment, a step further. In selecting a murder jury each prospective juror is asked if he has a conscientious objection to returning a death penalty verdict. If so, such a person is summarily excused as unqualified. No injustice obtains from this practice, since a private citizen has a right to his own opinion.

But this does not apply to judges and governors who have the duty of sentencing and the right of commutation, since their consciences must be guided by the law which they have sworn to uphold. Therefore, if a judge or state governor has such a conscientious objection to the death penalty that he 'creeps through the serpentine windings of utilitarianism to discover some advantage that may discharge him from the justice of punishment or even from the due measure of it,' then such a judge or governor has disqualified himself, and ought, in all justice to the commonwealth he serves, to vacate his lofty position and return it to the people to whom it belongs. Then, as a private citizen, he can campaign to his heart's content for the abolition of whatever law he doesn't happen to like. In the meantime, however, he ought not attempt to substitute the minority decisions of our Supreme Courts for majority decisions or be persuaded by the opinions of condemned criminals on murderer's row. Further, to incessantly inveigh from high office against the law of the land, particularly a law ingrained in the tradition of our Judea-Christian culture, smacks of arbitrary dictation. The business of government is justice, not pity—however self-consoling.

Life imprisonment

In most of our states life imprisonment simply does not exist. In truth and justice the term ought to be discarded since it does not mean what it says. In the State of California, for example, the State Constitution provides that the governor, under his commutation powers, may set aside the words 'without parole' with respect to life imprisonment. It would take a constitutional amendment to abolish that power. In other states life imprisonment means merely a varying number of years.

Death penalty seldom used

The argument that the death penalty is seldom used argues for its retention, not its abolition. It proves that juries and courts are exercising extreme leniency, even with vicious murderers. Yet, there are certain heinous crimes regarding which the very stones would cry out for the death penalty were it abolished. Therefore, it should be retained as just punishment and reparation for these and as a deterrent for other malignant criminals. It would be a better argument for the abolitionists if they could say that the death penalty was capriciously or routinely being returned for every homicide.

Specious arguments

Two of the reasons advanced for the abolition of the death penalty have no validity whatsoever. One is an attempt to equate human slavery with capital punishment. The argument is this: slavery was once rampant, but now an enlightened society favours its abolition; therefore, we ought to do away with capital punishment, since we 'moderns' are more 'enlightened' than our forebears.

Firstly, slavery never was, or never will be, morally right or justifiable or just. The death penalty is morally right and justifiable and just. So these sophists are merely advancing a completely false and odious comparison. Here is another 'beaut' from a university psychiatrist: the death penalty could be society's way of 'projecting its own crime into the criminal.' Now, I submit that the longer we permit this type of nonsense to be spread abroad, the more ridiculous our nation is going to appear in the eyes of the world. I understand that there is a growing resentment among those in the medical profession against this type of gobble-de-gook, and about time.

It is obvious to anyone who believes in the moral and natural law (as clearly stated in the law of the land) that first degree murder requires personal premeditation and the full consent of the will, hence, its punishment should be meted out to the criminal or criminals personally responsible. To argue otherwise is to argue the unnatural, but admittedly, this is the day of the unnatural logician.

We argue that the unnatural in sex is natural and point to fables for proof. Thus, we have the Oedipus and Electra complexes, situations culled from Greek drama and foisted upon us as Freudian truisms. No use talking about free will, we just can't help ourselves. So today there is no crime, really, and no criminals—just 'complexes'. And these 'complexes' are so 'complex' we must all eventually succumb to their 'complexity'—and employ a psychoanalyst. (Physician, heal thyself!) Truly, it is possible for people, even with exceptionally high I.Q.s, to be nuttier than fruitcakes, or vice versa, as the case may be. We had better be careful in these 'modern' times (which condone the criminal immorality of ancient Greece and Rome) or we, too, will abandon our reason altogether. Mainly because of their sexual excesses, aberrations and perversions, St Paul told the Romans (First Epistle to the Romans) that they had gone blind and no longer knew the difference between right and wrong. Neither does this generation in many respects, and we will degenerate further if we continue to give ear to certain types of psychoanalytical professors and their automorphic automatons who impute to all of us (including themselves?) the guilt for the personal crimes of individual criminals.

Swift and certain punishment

Swift and certain punishment is assuredly a crime deterrent, but only when coupled with commensurate severity, otherwise the statement is an absurdity. Suppose a bank robber was very swiftly and very surely sentenced to five days in the county jail; or a rapist swiftly and certainly given a $25 fine. Would such punishment(?) be a deterrent to either the bank robber or the rapist? Surely, the deterrent value is in the severity as well as the swiftness and the certainty. However, if one had to choose but one of the three, then the severity of the punishment must needs be selected.

Once again, we must reiterate that some lawyers and courts and the criminals themselves have caused the 'swiftness and certainty' of justice to have almost vanished from the American scene. The same sources would now abolish the severity. Yet, those lawyers who, through capricious, dilatory tactics continually postpone justice are the very ones who prattle about swiftness and certainty as a substitute for severity. The Chessman case is a prize example of how lawyers, judges and a governor can foul up 'swift and certain' punishment. The irony of it is that Chessman and his attorneys and the present governor, who were responsible for the seemingly interminable postponements, now cry to the high heavens that such postponements are 'cruel and unusual punishment.' No wonder Hamlet cited the 'law's delay' as one of the problems that was driving him nuts. Chessman himself became so disgusted with the publicity-seeking antics of one lawyer who injected himself into the case that he fired him, publicly. However, this did not delay the redoubtable attorney, and he is still trying to make a career of the case. Wonder what further 'deterrent' he needs?

Individual states and capital punishment

A study of the statistics on murder in the forty-eight states in 1958 produced some interesting results with respect to the capital crime. The proponents for abolition make much of the fact that there were seven states in 1958 (nine since the admission of Alaska and Hawaii) which have abolished capital punishment. These proponents make no mention of the fact that eight other states in the Union once abolished capital punishment and have returned to it.

The states which abolished capital punishment and after an unhappy experience restored it are: Kansas, Iowa, Colorado, Washington, Oregon, Arizona, Missouri, and Tennessee. It is noted that three of these states border on California: Arizona, contiguous to the southeast; Oregon, contiguous to the north on the coast; and Washington, further north and also on the west coast. Since these comprise the area surrounding and abutting California, it is the most revealing and significantly important statistic for California residents. Of the states which have abolished capital punishment, two are now in New England: Maine and Rhode Island. Maine had one of the highest murder rates in New England in 1958, with an average of 2.5 per 100,000 population (all averages are quoted using this population figure). The six New England states have an average of 1.6, the lowest murder rate of any section of the country, yet only two of the six states have abolished the death penalty, and one of them has a rate half again as high as the average. New Hampshire, which has the death penalty, compares with the lowest, 0.7.

Seven midwestern states: Iowa, Kansas, Minnesota, Nebraska, North Dakota, South Dakota and Missouri, have an average of 2.2 murders for 1958. It is noted that three of these states returned to capital punishment after having abolished it, and two of the seven still have no capital punishment.

In the eleven far western states, the average percentage in 1958 was 3.7 per cent, oddly enough the exact percentage for the State of California. Four of these states returned to the death penalty. The other seven states have always had capital punishment.

Eleven north-eastern states had an average of 3.1 murders in 1958.

The highest murder rate of the geographical groups of states was the southern group of thirteen states. They had the exceptionally high rate of 9.0. Admittedly, the South has a problem, but the removal of the death penalty would only aggravate it. Of these states only Tennessee ever tried to get along without capital punishment and has since returned to it.

It would appear that the permeance of racial, ethnic and religio-political cultures influence crime rates, including murder, in the various geographical sections or our country. Common sense dictates that more severe punitive sanctions are necessary in those states or sections where serious crime is more prevalent. Conversely where the crime is minimal because of the law-abiding nature of the people, murder is less frequent. Thus it is that the New England states have a low murder rate while the South has an unusually high rate. It would be the height of folly therefore to advocate the removal of the death penalty throughout the Southern states where the crime of murder is a serious threat.

Where crime and murder are at a low level and where community life is governed by respect and reverence for law, rather than by its enforcement, then severe punitive measures may be relaxed, but not abolished. (Such a state presages the millennium.) On the other hand, where crime and murder are a serious problem, then the removal of stringent punitive measures further aggravates it. The eight states which re-enacted the death penalty after a trial period without it, discovered this to their own dismay.

The seven states within the corporate United States which do not have the death penalty are among the smallest, in territory and/or population: Delaware, Maine, Michigan, Minnesota, North Dakota, Rhode Island, and Wisconsin. There is among them only one really large state, Michigan, whose 1958 population of 7,865,547 exceeds by more than a half-million the combined total of the six other states. Michigan's 1958 murder rate per 100,000 population was 3.1, not only the highest of these seven states, but higher than both Pennsylvania and New York, two or the three most populous states in the Union—with over eleven to sixteen million respectively. California, in the top three, has approximately twice the population of Michigan. New York has a 2.8 rate and Pennsylvania 2.5. The experience has been that the larger states with crime problems have found it necessary to return to the death penalty. And to re-emphasise, three of these states either border on California, or are on the west coast, or both.

California officers murdered on duty

I do not have the figures for the other states, but in California a review of the number of police officers killed in line of duty during the past ten years is of significance. From 1950 through 1959 there have been thirty-five law enforcement officers shot and killed while performing law enforcement duties, i.e., protecting the lives and property of California citizens. Even more alarming is the fact that of the thirty-five, approximately twice as many were murdered during the latter half of the decade than were killed during the first half. Twelve were killed from 1950 through 1954 and twenty-three from 1955 through 1959. Jn the last three years seventeen of these twenty-three were murdered while on duty.

At a time in our national and state history when crime is increasing alarmingly and when the murder of police officers in the State of California is reaching new heights, we have powerful figures and groups advocating the abolition of capital punishment—almost an invitation for murderous thugs to kill more police officers whose duty it is to protect (even at the expense of their own lives) the very citizens who advocate leniency for their murderers. Where is the reciprocal regard for the life of a police officer in the minds and hearts of these paragons of Christian charity, in or out of the governor's office, in or out of our courtrooms, on or off our judicial benches, or in or out of the Humpty-Dumpty (egghead) claque in politics, entertainment, television, journalism, and education? (By 'eggheads' I do not mean authentic intellectuals, but the poseurs.)

Perhaps we are arriving at a governmental philosophy which considers the lives of police officers expendable, but not so the lives of the vicious criminals who murder them. Rather, we must protect the latter, since to punish them too severely would be 'projecting society's crime into the criminal.' Would it not be more sensible and accurate to state that 'society' is to blame for the murder of its police officers unless it insists upon the retention of the death penalty as a protection for its own protectors, ergo, society itself? Unmistakably, without militant police protection the whole of society would overnight become a criminal jungle.

Conclusion

Of course, the overwhelming statistic (for those who wish to decide on statistics alone) is that forty-one of the fifty states and the majority of the nations in the world have the death penalty.

However, even though statistics, per se, unquestionably favour the retention of the death penalty, mere numbers, pro and con, ought not be the deciding factor. The deciding factor should be the consideration of justice — the primary, if not the sole business of government. All of the erudition, wisdom, experience, and knowledge of history reveals that the death penalty is morally and legally just. For the just man or nation this should be sufficient. Even so, justice is still justice, if no man is just — were it not so, God would have told us.

21

Crime increase a threat
to all citizens

P.R. Biggin

Percival Robert Biggin was for many years the stipendiary magistrate for the Wimmera, based at Horsham. He became well known for the strength and vigour of his convictions (see Lloyd v. Biggin (1962) Victorian Reports p. 593, per Smith J). Born in 1897, his date of death has proved elusive. The following article was published in *The Wimmera Mail-Times* of Horsham on 6 May 1966.

* * *

On one day during the past week, six men were remanded in the Melbourne City Court on eight charges of murder.

The following day, the Chief Commissioner of Police made a sensational public protest against the trivial and ineffective penalties habitually imposed by the criminal courts in Victoria.

It was obviously the utterance of a man, charged with the heavy responsibility for the lives and property of the Victorian public, who had been provoked beyond endurance. The two incidents combine to lend great force to your editorial of 25 April, in which you reflect upon the current attitude to murderers, and with which, let me here say, I heartily agree.

Nothing is more characteristic of the times in Australia, and particularly in Victoria, than the startling increase in violent and heinous crime, which has occurred during the last twenty years.

Every issue of the daily press reports the commission of the most serious crimes in the calendar, from murder to criminal assaults, from armed hold-ups to huge financial defalcations.

In the lower scale of crime, the larceny or illegal use of motor cars has swelled to such proportions that it is virtually uncontrolled as is also the commission of vandalism and wilful destruction of property.

If it is ever possible for the urgency of an issue to move the public to action, this is surely such a one.

Crime has already attained such proportions that it threatens every citizen in the State, and it is increasing annually.

This, in a period of the greatest and most general prosperity that this country has ever known.

So far from there being any guarantee of an indefinite continuity of this prosperity, it is practically certain that in due course the economic pendulum will swing back, as it has always done in the past.

With the incidence of crime at its present level, in times of prosperity and full employment, what is it likely to be in a time of depression and unemployment?

Reality

It is not a pleasant prospect to contemplate, but it should not require much reflection to see the reality of it. Propaganda has induced a frantic obsession with communism, to such a degree that we do not hesitate to conscript our youth and send them off to fight in an undeclared war, against people who, so far at any rate, have neither harmed us nor have threatened to do so.

Without any desire to be sensational, and with due regard to such reputation I may have with the people of this community, I say that a vastly graver and more immediate menace to Australia is growing up right here within our own shores.

While rampant crime does not constitute the whole of that danger, it is already a major component, and may well become the dominant element unless it be contained in time.

Many antecedent factors play their part in the making of a criminal, but with these I am not here concerned.

The question which arises is, what has caused an eruption of crime within a limited period of time in a State which was formerly most law-abiding?

Immigration is no answer, for two reasons—firstly, criminality has increased in vastly greater proportion than has the population; and secondly, there is no evidence of a greater degree of crime among immigrants than among the indigenous population—quite the reverse, in fact.

Predominant

There is therefore no escaping the conclusion that at least the predominant cause is that pointed to by the Chief Commissioner of Police, the abject failure of the criminal courts to deter crime by the application of adequate penalties, which they are amply empowered by law to impose.

At one time, the criminal law was something to be reckoned with by any intending enemy of society. It is no longer so.

Yet the law itself has not changed. It is in its application that it has broken down. Instead of straight gaol terms, it is now the practice to release on bond even criminals with lists of prior convictions, or to allow probation after serving a few months in gaol for an offence that may have ruined a life.

The performances of the so-called criminal courts, especially the courts of general sessions, today amount to nothing short of condonation of crime, at the cost of the people whom it is their duty to protect. Society is now suffering the consequences.

How to explain this reversal of form? One factor is undoubtedly a general sympathy with criminals. The sturdy, uncomprising attitudes of our forefathers in this connexion have gone with the wind.

We have never recovered from the perversion of moral values resulting from two world wars in one generation.

In the subconsciousness of every individual vis-à-vis the criminal there lurks the feeling 'There, but for the grace of God, (or the luck of the game) go I.'

This insidious influence manifests itself in many ways, under many disguises. It prompts the juryman to say 'not guilty' where the evidence clearly says otherwise.

It encourages the judge or magistrate to be a 'good fellow,' go along with the specious submissions of defending counsel, and give a bond in defiance of the clear intent of the statute and in disregard of the public interest.

It persuades witnesses not to come forward, or at the most to water down their evidence. It urges prosecutors to take it easy and not 'put the boots in.'

I doubt whether even that saviour of last resort, the psychiatrist, is immune.

Basing his opinion on nothing more substantial than the blandishments of a cunning criminal, he is ever ready to explain the crime in terms of 'schizophrenia', 'compulsive urge' or like jargon, with the clear inference that the perpetrator is himself the victim of a cruel fate, and cannot in fairness be held responsible.

It might be, if psychiatry were directed into a more useful channel, that it could demonstrate a connexion between this morbid sympathy and the spurious humanitarianism of the times.

Thus might be explained the persistent abortive attempts to 'reform' vicious criminals who have long since passed the point of no return.

Under the leniency of our law, the man who stands convicted of a serious crime almost invariably has a long criminal history reaching back to the Children's Court.

He has already been given repeated chances, and is now about as likely to change his form as the leopard his spots. Yet the optimist on the bench still thinks he can 'reform' him by giving him another bond, or at most a sentence vitiated by a ridiculous parole clause.

So another wolf is let loose on the fold for the unfortunate police to hunt down all over again. It is no wonder there is a chronic shortage of police.

The psychiatrist might well find a rewarding area of study in those otherwise intelligent people who hysterically oppose capital and corporal punishment.

With murder running at the rate of one a week, against a pre-war rate of three or four a year, why do these people persist in their patently silly claim that hanging does not deter murderers?

How can they still their voices about the wholesale, hideous slaughter of human beings with the bayonet and the napalm bomb, yet hesitate not to abuse the process of the law and humiliate the government of the State in order to save from a humane death the vilest murderer who had ever fouled the history of Victoria? A man who had violated and brutally murdered a poor, helpless old woman?

How can they accept the pain and shock and horror occasioned by criminal assaults, yet oppose the use of the lash on the carcasses of the animals responsible?

It is high time that all responsible people repudiated these psychopaths and stood out boldly behind their own convictions. There is no place for the weakling or the theorist in dealing with crime. It is something which stands outside of all benign human relationships.

The criminal is a beast in human form. He is a self-declared and ruthless enemy of society.

To tolerate him involves the inevitable concomitant of sacrificing innocent people to his animal urges.

That is the simple choice with which society is faced, and I cannot imagine how anyone who calls himself a man can find any ground for hesitation.

Back in the eighteenth century a celebrated English judge remarked, 'He threatens the innocent who spares the guilty.' Surely never was judicial wisdom more dramatically vindicated, and in our own time.

So we come to Hamlet's question, 'Whether 'tis nobler in the mind to suffer, or to take arms against a sea of troubles, and by opposing, end them.'

It remains to be seen how far the national rot has gone. But one iron fact will stand—we will always get the social conditions we deserve.

Let all true citizens stand up and be counted.

22

Crime and punishment

Editoral, *Geelong Advertiser*

The *Geelong Advertiser* is the oldest paper with a continuous publishing history in Victoria. As is pointed out in Part IV below, many rural areas retained strong retentionist views, and the editorial that was published in the newspaper on Saturday 8 April 1967 may perhaps be regarded as a reasonable example of similar editorials in other country newspapers.

* * *

If all policies of the Country Party in this State were as sound as those which, in relation to the retention of capital punishment and the re-introduction of the birch for persons convicted of armed hold-ups and robbery with violence, were approved this week at the Mildura conference, then the party might well expect to hold more seats than it does at present in the Victorian Parliament. When, recently, a campaign was waged to save Ronald Joseph Ryan, convicted of the murder of a Pentridge Gaol warder, from the gallows, it was made to appear that his hanging would be against the wishes of a majority of Victorians. That was merely an assumption, but, bolstered by a spate of much publicised protests, it created a magnified impression. If the opinions of all Victorians on the decision to hang Ryan were tested, it might well be proved that most were in agreement with the carrying out of the death sentence.

The Country Party conference passed three resolutions supporting retention of capital punishment, rejected one for abolition, and defeated a proposal for a referendum on the question. That summarises the official attitude of only one political party—an attitude which undoubtedly is widely approved. It should be remembered, too, that it was the Bolte government that was unwilling to commute the sentence to imprisonment, and it can be taken for granted that by far the greater proportion of Liberal voters endorsed that stand.

Matter of degree

As Victorians have good reason to know, the provision in the law for capital punishment does not mean that every criminal on whom the death sentence has been passed will be executed. In fact, only in exceptional circumstances is the supreme penalty exacted on persons who are found guilty of capital offences. But if the provision were excised from the Statute book, then the maximum penalty that could be imposed on a person convicted of a capital crime would be imprisonment. In those circumstances not even a murderer of the most diabolical type, his guilt proven, would need to fear that he might have to pay with his life.

After the recent hanging, the clamour for the abolition of the death penalty quickly subsided. If the cause is so worthy, is it not reasonable to expect it to be pursued with undiminished fervour in the hope of attaining the objective before the full force of the law is about to be applied in another instance? The delegates at Mildura did well to make their decision in an atmosphere undisturbed by emotionalism.

Public alarm

Lately, the public has had reason for its alarm at the prevalence of armed hold-ups, robbery with violence, and brutal attacks by packs of young thugs on unoffending individuals. Despite the unceasing efforts of the police to maintain good order in the community, and the penalties the courts inflict on the conviction of offenders, violence is increasing, and public uneasiness likewise.

Though birching as a punishment for savage crime has been abolished in Victoria for a long time, many citizens like those who attended the Country Party conference, feel that the time is overdue for its revival. Numbers of them would go further than the conference did and would include vicious assaults on innocent persons in the list of crimes for which birchings could be stipulated.

It is strange that though Victorian penal history bears witness to the use of the cat-o'-nine-tails on a notoriously dangerous and unrepentant prisoner a few years ago, a much longer period has elapsed since the last birching. Yet birching is a much milder form of punishment. According to a former consultant psychiatrist to the New South Wales Department of Justice, use of the birch results in a loss of face and 'dignity' for hoodlums. 'They feel as though they have been treated as naughty children,' he said.

The abhorrence with which good citizens regard the infliction of corporal punishment on their fellow men, even though it is the reward for armed hold-ups, robbery with violence, or savage, unprovoked attacks, is understandable. Nevertheless, if lawlessness of that kind is impossible to control by the use of existing methods, then in the interests of the public generally there must be recourse to measures which alone will serve to bring about urgently needed improvement.

Part IV

The Reality

23

Hanged by the neck

Arthur Koestler & C.H. Rolph

The intention of this Part is to explain in some detail the precise act of capital punishment, discussed earlier in its abstract implications. The details are so remote from human experience that reportage of the reality has a shocking impact. It may be said by some retentionists that they do have some idea of what is involved—in which case these extracts are for others who may not know.

Hanged by the Neck is from Koestler and Rolph's book of the same name, published in 1961.

* * *

There have been some notable advances. In the 1880s the hangman was still occasionally, and of course by inadvertence, pulling prisoners' heads off. Sometimes, on the other hand, he failed to kill his man even after three tries. (To appreciate this picture fully, you need to imagine the process, twice repeated, of unhooking the prisoner, getting him up from the pit, and rearranging him on the scaffold for the next drop.)

The Home Office have always been able to phrase this kind of thing more decently. In their Memorandum of evidence to the 1949 Royal Commission on Capital Punishment they put it this way:

In 1885 an unfortunate case occurred at Exeter Prison in which, owing to a defect in the apparatus, three attempts to execute a man named Lee were unsuccessful: his sentence was subsequently commuted. Cases had

215

also occurred in which the effect of hanging was that the prisoner was decapitated.

That sounds better? You could hardly have a nobler example of the true function of words, namely the partial concealment of fundamentals. The phrase 'capital punishment' itself is a less obvious instance—less obvious because we have got so used to it. It means (in England) dislocating a man's neck by tying a six foot rope round it and suddenly dropping him through a trap-door with his arms and legs tied. If his neck happened not to break—it is certain at least to dislocate—then he would strangle, which takes longer and turns his face dark blue. In either case he often defecates, since people usually want to do this when they are frightened, and the huge shock to his nervous system when the rope tightens removes the last vestige of self-control, together with the social need for it.

This is not a nice picture and few of us care to be reminded of it. Many of us can think calmly enough of capital punishment, because the phrase embodies what *The Times* would call 'a decent reticence'. The reticence has been growing decently for about a century, beginning in 1868 with the decision to hang people in private instead of making it a public spectacle. Its most recent manifestation has been the abolition of the notice that used to be posted on the gates of the prison, the little symbolic square of paper that had taken the place of the pillory, the stocks, the gibbet, and Tyburn Tree.

All these things are done in our name. Not only the neck breaking, the strangling, the occasional bungling, and the mess, but the degradation of the men who have to do the job for us (and who actually told the Royal Commission that they did not feel in the least degraded). The oddly assorted crowd outside the prison on execution mornings are our representatives too, self-appointed though they be. There they are at nine o'clock in the morning, sometimes in the fog, sometimes in the rain, to take their hats off and hush their children at the moment when, inside the prison, a handful of grim men kill another man for money—your money.

Not all of them are people who would have gone, in former years, to see a public execution and in a mood for public spectacle.

Some of them are reformers, who might have done so to make an anti-death-penalty 'demonstration' in front of witnesses seemingly most in need of a change of heart. Some of them go there to pray for the man being killed and for those killing him. Some of them are relatives and friends of the man being killed. And it is these people who, on occasion, supply the most poignant commentary on the whole process by bringing a wreath, a wreath of flowers purchased and carried to the prison to commemorate a man who is not yet dead. They wait until the killing can be presumed to have been done (there is no longer any tolling of a bell, no black flag is hoisted—we have made notable advances), and until the little crowd has melted away; and then they ring the gate-bell and hand in the wreath.

To buy a wreath for a man who is not yet dead is to acknowledge and share the freezing certainty that is in the mind of the prisoner himself, the quality of which was unforgettably imagined by Dostoyevsky in *The Idiot*:

> But the chief and worst pain may not be in the bodily suffering but in one's knowing for certain that in an hour, and then in ten minutes, and then in half a minute, and then now, at the very moment, the soul will leave the body and that one will cease to be a man, and that that's bound to happen; the worst part of it is that it's certain. When you lay your head down under the knife and hear the knife slide over your head, that quarter of a second is the most terrible of all. You know this is not only my fancy, many people have said the same. I believe that so thoroughly that I'll tell you what I think. To kill for murder is a punishment incomparably worse than the crime itself. Murder by legal sentence is immeasurably more terrible than murder by brigands. Anyone murdered by brigands, whose throat is cut at night in a wood, or something of that sort, must surely hope to escape till the very last minute. There have been instances when a man has still hoped for escape, running or begging for mercy after his throat was cut. But in the other case all that last hope, which makes dying ten times as easy, is taken away for certain. There is the sentence, and the whole torture lies in the fact that there is certainly no escape, and there is no torture in the world more terrible. You may

lead a soldier out and set him facing the cannon in battle and fire at him and he'll still hope; but read a sentence of certain death over the same soldier, and he will go out of his mind or burst into tears. Who can tell whether human nature is able to bear this madness? Why this hideous, useless, unnecessary outrage? Perhaps there is some man who has been sentenced to death, been exposed to this torture, and has been told 'you can go, you are pardoned'. Perhaps such a man could tell us. It was of this torture and of this agony that Christ spoke, too. No, you can't treat a man like that!

But probably Dostoyevsky's man was not allowed the ineffable comfort of dominoes. Ours are.

Immediately a prisoner sentenced to death returns from court, [the Home Office told the 1949 Royal Commission] he is placed in a condemned cell and is watched day and night by two officers. Amenities [sic] such as cards, chess, dominoes, etc., are provided in the cell, and the officers are encouraged to—and in fact invariably do—join the prisoner in these games. [These games!] Newspapers and books are also provided.

Thus his mental health is carefully tended. His quite reasonable distress that soon 'the soul will leave the body' is soothed away. His bodily health is nurtured, too. One would rather not hang a man who has a high temperature, or diarrhoea, or paroxysms of coughing inside the white bag on the scaffold, or a raging duodenal ulcer, or general debility. He must be able to stand, and place his feet one on each side of the crack between the trap-doors; he has his own part to play and must be kept up to it. Therefore:

Food is supplied from the main prison kitchen, the prisoner being placed on hospital diet, with such additions as the Medical Officer considers advisable. A pint of beer or stout is supplied daily on request, and ten cigarettes or half an ounce of pipe tobacco are allowed unless there are medical reasons to the contrary [the gallows must not be cheated].

Despite all this, he may be ill on the last morning: ailments like migraine, epilepsy, colic, biliousness cannot always be staved off. He may even be a foreigner—the hangman told the Royal Commission of 1949 that the only victim who had ever spoiled the show for him was 'not an Englishman, he was a spy and he kicked up rough'. But no execution has ever been postponed because the man was ill or foreign: he won't be ill, or even foreign, for long.

Mr Albert Pierrepoint, our own executioner, was asked about this by Sir Alexander Maxwell when he gave evidence to the 1949 Royal Commission:

'What happens if a prisoner faints at the last minute?

'They carry him to the scaffold.'

'But what happens if he gets on to the scaffold and then faints?'

'He has to go just the same. They pull the lever, and away he goes.'

'Supposing he faints before you get him to the scaffold?'

'We would have to carry him there.'

'And put the rope round his neck?'

'Yes. There is an officer on each plank holding him up. There's a rope for the officer to hold on to, and he stands on the plank and holds him up.'

Mr H.N. Gedge, who was then Acting Under-Sheriff (unpaid) for the County of London, was asked by Sir Ernest Gowers, the Royal Commission's chairman, whether men were sometimes hanged sitting on a chair, because of illness or disability. 'That has happened in London,' said Mr Gedge, 'because a man collapsed and it was the only way of getting him on the drop.' He implied that this had happened only once, but he may not have had a very good memory. He told Sir Alexander Maxwell, for example, that the 'unfortunate women officers' who had to be present at the execution of a woman 'showed not a sign of emotion', and yet Mr Pierrepoint said on the same day that they were not even present to show any:

'You said that women, when they are going to be hanged, are quite brave?' he was asked by Sir William Jones.

'Very brave,' said Mr Pierrepoint.

'What is the attitude of the women officers who have to attend to them?'

'The women don't see the execution,' Mr Pierrepoint replied.

'The men take over out of the cell, just before the execution.'

'So that there is no women present at the actual execution?'

'No. They stay in the cell and the women don't witness the execution.'

Mr Pierrepoint's evidence to the Royal Commission must have made the Establishment cough nervously; but they allowed these bits to be published. Normally they are as deeply concerned to keep the public in the dark about all this as they are to root out communists at Holy Loch or Harwell. The same Act of Parliament—the Official Secrets Act, 1911—covers them all:

> If any person having in his possession any information which he has obtained or to which he has had access owing to his position as a person who holds or has held office under Her Majesty, communicates the information to someone other than a person to whom he is authorised to communicate it … he is liable to two years' imprisonment.

In 1926 Major F.W. Hastings Blake, former Governor of Pentonville Prison, published a book about his prison experiences, and was prosecuted under the Official Secrets Act. What dire secrets he had disclosed never became widely known, but during his trial Mr Roland Oliver, KC, his Counsel, read out in open Court the following extract from a Home Office instruction to prison governors dated 10 January 1925 about executions:

> Any reference to the manner in which an execution has been carried out should be confined to as few words as possible, e.g. 'it was carried out expeditiously and without a hitch'. No record should be taken as to the number of seconds, and, if pressed for details of this kind, the Governor should say he cannot give them as he did not time the proceedings, but 'a very short interval elapsed' or some general expression of opinion to the same effect.

On 23 June 1926 the Home Secretary was asked in the House of Commons whether he would not publish the whole instruction of which the foregoing is a small part. He said:

> It would be most undesirable and entirely contrary to established
> practice to make the terms of such instructions public. The less said at
> the inquest [on an executed prisoner], either by Governors or anyone
> else, the better. It is preferable to draw a veil over these cases.

Thirty years later, one of us wrote a book that reproduced the
same passage and added:

> The truth is that some prisoners struggle both in the condemned cell
> and under the noose, that some have to be carried tied to a chair, others
> dragged to the trap, limp, bowels open, arms pinioned to the back, like
> animals; and that still other things happen which should happen only in
> nightmare dreams.[1]

All this is true. But when some extracts from this book were
published in the *Observer* in March 1956, including the passage from
a Home Office circular to prison governors already quoted, they
precipitated a major row. In the House of Lords on 8 March Lord
Waverley (Home Secretary in 1939–40 as Sir John Anderson) asked
the government whether they had any statement to make about
the article. They had. The article, said Lord Mancroft, Home Office
under-secretary, 'purported to quote' a 'confidential instruction to
prison Governors about executions', but it omitted important parts
and gave 'an entirely misleading impression'. Lord Mancroft then gave
the words it had omitted: 'If there has been any hitch or unusual event
the fact must, of course, be stated, and a full explanation given If there
has been any undue delay it must be stated, and an explanation given.'
But this had never before been made public. On 23 June 1927 Sir
William Joynson-Hicks, Home Secretary, said that to do so 'would be
most undesirable and entirely contrary to established practice'. Did
the Home Office instruction include suggestions, asked Mr Pethick-
Lawrence, 'that the words used by the Governor should be as few

---

1   Arthur Koestler, *Reflections on Hanging*, London 1956.

as possible and that he should not give the length of time of the execution'? Enough supplementary questions, the Home Secretary replied, would get out of him the exact terms of the instructions, 'and I think it is undesirable to give that'. Thirty years later, when Lord Mancroft had told the House of Lords that the *Observer* article gave 'an entirely misleading impression', the *Observer* asked the Home Office for the full text of the instructions. The request was refused.

The few sentences that were publicly known, as a result of the Major Blake trial, had been published in the literature of the National Council for the Abolition of the Death Penalty; and when that Council was merged in the Howard League for Penal Reform, the sentences were incorporated in Howard League literature as the only available version. 'The passages now given in the House of Lords,' said the Howard League at the time of the *Observer* row, 'will, of course, be inserted: but since partial information can never be satisfactory, one trusts the Home Office will now publish the full text of the instruction.'

The Home Office never did. When he made his House of Lords statement, Lord Mancroft had assumed that the author of the book was in possession of the full Home Office instruction to governors and had 'picked over' that document for the sentences which best suited his case. 'I was wrong,' said Lord Mancroft on 8 March, 'and I have apologised.' But the instructions, he said, were 'not confined to the points to which it has been thought right to make a correction'. We still do not know what they are. Any prison officer who divulged them (although Lord Mancroft thought they had already been officially divulged) would probably be prosecuted under the Official Secrets Act, as though he had betrayed his country instead of having betrayed the small community that does helpless men and women to death at nine o'clock in the morning.

There is reason to believe, moreover, that not all Mr Pierrepoint's matter-of-fact disclosures were allowed to get into the printed 'minutes of evidence' given to the 1949 Royal Commission. You will find it difficult to get a sight even of those that did. Her Majesty's Stationery Office will tell you that the report of the evidence for that day (the twenty-eighth of the hearing) is out of print. It is the only day's evidence that is. Probably this kind of thing is not considered fit reading for you. Sir Ernest Gowers, the Chairman of the Commission (who subsequently declared himself to have turned against the death penalty), is here questioning Mr Albert Pierrepoint:

'Have you ever known a case where you have not given exactly the right drop and have either nearly decapitated him or strangled him instead of dislocating his neck?'

'I have never seen any signs of it' [i.e. presumably, of the man's head being off].

'Never?'

'Never.'

'The knot must always be under the angle of the left jaw?'

'Yes.'

'That's very important, is it?'

'Very important.'

'Why is it very important?'

'If you have the same knot on the right-hand side, it comes back behind the neck, and throws the neck forward, which would make a strangulation. If you put it on the left side it finishes up in front and throws the chin back and breaks the spinal cord.'

You have to guess that this is because the rope is ringed and noosed that way. But Mr Pierrepoint must know—he had, he said, been the executioner of 'some hundreds' of people; in fact, he added proudly, 'I have seen more executions than anybody living.'

'You don't turn a hair?' the Chairman asked him. 'No.'

'Have you had any experience of judging what the general opinion of ordinary people in England is about capital punishment? I imagine that people must talk to you about your duties?' [After all, he was a licensee.]

'Yes, but I refuse to speak about it. It is something I think should be secret, myself. It's sacred to me, really.' [If you find this hard to believe you can confirm it in the State Papers room at the British Museum, where it is preserved for the entertainment of posterity.]

'Then have you had no special opportunity of judging what people think on these things?'

'I have thought that, if I say anything either way, they will say

"It's his job", and think I'm biased towards it. So I keep quiet.' [Thus enabling anyone so minded to assume that he was opposed to the death penalty and just another round peg in a square hole.] A man must live … 'I'm not in a position to judge, because if I agreed with it they would think, naturally, that it was because I wanted to carry on my job.'

Naturally. Still, it seemed likely that he agreed with it. The Home Office witnesses told the Royal Commission that throughout the years the Prison Commissioners receive on an average five applications every week for the post of hangman; and they seem likely to be persons who agree with it, too. The job is never advertised. Mr Pierrepoint took over from his uncle, and the uncle had taken over from his father. 'It's in the family, really,' he said. But he had to apply for it, in the ordinary way. (Pause here a moment and try to imagine yourself doing that. Then reflect that, week after week, five people reach for their pens and do it. What do they say? 'I respectfully apply … I am strong, and do not easily feel sick … I am used to simple machinery … I approve of capital punishment . . . Good references, punctual.' Perhaps even 'I am a regular churchgoer', or 'a member of the Band of Hope'.)

Mr Pierrepoint said he was a Manchester publican. When he was appointed as an assistant executioner he went to a killing school for a week ('Everybody has to have a week's training in prison') carrying out dummy executions with weighted sacks, and seeing how quick they can be in pinioning a man's arms behind him with a strap, so that he can't reach up and take his weight off the rope, and then tying his knees together so that he can't support himself against the sides of the 'drop' with outstretched legs.

Capital punishment, we call it. Mr Acting Under-Sheriff Gedge was asked by Sir Ernest Gowers whether he found it all extremely distasteful. 'My only concern', said Mr Gedge, 'is to be awakened early enough in the morning.'

Dostoyevsky says somewhere that if in the last moment before being executed a man, however brave, were given the alternative of spending the rest of his days on the top of a bare rock with only enough space to sit on it, he would choose it with relief. The horror of the death penalty goes beyond the mere fear of death or pain or indignity. It is connected not with the brutality but with the macabre, cold-blooded politeness of the ceremony, in which the person whose neck is going to be broken is supposed to collaborate in a nice, sensible manner, as if it were a matter of a minor surgical operation. It is present in the delinquent's knowledge that in the embarrassed stares of the officials he is already mirrored as a dead man with a blue face and ruptured vertebrae; and that what for him is the final, violent termination of life is for them merely an unpleasant duty, followed by a sigh of relief and a plate of bacon and eggs. The Romans deprived their victim of the dignity of death by throwing him to the beasts in the arena with a clown's mask attached to his face; we put a white cap over his head, and, as a medical man disclosed in *The Lancet* on 20 August 1955, if the victim is a woman she is made to put on waterproof underwear on the morning of the execution.

When the operation is over, the victim is buried within the prison walls. By contrast with the custom in those American states which kill by other means than hanging, the body is not handed over to the relatives, for a technical reason which sums up the obscene ignominy of the whole thing: in the words of the Royal Commission Report, 'hanging … leaves the body with the neck elongated'.

If hanging is the modern form of the Godly butchery, the alternatives of the guillotine, of electrocution and the gas chamber are no better, and possibly worse, because the preliminaries take longer. Lethal injections can be relied on only if given intravenously — a procedure which necessitates the voluntary collaboration of the patient. The Royal Commission considered whether the condemned man should be offered this 'as an alternative, pleasanter method of execution', but rejected it for a number of reasons. One of these was:

the vacillation that might be evoked in a prisoner by having to make so crucial a decision … and the need to have the hangman waiting in the background in case his services should be required after all, gradually perhaps losing his skill from disuse.

Irony is a rare feature in Royal Commission reports.

24

A hanging

George Orwell

George Orwell was the pen-name of Eric Arthur Blair (1903–1950). Born in India and educated at Eton, he served with the Imperial police in Burma 1922–27, then became a journalist in France, England, and Spain. He was badly wounded in the Spanish Civil War. He wrote 556 essays, articles, and reviews, and several non-fiction books, and established his reputation as one of the greatest twentieth-century writers with *Animal Farm* (1946) and *Nineteen Eighty-Four* (1949).

This essay was published in 1931.

* * *

It was in Burma, a sodden morning of the rains. A sickly light, like yellow tinfoil, was slanting over the high walls into the jail yard. We were waiting outside the condemned cells, a row of sheds fronted with double bars, like small animal cages. Each cell measured about ten feet by ten and was quite bare within except for a plank bed and a pot for drinking water. In some of them brown, silent men were squatting at the inner bars, with their blankets draped round them. These were the condemned men, due to be hanged within the next week or two.

One prisoner had been brought out of his cell. He was a Hindu, a puny wisp of a man, with a shaven head and vague liquid eyes. He had a thick, sprouting moustache, absurdly too big for his body, rather like the moustache of a comic man on the films. Six tall Indian warders were guarding him and getting him ready for the gallows.

Two of them stood by with rifles and fixed bayonets, while the others handcuffed him, passed a chain through his handcuffs and fixed it to their belts, and lashed his arms tight to his sides. They crowded very close about him, with their hands always on him in a careful, caressing grip, as though all the while feeling him to make sure he was there. It was like men handling a fish which is still alive and may jump back into the water. But he stood quite unresisting, yielding his arms limply to the ropes, as though he hardly noticed what was happening.

Eight o'clock struck and a bugle call, desolately thin in the wet air, floated from the distant barracks. The superintendent of the jail, who was standing apart from the rest of us, moodily prodding the gravel with his stick, raised his head at the sound. He was an army doctor, with a grey toothbrush moustache and a gruff voice. 'For God's sake hurry up, Francis,' he said irritably. 'The man ought to have been dead by this time. Aren't you ready yet?'

Francis, the head jailer, a fat Dravidian in a white drill suit and gold spectacles, waved his black hand. 'Yes sir, yes sir,' he bubbled. 'All iss satisfactorily prepared. The hangman iss waiting. We shall proceed.'

'Well, quick march, then. The prisoners can't get their breakfast till this job's over.'

We set out for the gallows. Two warders marched on either side of the prisoner, with their rifles at the slope; two others marched close against him, gripping him by arm and shoulder, as though at once pushing and supporting him. The rest of us, magistrates and the like followed behind. Suddenly, when we had gone ten yards, the procession stopped short without any order or warning. A dreadful thing had happened—a dog, come goodness knows whence, had appeared in the yard. It came bounding among us with a loud volley of barks, and leapt round us wagging its whole body, wild with glee at finding so many human beings together. It was a large woolly dog, half Airedale, half pariah. For a moment it pranced round us, and then, before anyone could stop it, it had made a dash for the prisoner, jumping up tried to lick his face. Everyone stood aghast, too taken aback even to grab at the dog.

'Who let that bloody brute in here'?' said the superintendent angrily. 'Catch it, someone!'

A warder detached from the escort, charged clumsily after the dog, but it danced and gambolled just out of his reach, taking everything as part of the game. A young Eurasian jailer picked up a handful of gravel and tried to stone the dog away, but it dodged the stones and came after us again. Its yaps echoed from the jail walls. The prisoner, in the grasp of the two warders, looked on incuriously, as though this was another formality of the hanging. It was several minutes before someone managed to catch the dog. Then we put my handkerchief through its collar and moved off once more, with the dog still straining and whimpering.

It was about forty yards to the gallows. I watched the bare brown back of the prisoner marching in front of me. He walked clumsily with his bound arms, but quite steadily, with that bobbing gait of the Indian who never straightens his knees. At each step his muscles slid neatly into place, the lock of hair on his scalp danced up and down, his feet printed themselves on the wet gravel. And once, in spite of the men who gripped him by each shoulder, he stepped slightly aside to avoid a puddle on the path.

It is curious, but till that moment I had never realised what it means to destroy a healthy, conscious man. When I saw the prisoner step aside to avoid the puddle I saw the mystery, the unspeakable wrongness, of cutting a life short when it is in full tide. This man was not dying, he was alive just as we are alive. All the organs of his body were working—bowels digesting food, skin renewing itself, nails growing, tissues forming—all toiling away in solemn foolery. His nails would still be growing when he stood on the drop, when he was falling through the air with a tenth-of-a-second to live. His eyes saw the yellow gravel and the grey walls, and his brain still remembered, foresaw, reasoned—reasoned even about puddles. He and we were a party of men walking together, seeing, hearing, feeling, understanding the same world; and in two minutes, with a sudden snap, one of us would be gone—one mind less, one world less.

The gallows stood in a small yard, separate from the main grounds of the prison, and overgrown with tall prickly weeds. It was a brick erection like three sides of a shed, with planking on top, and above that two beams and a crossbar with the rope dangling. The hangman, a grey-haired convict in the white uniform of the prison, was waiting beside his machine. He greeted us with a servile crouch as we entered. At a word from Francis the two warders, gripping the prisoner more closely than ever, half-led, half-pushed him to the gallows and helped him clumsily up the ladder. Then the hangman climbed up and fixed the rope round the prisoner's neck. We stood waiting, five yards away. The warders had formed in a rough circle round the gallows. And then, when the noose was fixed, the prisoner began crying out to his god. It was a high, reiterated cry of 'Ram! Ram! Ram! Ram!' not urgent and fearful like a prayer or cry for help, but steady, rhythmical, almost like the tolling of a bell. The dog answered the sound with a whine. The hangman, still standing on the gallows, produced a small cotton bag like a flour bag and drew it down over the prisoner's face. But the sound, muffled by the cloth, still persisted, over and over again: 'Ram! Ram! Ram! Ram! Ram!'

The hangman climbed down and stood ready, holding the lever. Minutes seemed to pass. The steady, muffled crying from the prisoner went on and on, 'Ram! Ram! Ram!' never faltering for an instant. The superintendent, his head on his chest, was slowly poking the ground with his stick; perhaps he was counting the cries, allowing the prisoner a fixed number — fifty, perhaps, or a hundred. Everyone had changed colour. The Indians had gone grey like bad coffee, and one of two of the bayonets were wavering. We looked at the lashed, hooded man on the drop, and listened to his cries — each cry another second of life; the same thought was in all our minds: oh, kill him quickly, get it over, stop that abominable noise!

Suddenly the superintendent made up his mind. Throwing up his head he made a swift motion with his stick. 'Chalo!' he shouted almost fiercely.

There was a clanking noise, and then dead silence. The prisoner had vanished, and the rope was twisting on itself. I let go of the dog, and it galloped immediately to the back of the gallows; but when it got there it stopped short, barked, and then retreated into a corner of the yard, where it stood among the weeds, looking timorously out at us. We went round the gallows to inspect the prisoner's body. He was dangling with his toes pointed straight downwards, very slowly revolving, as dead as a stone.

The superintendent reached out with his stick and poked the bare brown body; it oscillated slightly. 'He's all right,' said the superintendent. He backed out from under the gallows, and blew out a deep breath. The moody look had gone out of his face quite suddenly. He glanced at his wrist-watch. 'Eight minutes past eight. Well, that's all for this morning, thank God.'

The warders unfixed bayonets and marched away. The dog, sobered and conscious of having misbehaved itself, slipped after them. We walked out of the gallows yard, past the condemned cells with their waiting prisoners, into the big central yard of the prison. The convicts, under the command of warders armed with lathis, were already receiving their breakfast. They squatted in long rows, each man holding a tin pannikin, while two warders with buckets marched round ladling out rice; it seemed quite a homely, jolly scene, after the hanging. An enormous relief had come upon us now that the job was done. One felt an impulse to sing, to break into a run, to snigger. All at once everyone began chattering gaily.

The Eurasian boy walking beside me nodded towards the way we had come, with a knowing smile: 'Do you know, sir, our friend (he meant the dead man) when he heard his appeal had been dismissed, he pissed on the floor of his cell. From fright. Kindly take one of my cigarettes, sir. Do you not admire my new silver case, sir? From the boxwallah, two rupees eight annas. Classy European style.'

Several people laughed—at what, nobody seemed certain. Francis was walking by the superintendent, talking garrulously: 'Well, sir, all hass passed off with the utmost satisfactoriness. It was all finished—flick! like that. It iss not always so—oah, no! I have known cases where the doctor wass obliged to go beneath the gallows and pull the prissoner's legs to ensure decease. Most disagreeable!'

'Wriggling about, eh? That's bad,' said the superintendent. 'Ach, sir, it iss worse when they become refractory! One man, I recall, clung to the bars of hiss cage when we went to take him out. You will scarcely credit, sir, that it took six warders to dislodge him, three pulling at each leg. We reasoned with him. "My dear fellow," we said, "think of all the pain and trouble you are causing to us!" But no, he would not listen! Ach, he wass very troublesome!'

I found that I was laughing quite loudly. Everyone was laughing. Even the superintendent grinned in a tolerant way. 'You'd better all come out and have a drink,' he said quite genially. 'I've got a bottle of whisky in the car. We could do with it.'

We went through the big double gates of the prison into the road. 'Pulling at his legs!' exclaimed a Burmese magistrate suddenly, and burst into a loud chuckling. We all began laughing again. At that moment Francis' anecdote seemed extraordinarily funny. We all had a drink together, native and European alike, quite amicably. The dead man was a hundred yards away.

25

An execution

Peter Lewis

The following powerful account of a hanging in Canada appeared in the *New Statesman* for 21 April 1961. I have failed to identify a Canadian author of that name, and I speculate that the writer may have been the widely travelled English journalist and critic Peter Lewis (1928–2016).

* * *

We arrived at the prison at 11.30 pm. At the guardhouse outside, we showed our cards and were allowed in. Two guards searched us indifferently. They told us to wait until the telephone rang, with permission to pass to the main part of the building.

One guard's breath smelled of whisky. His face was swollen. He looked at me and cocked his head towards the sound of the rain pattering on the roof.

'Bad night for a hanging,' he commented. The telephone rang. We passed a lighted courtyard and mounted the four marble steps through the main door. The hallway was extravagantly lit, with a cold floor and oak doors to either side. It seemed like the reception hall of a hospital, even to the young picture of the Queen. But there were guards in uniform at every 15 paces.

'You're the newspaper boys? Show me your passes,' one of them demanded. He looked us over, then pointed to an open door.

Inside, in deep silence, sat a dozen men. They were ranged on benches on each side of the room. 'The inquest jury,' the other reporter whispered. We took a place on the bench. The jurymen were mostly middle-aged. They had been chosen and committed, as responsible citizens of the province of British Columbia, to present themselves, to witness and attest to the execution of the murderer. They were dressed in dark suits. They appeared uncomfortable and tense, seemingly too nervous to speak to one another.

Five minutes passed. We heard steps coming along the corridor, then moving off again. I noticed one of the witnesses was having trouble in breathing. His face was flushed and he was gasping. Suddenly a man appeared in the doorway. He was broad-shouldered, blond and dressed in a brown suit. As he stepped to the centre of the room, he glanced at the seated figures.

'I am the warden,' he said, holding up his hand for attention. 'We'll wait for a minute, then go upstairs. When I give the signal follow me in single file.'

The murderer was a Ukranian, aged sixty-four. He had been condemned to death for killing his wife. He had shot her after discovering that she had been unfaithful to him. Somewhere in this building, hidden from us, he was now living his last minutes.

'If you're ready we will go now,' the warden said. His words were followed by a scraping and shuffling as we stood. Avoiding each other's eyes, we formed a line and filed from the room. In the hallway, our party was joined by several guards. Presently we halted, waiting for an iron door to be swung open. We began to climb a steel staircase.

Immediately behind me was the man whose irregular breathing I had noticed earlier. His step was unsteady. I glanced back, seeing he was managing the stairs only with great effort. He had closed his eyes, and he pressed a handkerchief to one side of his red face.

We reached a dim whitewashed corridor, at the end of which a door stood open. This was our destination, the execution shed. We hastened our step. The shed was lit by powerful lamps. It was low-roofed and narrow, but very long, perhaps sixty feet. The walls were painted in gunmetal grey. The first thing that struck me was the sour odour of new paint, the air of crude cleanliness in the room.

Once completely in the doorway, however, my eyes fell on the only important fixtures in sight: the trap-door and rope. These were half-way along the room, close to the wall. Seven uniformed policemen stood a curious guard, each with his back to the trap-door. They were wordless and their faces without expression.

Eight feet above the trap-door, neatly tied and looped to the ceiling, was the executioner's rope, which seemed fresh and white.

The trap-door was level with the cement floor, not mounted as I had assumed it would be. (I was told later the space underneath, into which the murderer dropped, had once been an elevator shaft; that in most prisons executions were now arranged like this, doing away with the use of a scaffold.) The trap-door was constructed in wood, and around its edges ran a strip of steel.

At the extreme end of the windowless chamber was a platform, raised slightly from the floor. This was the witnesses' stand. We were led towards it, and in confusion we took our places, pressing close to one another to find a position. I was jostled into the second row. By being elevated thus we could see the execution site only too well. Perhaps three minutes passed. The only sound was the breathing of those around me. The red-faced man was somewhere in the back row, out of my vision, yet his sharp ugly gasps dominated the other noises.

Through the doorway emerged a squat figure in a brown suit. He strode to the side of the trap-door and guards. He was about fifty and his gross features were encased in a turnip-like yellow skin. In his left hand he carried two leather straps. With the other he began to fiddle with the rope. He was the hangman.

Before I recovered from the shock of his appearance, I heard the shuffle of many feet along the unseen corridor. The footsteps grew nearer. I made out a soft mumbling noise, then the first figures were in the doorway, exposed to the brittle light.

For an instant I did not see the condemned man. He was hidden in the knot of guards and men in civilian dress, among whom stood the warden. (He had stolen away from our group earlier, unnoticed.) There was a priest in a cassock, reading from a breviary.

Then the guards parted, seeming to eject a man from their midst, the murderer. He was a little man and he blinked and peered about him. He was dressed in dark prison trousers, and his old head drooped forward from his shoulders. He wore a faded blue shirt, the collar of which was opened.

A strap pinioned his arms behind his back. He wore only woollen stockings on his feet. In the centre of his mouth was a lighted cigarette, a quarter smoked. He appeared not terrified. When his eyes had grown used to the light, he inspected the faces of the men nearest him, then looked at the trap-door and the rope. He turned his head towards the witness stand, taking us in with an air of grave frank curiosity.

Although someone seemed to be guiding him, the grey-haired murderer moved ahead willingly but slowly, as if insisting on setting the pace himself. With this last gesture of independence, he moved upright and self-absorbed to the edge of the trap-door.

He puffed mildly on his cigarette and looked with renewed interest at us. The warden whispered something in his ear. He appeared to take seconds to comprehend, his old face creased and pondering. At last he shook his head negatively. Suddenly the hangman appeared at the murderer's back and pushed him to the centre of the trap. He set to work energetically, bending almost double to lash the old man's legs together with the straps. As he worked, straining to tighten the leather, the murderer's body bobbed and swayed. The expression on his face did not alter, even as the hangman finished his job and half pushed, half dragged him to position under the rope. He smoked his cigarette unprotestingly, as if somehow he were not connected with what was being done to him.

He continued to examine our group, with an air of intense curiosity. I stiffened and my knees felt suddenly very weak, for he was looking directly at me. His eyes had centred on my chest, where I was clutching a notebook. He spoke all at once. So softly I could not be sure it was a voice. From far off the words touched me, touched the others. 'You should have given me a fair trial. I did not have a fair trial.' But it was lifeless, without spite. The words were impossibly futile, almost as if he were uttering them, not for his own benefit, but to recite what was expected of him.

What happened next was finished in perhaps ten seconds.

The murderer's white face looked dumbly at us. The cigarette still rested in the centre of his mouth. His blue eyes did not blink. Swiftly the executioner came from behind. His hand snaked around and tore the condemned man's cigarette from his mouth, flinging it brutally aside. With his free hand the executioner pulled a white hood from his pocket. He unfurled it as though it were a great silk handkerchief, and stood on his toes. He dropped the hood over the murderer's face.

For one instant, between the time his cigarette was snatched and the hood had descended, the murderer's face was taken by pained bewilderment. He had at last understood. Then his features vanished.

The hangman reached higher still, and unhooked the rope coiled above the condemned man's head. With incredible speed he adjusted the noose, securing the knot at the back of the neck, and next he seemed to propel himself backwards, his foot reaching for a lever on the floor.

The hooded body wavered.

There was a violent deadly crack, the trap-door opening. Instantly the murderer's body dropped from sight. The rope spun after it into blackness. The rope jerked.

A moment of impossible terror. My left knee moved by itself, kicking upwards. A numbness came over me.

The snap of the trap-door's spring lingered in the room for many moments. Somehow I felt it important to look at my watch. It was 12.06.

When I returned my eyes to the room I became aware of the priest, standing at the edge of the open pit. He was making the sign of the cross, only a few feet from where the rope swayed stiffly into the darkness. Everyone in the room became animated coughing and shuffling towards the doorway. I felt the other men around me beginning to stir. I let myself be pushed into motion.

The sound of the trap-door had resounded through the jail. Many prisoners from the block closest the execution chamber had set to screaming and clanking metal objects together. As I descended the staircase, I heard them chanting in unison, one young voice rising above the rest: 'Hang the bloody hangman. Hang the bloody hangman …' Once downstairs, we were herded into the room we had occupied earlier. The jury members were told they would have to view the body, so as to certify death. For 15 minutes we waited, hardly talking. They were called by the prison doctor to another room.

With my fellow reporter I wandered into the outer corridor. There we found the prison warden. As we talked with him, a stout brown-suited figure passed, carrying four leather straps over his arm. He ignored our stares.

'He's made his 200 dollars,' said the other reporter, hostilely.

'Yes,' replied the warden. 'He's often here. He'll be back in three weeks' time.' Then he added, 'I suppose there's got to be someone to do it.'

The warden excused himself. A few minutes later he was back, holding a slip of paper. Behind him, along the corridor, I caught a glimpse of a stretcher being wheeled hurriedly out of one doorway, then into another. The body was covered by a grey sheet. Only the feet protruded, in their woollen socks.

'Pronounced dead at 12.24,' said the warden.

We wrote the time in our notebooks. The warden looked closely at us.

'Don't mention the times. They die instantly, but their heart continues to beat for quite a long time. The public wouldn't understand.'

26

The death of Ronald Ryan

Patrick Tennison

Patrick Tennison (1928–1988), born in Queensland, was a journalist and broadcaster with extensive television experience. The London correspondent for the Herald & Weekly Times newspapers 1959–61, he became Australian correspondent for several overseas journals.

He witnessed Ronald Ryan's hanging as a representative of *The Australian*.

* * *

The life that was Ronald Ryan's was taken from him yesterday.

He died silently, His face white but impassive. His thin lips together, but not clenched.

You get weird mental impressions. His face was strangely like a small child who had composed himself into calm bravery just before the doctor gives a needle.

Only once did this change. The hangman readying the knot jolted his head with the rope. Ryan turned his head slightly towards him. That was all.

The hangman stepped back, the body fell from view. The rope dragged taut and swayed just slightly. The voice of the priest was heard reading his prayers.

I was one of 14 newsmen-witnesses representing the public.

We were marshalled first into a long visitors' room with plastic flowers. An official warning was given: No cameras or tape recorders—'that wouldn't be cricket.' No smoking once inside either.

Then the clock took over. At 10 minutes to eight we were led to D block. Our bodies were counted on the way, tallied at the door.

A last impression going through the door: A lot of birds singing.

Inside small fluorescent lights helped the bits of sunglow seeping through roof windows. A rope was held back up 40 feet from a green canvas-like screen. On a catwalk above, the noose lay neatly placed on a railing. Its rope ended on the thick beam above, tied around the beam in six loops.

Two minutes to eight. The prison officials' party walked on the tier catwalk above to Ryan's cell. The hangman suddenly walked quickly under the scaffold and entered behind them. A big, dark green cap—like English Soccer fans wear—pulled down low around his head. Big sun goggles over his eyes.

Forty seconds before eight. Ryan emerged. Five long paces from his cell door to the noose. Dull blue prison denims. Hands tied behind his back. A grey cloth on his head.

As the hangman fixed his rope, you could see wispy grey hair under his cap on his neck. It was a redly sunburnt neck.

Ryan, white, immobile, passive, as a wide flap from the cloth on his head was dropped over his face.

The trap door opened efficiently at eight.

Part V

The Decline and Fall of the Death Penalty in the English-speaking World

27

A survey

Barry Jones

The United Kingdom

The long campaign for abolition began in the nineteenth century when the reformers Romilly, Montagu, Bentham, Mill, and the Howard League argued for limitation of the death penalty. The abolition of public executions in 1869 was felt to be an advance — but in the light of later experience the abolition of public executions may have been a major factor in retarding total abolition.

In 1925 Roy Calvert (1898–1933) founded the National Council for the Abolition of the Death Penalty, and his book *Capital Punishment in the Twentieth Century* (1927) was the standard abolitionist text for many years.

The United Kingdom had three serious government-sponsored investigations into the death penalty — the Royal Commission of 1864–66, the Parliamentary Select Committee of 1929–30, and the Royal Commission of 1949–53. The Royal Commission of 1864–66 recommended in its report that there should be grades of murder. Five of its twelve members, however, said that they were in favour of the complete abolition of capital punishment. The report of the Select Committee 1929–30, which recommended abolition for a trial period, was signed by a majority of its members but was not unanimous; the minority never drafted any alternative report. In 1938 the House of Commons passed a resolution proposing abolition for a trial period of five years. The government did not proceed with the experiment.

The Royal Commission 1949–53, chaired by Sir Ernest Gowers (see above), was asked 'to consider and report whether capital punishment should be limited or modified and if so to what extent and by what means', but abolition was excluded from its terms of reference.

The effect of the main part of the Gowers report is that there is no way substantially to limit capital punishment except, in effect, to leave it to the jury to decide in each case. There are grave disadvantages about this course, as the Royal Commissioners appreciated, and, in the concluding words of the main part of their report, they said,

> its disadvantages may be thought to outweigh its merits. If this view were to prevail, the conclusion to our mind would be inescapable that in this country a stage has been reached where little more can be done effectively to limit the liability to suffer the death penalty, and that the real issue is now whether capital punishment should be retained or abolished.[1]

In 1948 the House of Commons inserted a clause in the Criminal Justice Bill suspending the death penalty for five years. Despite the large Labour majority in the House of Commons, in a free vote the abolitionist clause was carried by only twenty-three votes. In the House of Lords the clause was decisively rejected (181–28): the Law Lords were uniformly retentionist, as were most Bishops. Gallup Polls reported 68 per cent support for hanging.

Nevertheless, the death penalty was suspended for most of 1948—and the reported homicide rate was not demonstrably affected either way.

The controversy over the Criminal Justice Bill led to the appointment of the Gowers Commission reported above, and to the revival of the National Campaign for the Abolition of Capital Punishment, among whose leading lights were Gerald Gardiner, QC, Sydney Silverman, MP, Arthur Koestler, and C. H. Rolph.

In February 1956 the House of Commons carried by a majority of forty-six a resolution calling on the government 'to introduce forthwith legislation for the abolition or suspension of capital

---

1   Gerald Gardiner, QC, *Capital Punishment as a Deterrent: and the Alternative*, Gollancz, London 1956, pp. 22–23, slightly abridged.

punishment'. In June 1956 the Death Penalty (Abolition) Bill passed the House of Commons but was rejected by the House of Lords in July. In March the government, with the whips on, passed the Homicide Act 1957, and the first execution for over eighteen months occurred in July that year. In the eighteen months after executions recommenced there were more murders than in the eighteen months before the Act, when there were no executions.

Part II of the Act established a system of grades or degrees of murder and restricted capital punishment to those guilty of 'capital murders'. Sections 5 and 6 constituted as 'capital murders':

a. any done in the course or furtherance of theft;
b. any done by shooting or by causing an explosion;
c. any done in the course or for the purpose of resisting or avoiding or preventing a lawful arrest, or of effecting or assisting an escape or rescue from legal custody;
d. any murder of a police officer acting in the execution of his duty or of a person assisting a police officer so acting;
e. any murder by a prisoner of a prison officer acting in the execution of his duty or of a person assisting him;
f. any second murder by the same person if done 'on a different occasion' in Great Britain.

The effect was that:

1. If a man killed his wife with the nearest weapon to hand, it was capital murder if the weapon was a gun, but non-capital murder if it was a hatchet.
2. If a man raped a girl, strangled her, and took her handbag, it was capital murder, but if he did not take the handbag it was non-capital.
3. If a woman had left a man money in her will and, with premeditation he poisoned her for the money, this was non-capital murder.[2]

---

2   Ibid., pp. 5–6. The material on the three last pages has been drawn very largely, with permission, from Lord Gardiner's book.

Commenting on the Homicide Act, the Lord Chief Justice, Lord Parker of Waddington, told the House of Lords in 1965:

> Looking back to eleven (sic] years ago, if anybody had suggested that I should come out as a full-blooded abolitionist I should have been surprised. But during that time, and particularly during the last seven years when I have held my office, I have seen the complete absurdities that have been produced, and have become completely disgusted at the results. I suppose poisoning is the most cold-blooded and deliberate of murders, yet you do not hang. You can poison your wife for months or years, and the most you can get is life imprisonment, unless you marry again and do it a second time. The taking of a note or a coin may make the difference between capital and noncapital murder ...
>
> Judges as a body are supposed to be very reactionary. I do not myself think that is true today. They sit in court; they see where the shoe pinches; they see where justice does not appear to be done, and when it is not done. And I think I can say that all the judges are quite disgusted with the results produced by the Homicide Act.

General public concern about the death penalty was aroused less by sociological analysis or philosophical insight than by a series of cases exposing the arbitrary and irrevocable nature of the penalty.

Outstanding among these were the cases of Timothy Evans, Derek Bentley and Ruth Ellis:[3]

> TIMOTHY EVANS, 25, lorry driver, illiterate and mentally backward, charged with murdering his child. Evans' counsel accused prosecution witness Christie of murdering Mrs Evans and the child. (Christie was later found to have murdered seven women in circumstances identical with those of Mrs Evans' death: the probability that he killed Evans' child too, because its presence was inimical to his own defence, is now almost universally accepted.) Hanged on 8 November 1949. (He was granted a posthumous pardon and re-buried in consecrated ground in 1966.)

---

3   Case notes taken from Arthur Koestler and C. H. Rolph, *Hanged by the Neck*, Penguin Books, London 1961, pp. 107, 121, 127.

DEREK BENTLEY, 19, grade 4 mentally impaired, was found guilty as an accomplice in the shooting of a policeman by 16-year old Christopher Craig. Recommendation to mercy by jury. Two hundred Members of Parliament, including ten former Ministers, placed a Motion upon the Order Paper: 'That this House respectfully dissents from the opinion of the Home Secretary that there are not sufficient grounds on which to advise the exercise of Her Majesty's mercy in the case of Derek Bentley.' Hanged on 28 January 1953.

RUTH ELLIS, 28, model, of South Kensington, mother of two children. Murder by shooting of David Blakely, 25, engineer, of Penn, Buckinghamshire. Her two marriages had been dissolved, and in 1953 she lived for a few months with Blakely. The latter wanted to break off even this relationship with her in favour of another woman, and she shot him one day in the street as he got out of his car, having waited for him intending to do so. She acknowledged all this. It was pleaded on her behalf that she was 'hysterical, and emotionally immature'. She had very recently had a miscarriage. Recommendation to mercy by the jury. No appeal. Hanged at Holloway Prison, 12 July 1955.

In addition to these there were many cases of persons hanged after recommendations, or strong recommendations, to mercy, in circumstances where the persons convicted appeared to have been insane in every sense except in terms of the M'Naghton Rules.

> The result has been a tragic procession to the gallows of psychopaths, epileptics, mental defectives, hysterics, sex maniacs, depressives, and people on the border of paranoia and schizophrenia.[4]

Of the forty-eight people sentenced to death for capital murder between March 1957 and December 1964, nineteen (that is, 40 per cent) were reprieved. The last hangings took place on 13 August 1964 when Gwynne Owen Evans (aged twenty-four) and Peter Anthony Allen (aged twenty-one), both mentally defective, were executed for

---

4   Koestler and Rolph, op. cit., p. 135.

bashing a man to death in the course of robbery.

The Wilson Labour government, elected in October 1964, announced that it would find time for a private members' Bill on the question of abolition and allow a 'free' or 'conscience' vote. In the meantime the Home Secretary (Sir Frank Soskice) reprieved all prisoners already sentenced to death under the Homicide Act—although he was quick to explain that each case had been examined on its merits, and he was not making a wholesale use (or misuse) of the dispensing power.

Sydney Silverman, MP, introduced the Murder (Abolition of Death Penalty) Bill on 4 December 1964. The Bill was confined to murder only—the other capital offences (treason and piracy) adding an unnecessary complication to the whole issue. He concluded a cautious, low-key speech with these words:

> I can well understand people saying that in the face of all our anxieties it may not matter whether we execute or do not execute two or three wretched murderers each year. It is impossible to argue that the non-execution of two people in England every year can make a very great contribution to improving a dark and menaced world. Yet we could light this small candle and see how far the tiny glimmer can penetrate the gloom.

A surprising convert to abolition was Henry Brooke, MP, the former Tory Home Secretary (later Lord Brooke of Cumnor):

> I am greatly influenced, and I was before I left the Home Office, because I called for the figures while I was there, by the figures set out in Table 6 at columns 247–8 of Hansard of 11 December. In that table, all murders from January 1952 to March 1957, are analyzed. Those were the years before the Homicide Act. It is ascertained that 14.4 per cent of all those pre-Homicide Act murders would have been capital murder had the Homicide Act definition then been in effect.
>
> It seems to me that, if the unique deterrent argument were valid, there should have been a substantial fall in that percentage after the

Homicide Act. Until then, the deterrent for murders which were to be non-capital and murders which were capital was the same. From March 1957 onwards, the special deterrent of the risk of death remained only for capital murders and it was removed for non-capital murders. Yet, although one would on grounds of logic, if the unique deterrent argument were sound, expect the percentage to fall materially, one finds, on examining the figures since 1957, that it has fallen hardly perceptibly. Before the Homicide Act, the percentages were 14.4 per cent capital and 85.6 per cent non-capital. Since the Homicide Act, the percentages have been 13.5 capital and 86.5 non-capital. I do not see in those figures support, still less proof, of the argument that the death penalty is a uniquely powerful deterrent.[5]

Brigadier Terence Clarke, Tory MP for Portsmouth West, an ardent retentionist, declared that Home Secretaries 'become so wet that they ought to be hanged themselves' and that a few of his younger Conservative colleagues 'were about as wet as the last three Home Secretaries' and were 'going to abolish this deterrent and allow our constituents to be raped, shot, and murdered'.

Attempts to amend the Bill by providing the death penalty for a second murder were defeated. In all British penal records since 1840, there are only two cases where a man convicted of murder and reprieved from the death sentence has ever been convicted of a second murder (Walter Graham Rowland executed in February 1947 but now thought to have been innocent of the second crime; Christopher Simcox, a cripple who murdered his two wives: the second wife was the first wife's sister and married him in full knowledge—he was reprieved in 1964). In addition a lifer, Peter Dunford, convicted of murder at seventeen—and thus ineligible to hang—killed another prisoner in gaol (1965).

However, on Henry Brooke's amendment, the Bill was passed for a five-year trial period. To be extended it had to be endorsed by resolution of both Houses in 1970. The Bill passed its second reading in the Commons by 200 votes to ninety-eight. The House of Lords,

---

5   Official Report, Commons, vol. 704 (no. 38), col. 909, 21 December 1964.

formerly the graveyard of all abolitionist Bills, debated the Murder Bill in July 1965.

Baroness Wootton, who moved the Bill, attacked the anomalies of the Homicide Act and quoted the view of the Gowers Commission on degrees of murder:

> We began our enquiry with a determination to succeed where so many have failed, and to discover some effective method of classifying murderers so as to confine the death penalty to the more heinous ... We conclude with regret that the object of our quest is chimerical and that it must be abandoned.[6]

Opponents of the Bill, notably the former Lords Chancellor Dilhorne and Kilmuir, forecast that abolition might lead to an alarming increase in murder and the arming of police.

Dr Michael Ramsay, Archbishop of Canterbury, considered that,

> it just is not shown that the death penalty is a uniquely powerful deterrent ... A sentence of life imprisonment is a terrible sentence, deterrent in effect, and capable of issuing in a wise, stern and human penology, and [I believe] that to abolish the death penalty in this country will set us in the way of progress ... and rid us from the wrong of a system which punishes killing by a penalty which helps to devalue human life.[7]

The Lord Chancellor, Lord Gardiner, closed the debate by appealing for the question of abolition to be divorced from party political bias. He argued that fears of an alarming increase in homicide after abolition were likely to be ill-founded.

> Broadly speaking, when one looks at the ten years before the war, 1930 to 1939, and the decade after the war, 1950 to 1959, the number of burglaries and housebreakings went up by about 250 per cent; rape and

---

6   *The Parliamentary Debates (Hansard)*, 5th Series, Volume. House of Lords, 1965, col. 455 ff
7   Ibid., col. 611–18.

other offences against women, by about 400 per cent, and wounding, by about 700 per cent—and these figures are rather worse now.

One would think that if the rate of crime goes up, particularly crimes of violence, the rate of murder must go up, too. But your Lordships will remember that my noble and learned friend the Lord Chief Justice said yesterday that that does not seem to happen. One can look at crime figures only by relating the number of crimes to the population, and per million of population the murder rate is virtually fixed. The other figures have gone up by as much as 700 per cent while, though murders go up one year and down the next, if we take any decade during this century, they are never less than 3½ or more than 4½ per million of the population. The worst ten years were the first ten years of the century; the next worse were the ten years just after the war, and the best were just before the war. Why murder does not increase when there are these enormous increases in other crimes, particularly crimes of violence, is very strange; but that is what happens. It is almost as if one cannot make the murder rate increase or decrease.

Then it is said that this is not the right time to do it, because of the increase in crime and so forth. I am perhaps in a fairly special position in your Lordships' House—at least, I imagine so—because I have read, more than once, every debate which has taken place in your Lordships' House on this subject since 1810. I can assure your Lordships that there has never been a debate in which it has not been said, 'This is not the right time.' I am afraid that this is something rather like the remuneration of the superior Judiciary. What I always feel is a little hard on the abolitionists is that this is always used both ways: that is to say, if crime is going up, it is said, 'Look at the awful way that crime is going up. Is this the time in which to chance so hazardous a venture?' If, on the other hand, crime is going down, it is said, 'Look how satisfactory the crime situation is. That shows how effective our deterrents are. What a mistake it would be to alter it at this time!'

What happened in 1948 was an exception, because then the two arguments were used by two noble and learned Lords in the same debate. But this was a record. One or them said: 'Is this the time at which to introduce this change in the law? The statistics which were given in another place by the Home Secretary have shown a great increase in crime.' The other noble and learned Lord said: 'The number of crimes of murder in this country is very small. I ask your Lordships to take the view that when things are going so well as regards the number of murderers this is not the time to make this change.' If two noble and learned Lords can put these arguments forward in the same debate, then I think it shows that it will never be the right time.

Lord Gardiner continued by restating much of the US and European material already printed in this book. He concluded with these words:

When Samuel Romilly started this he did not know what the result of abolishing capital punishment was going to be, here or elsewhere, because it had not been done, and he never used more than two arguments—namely, first, 'You think crime will increase if you abolish it, but it will not, because, you see, the great deterrent to crime is not severity of punishment but certainty of conviction, and you will find the conviction rate will go up.' Secondly, he said, 'We all underrate the effect of the example set by the State.' I have always been convinced that he was right, and I have agreed with John Bright when he said, 'A deep reverence for human life is worth more than a thousand executions in the prevention of murder. And it is in fact the great security of human life. The law of capital punishment, while pretending to support this reverence, does in fact tend to destroy it.[8]

The Bill was carried on 20 July 1965 by 204 votes to 104. This was a dramatic reversal of 1948: the Archbishop of Canterbury and eleven Bishops voted for the Bill and none against. Of eight present or former Law Lords voting, six were for abolition, two for retention—and by 1967 Lord Denning, Master of the Rolls, originally a retentionist, had announced that he would not vote for restoration. Former Lord Chief Justice Goddard, 88, remained intransigently retentionist.

Earl Attlee, Baroness Spencer-Churchill (Sir Winston's widow), and Baroness Asquith (the Liberal PM's daughter) joined many

---

8   Ibid., col. 695–712.

ex-Tory ministers in voting for abolition.

On 8 November 1965 the relevant section of the Bill became law: 'No person shall suffer death for murder'.

In its issue for 7 July 1967, *Time* magazine reported on the operation of the Murder (Abolition of Death Penalty) Act (1965):

Life without the hangman

Great Britain did away with the death penalty in murder cases in November 1965. Almost by reflex, advocates of capital punishment then argued that without the deterrence of executions, the number of killings would soar. For those who judge by headlines, it looked for a while as if the critics might be right. British papers seemed to overflow with stories about THREE POLICEMEN SHOT DEAD and TWO LITTLE GIRLS MURDERED. Pressure groups, including the police, began demanding the return of the hangman. The demand seems to have been premature. According to recently announced figures for 1966, there were only 173 murders in England, Scotland and Wales—compared with 183 and 180 in the two previous years.[9]

Despite abolition of the death penalty for murder in 1965, it remained theoretically applicable for some other crimes: arson in royal dockyards until 1971, espionage until 1981, treason and piracy with violence until the Crime and Disorder Act 1998. Beheading had been abolished as a penalty for treason in 1973.

As prime minister, Margaret Thatcher, 'the Iron Lady', had shown some interest in restoring the death penalty but she could not convince her colleagues. This was despite acts of violence by the Provisional IRA: the car-bombing of Airey Neave, MP, at Westminster in March 1979, blowing up Lord Mountbatten's boat in Sligo in August 1979, and the bomb explosion in October 1984 at the Grand Hotel, Brighton, at the time of the Conservative Party Conference

---

9   There were no executions in Scotland between 1928 and 1945. In this period the average number of murders known to police was 2.52 per million in Scotland compared with 3.89 in England and Wales. (See Christopher Hibbert's *The Roots of Evil*.)

in which five were killed and thirty-one injured. Mrs Thatcher was the primary target.

In the United Kingdom, in June 1988 the House of Commons defeated by 341 votes to 219 a motion for the restoration of the death penalty. This was the nineteenth attempt at restoration since 1965, and the fifth since 1979. (The 1987 motion was lost by 112 votes).

The largest number of deaths recorded in modern penology are attributed to the English physicians Dr John Bodkin Adams (1899–1983), 163 of whose patients (most of them generous to Adams in their wills) died suspiciously, and Dr Harold Shipman (1946–2004), known to his friends as Fred, whose total was about 250. Adams' patients had died when the death penalty was in force. However, when he was tried in 1957 there were ambiguities and incompetence in the prosecution case, and after a penetrating charge to the jury by the judge, Patrick (later Lord) Devlin, he was acquitted. Devlin later described Adams as 'a mercenary mercy killer'. Shipman was convicted of fifteen murders in 2000, and was sentenced to life imprisonment without parole, but hanged himself in prison.

Australia

After the Commonwealth of Australia was established in 1901 the only executions under Commonwealth law were in the Northern Territory (see below).

There were no executions of Australian soldiers for cowardice or desertion during World Wars I and II, in sharp contrast to the United Kingdom, Canada, and New Zealand.

Hangings of first nations people in Papua New Guinea in 1943–44 by the Australian Imperial Force (AIF) were a well-kept secret, even from the Commonwealth government (see p. 7). After World War II ended, Australian war crimes tribunals tried 924 Japanese in Rabaul, Singapore, Darwin, Manus, and Borneo for atrocious cruelties in prisoner-of-war camps, and 148 of those convicted were executed.

Australia provided Justice William Webb, from the High Court, to preside in Tokyo at the International Military Tribunal for the Far

East 1946–48, in which twenty-eight high officials were charged and seven hanged.

The Death Penalty Abolition Bill (1973), given a high priority by Gough Whitlam and his attorney-general, Lionel Murphy, abolished capital punishment under Commonwealth law for all offences, including treason. In the House of Representatives, in a free vote, it was carried by seventy-three votes to twenty-seven. 'Yes' votes from the Opposition included Billy Snedden, John Gorton, Jim Killen, and Ian Viner. Malcolm Fraser and Ian Sinclair voted 'No', with most of the Country Party. Absentees included William McMahon, Doug Anthony, Andrew Peacock, and Don Chipp. After passing the Senate, the Bill became law in September 1973.

Malcolm Fraser, at the Melbourne launch of my autobiography *A Thinking Reed* (2006), quoted movingly from my chapter on the death penalty. Ian Sinclair changed his mind, too.

In 2010 the prohibition on the death penalty was extended to state laws with the Commonwealth Crimes Legislation Amendment (Torture Prohibition and Death Penalty Abolition) Act 2010. This Act was to ensure that the death penalty could not be reintroduced by any state in Australia. Additionally, former High Court Justice Michael Kirby noted that the International Covenant on Civil and Political Rights Protocol 'represents an obstacle to any attempt on the part of a state or territory of Australia to restore capital punishment'.

New South Wales

The oldest and most populous of the states, from 1788 to 1900 New South Wales conducted about 1,000 executions, more than any other state. However, in the twentieth century there were more hangings in Western Australia.

In March 1868, in Sydney, in the first royal tour of Australia, Prince Alfred, Duke of Edinburgh, a son of Queen Victoria, was shot in the back by Henry O'Farrell, Irish born, paranoid, epileptic, and a failed aspirant for the priesthood. O'Farrell was speedily tried for attempted murder, convicted, sentenced to death, and hanged in

April. The prince, who was only slightly wounded and made a full recovery, interceded for O'Farrell's life, but this was the only request he made that was denied.

Within a week of the shooting, Sir John Robertson's ministry had secured passage of the Treason Felony Act, extending the death penalty to a variety of offences. There was no minimum age for hanging. This law remained on the statute books until 1955, and the prerogative of mercy was exercised as the result of political-administrative decisions by cabinet.

Decisions to hang were not subject to judicial review. After the formation of the Australian Labor Party (ALP) in the 1890s, the granting or withholding of commutation was inevitably determined on political lines. The fate of murderers was a matter of 'political football'. The ALP adopted an abolitionist plank in its earliest history, more from emotional conviction than from an examination of evidence or close sociological analysis. The main factor was probably the view that judges, lawyers, and the state ought not to be able to hold the power of life and death over victims of society—even criminal victims.

All death sentences were accordingly commuted under New South Wales Labor governments (see table 'Hangings in Australia').

In New South Wales in December 1916, two members of the Industrial Workers of the World, Robert Kennedy and Frank Franz, were hanged for the murder of a policeman in Bathurst Gaol under the Treason Felony Act, largely on the disputed evidence of an accomplice. This followed bitter controversy over conscription for overseas service and a split in the ALP. The then premier, William Holman, had been expelled from the Labor Party, formed a coalition with conservatives, and within weeks ordered the double hanging.

Two more executions took place while Holman was premier: one in May 1917, and the other in June, both at Long Bay Gaol.

Between 1917 and 1932, there were two executions, both in 1924, on the recommendation of the then Minister of Justice, Thomas John Ley, an ardent retentionist. In 1924 Ley specifically refused to reprieve Ernest Williams, a musician, who cut the throats of his three children because he could not bear to see them starve, although there was clear evidence of insanity.[10]

In March 1947 Ley, by then a resident of Great Britain and presumably still a retentionist, was convicted (with an accomplice) of the brutal murder and mutilation in a chalk-pit of a suspected rival in love. Ley and his accomplice were sentenced to death, only to be reprieved on the grounds of Ley's insanity. Ley died in Broadmoor.

In May 1936 Edwin John Hickey, aged seventeen, was hanged at Long Bay for having (at the age of sixteen) bashed Conciliation Commissioner Montagu Henwood to death with a water bottle as he sat sleeping in a train. There may have been some compelling reason to suggest that if the boy had been reprieved the whole fabric of law and order in New South Wales might have been in jeopardy. But if such evidence existed, the government kept it a well-hidden secret. The necessity for his death will remain a mystery.

Two New South Wales cases that aroused much discussion about the death penalty involved Frederick Lincoln McDermott and Lionel Keith Lawson. McDermott was convicted of an outback murder in 1947, and if the ALP had lost the state elections of that year he might well have been hanged. However in January 1952 a royal commission decided that McDermott had been wrongly convicted: he was released and compensated. Own the other side of the ledger was the case of Lawson, a well-known Sydney artist, who tied up and raped a number of models on a country excursion in May 1954. Under the old New South Wales law he was sentenced to death, a penalty soon commuted to 'life'. Lawson, an ideal prisoner, was released from prison in 1962. Within a few weeks he had shot a schoolmistress and a pupil both to death. Convicted of murder, he was sentenced to life imprisonment under the new law.

Although Labor held office in New South Wales from 1941 to 1965, it took fourteen years before Joe Cahill's government abolished the death penalty for murder in 1955, an issue pushed by two Ministers, Reg Downing and Billy Sheahan (who were cousins).

---

10   In November 1925, Ley narrowly defeated the sitting federal MP for Barton, Frederick McDonald, but accusations of bribery were raised, and McDonald sought the aid of Premier J.T. Lang to have the result declared void. In April 1926 McDonald disappeared.

Hangings in Australia 1901–67

Year	NSW	Vic	Qld	SA	WA	Tas	NT	Total
1901	3		5				1	9
1902		2						2
1903	3		2					5
1904	1	1		1				3
1905			2	1	3		1	7
1906	1		3	1	1			6
1907	3		1		1			5
1908		1		1	2			4
1909			2		1			3
1910			1	3	1			5
1911					2			2
1912	1	1	1					3
1913			2		1		1	4
1914					1	1		2
1915					1			1
1916	2	2						4
1917	2							2
1918		2						2
1919				1				1
1920				1				1
1922		1			1	1		3
1924	2	1						3
1926					3			3
1927				2	1			3
1929				1				1
1930					1			1
1931					1			1
1932	1	1						2
1936	2	2						4
1938	1							1
1939	1	2						3
1941	1							1
1942	1		1					2
1944				1				1
1946				1		1		2
1950				1				1
1951		3						3
1952					1		2	3
1953				1				1
1956				1				1
1958				1				1
1960					1			1
1961					1			1
1964				1	2			3
1967		1						1
Total	23	22	19	20	26	3	5	118

The twenty-one years in which there were no hanging are omitted.

The Liberal government elected in May 1965 showed no interest in restoring capital punishment, and accepted the status quo.

Due, apparently, to a collective lapse of memory, death remained as a penalty for some other offences (treason, piracy, and arson in naval dockyards) until 1985, when Neville Wran's Labor government removed the last vestiges from the Statute books in the Crimes (Death Penalty Abolition) Amendment Act. The legislation was introduced by Terry Sheahan, Billy's nephew.

Paradoxically, New South Wales, the second Australian state to abolish execution for murder, was the last to eliminate the death penalty from the statute books.

Victoria

There were 187 executions in Victoria, 165 of them in the nineteenth century. Until 1851 Victoria was known as the Port Phillip District, before separation from New South Wales.

The first two executions were the public hangings of Tunnerminnerwait and Maulboyheenner on 20 January 1842 at the Old Melbourne Gaol, after a trial in which they were denied the right to give evidence on their own behalf and Judge Willis declared them guilty before any evidence had been called. They had been defended by Redmond Barry.

Four more executions followed in 1842, of one more Indigenous Australian and three European settlers. In 1857 seven prisoners were hanged for murdering the sadistic inspector-general John Price.

Thirteen bushrangers were hanged (Ned Kelly was the last), most without murder being involved.[11]

The most celebrated of all Australian executions was that of Ned Kelly (1854–1880), convicted of killing a policeman, Thomas Lonigan, at Stringybark Creek in 1878. The judge who pronounced the death sentence was Sir Redmond Barry. He was hanged in the Old Melbourne Gaol, now a tourist destination, on 11 November

---

11　See Appendix A for the statutory provisions relating to the death penalty in Victoria..

1880. He has been the subject of five films (the first in 1906), an extensive literature (twenty-four non-fiction and four novels), and iconic paintings and lithographs by Sidney Nolan.

Until 1949 the Victorian Crimes Act prescribed death as the statutory penalty for twelve crimes, such as administering poison or wounding with intent to murder, for setting fire to a ship with intent to murder, for rape, for robbery and burglary with wounding, and for setting fire to a house with persons inside. From 1900, fifty-two people were sentenced to death for crimes other than murder, but only two had been executed.

Albert Edward McNamara was hanged in April 1902 for arson that had, apparently inadvertently, caused the death of his four-year-old son.

In September 1932, David Bennett, aged fifty-nine, was hanged for carnal knowledge of a four-year-old girl. He had spent most of his adult life in prison. Convicted of rape in Western Australia in 1911, he was flogged and sentenced to life imprisonment, being released a few years later when his guilt became doubtful. In 1917 he was sentenced in Melbourne to fifteen years for an armed robbery in company with his close friend Angus Murray—and in 1923 planned to escape with him. He committed his last crime almost immediately he had completed his sentence.

His friend Murray was the last person hanged at the Old Melbourne Gaol. A carpenter by trade, Bennett worked to instal the hanging beam in Pentridge and became the first person hanged there. The classical retentionist arguments about deterrence seem to have had little effect on Bennett.

The restriction on the death penalty was recommended by the Chief Justice's Law Reform Committee and carried by Parliament when Thomas Tuke Hollway's Liberal government was in office.

In Victoria the ALP has always been abolitionist, the Country Party fiercely retentionist, with the Liberal (formerly United Australia Party or Nationalist) Party sticking to the status quo, without demonstrably strong feelings either way. Decisions to hang seem to have depended on the composition of cabinet and the emotional reactions of individual ministers to the crime itself, with rural ministers arguing for retention, and urban ministers leaning towards abolition (or suspension—not quite the same as hanging).

The Victorian figures suggest a striking lack of correlation between executions (or their likelihood) and the maintenance of the death penalty.

Until 1949 rape was a hanging matter in Victoria. In the period 1945–49 there were eighty-four cases reported to the police, followed by forty-eight prosecutions, with a strikingly low conviction rate (due in part to the existence of the death penalty for a crime capable of such ambiguity in interpretation). In the period 1949–53, despite the rapid population rise, there were only eighty reported cases, with forty-six prosecutions.

This pattern is borne out in the record of reported homicides.

In 1961 there were sixty-one reported homicides in Victoria, but, as Creighton Burns pointed out, only forty-four people were actually charged, and all but five were acquitted of murder.[12]

By 1962 the reported homicides had fallen back to twenty-eight. The fall seems inexplicable, although in 1967 the Victorian deputy premier attributed it to cabinet's decision to hang Robert Peter Tait. That a decision taken in the last third of 1962, and, in any case, rescinded two months later should have this retrospective effect on homicide rates owes as much to clairvoyance (or wishful thinking) as to demonstrating a clear cause-and-effect relationship between capital punishment and the murder rate.

Year	Reported Homicides[13]	Government	Attitude to Death Penalty
1950	28	Country Party	Retentionist
1951	28	Country Party	Retentionist (triple hanging in February)
1952	30	Country Party	Retentionist
1953	23	Labor Party	Abolitionist
1954	19	Labor Party	Abolitionist
1955	24	Labor Party (until May)	Abolitionist
		Liberal Party (after May)	Retentionist
1956	33	Liberal Party	Retentionist

12   Creighton Burns, *The Tait Case,* Melbourne University Press, 1962, p. 14.
13   Stanley W. Johnston, *Criminal Homicide Rates in Australia*, Howard League, Melbourne 1962, p. 2.

Between 1919 and the advent of the Country Party government of Albert (later Sir Albert) Dunstan in 1935, there were only three hangings in Victoria: two for murder, and one for rape.

Colin Campbell Ross was hanged on 22 April 1922 for the murder, just off Melbourne's Eastern Market, of Alma Tirtschke, aged twelve. This became the subject of an important book by Kevin Morgan, *Gun Alley: Murder, Lies and Failure of Justice* (2005). Forensic evidence — hairs on a blanket — was central to the prosecution case. Ross died protesting his innocence. Decades later, after DNA became central to diagnosis, the fatal hairs were found not to be from Ross. Rob Hulls, the attorney-general, asked Chief Justice Marilyn Warren to review the case, and a panel of three judges examined the evidence and recommended a posthumous pardon, which was signed by the governor of Victoria, David de Kretzer (himself an eminent medical researcher) in May 2008.

In October 1923, Richard Buckley held up and shot a bank manager in the Melbourne suburb of Glenferrie, who later died. His accomplice, Angus Murray, was captured and sentenced to death, although the evidence showed that he was unarmed. Buckley escaped. Despite a large campaign organised by Jack Holloway, then Secretary of the Melbourne Trades Hall Council,[14] Murray was hanged in April 1924. (Buckley was recaptured in 1930, convicted, then reprieved by the Hogan Labor government. He was released in 1946 and died in September 1953.)

The Dunstan government hanged five men in its ten years in office — all for murder. Two of these, Arnold Sodeman (1936) and Thomas Johnstone (1939), appear to have been insane.

Tom Hollway's Liberal government 1947–50 hanged no one. The Country Party returned to power with Labor support in mid-1950. In December 1950 the premier, John (later Sir John) McDonald, announced that the death sentence would be carried out on Jean Lee (thirty-one), Robert Clayton (thirty-six), and Norman Andrews (thirty-eight), three criminals from Sydney (a point not without

14 Later a federal minister 1941–49, acting prime minister 1949, and a Privy Counsellor. Born in 1875, he became a patron of the Anti-Hanging Council (Victoria) in 1967 and died in the same year.

significance) for the brutal murder and mutilation in Carlton of a seventy-three-year old illegal bookmaker, 'Pop' Kent, during the Melbourne Cup season in 1949. After feeble protests from clergy and women's groups—and complete passivity from the press—the three were hanged at Pentridge Gaol on 19 February 1951 by the chief warder of Yatala Prison, South Australia.[15] The Labor government of John Cain, Sr, in office 1952–55, commuted all death sentences, but failed to introduce abolitionist legislation, lacking the numbers to pass a Bill through the Legislative Council.

Labor's leader in the Upper House, Jack Galbally,[16] became the most vocal abolitionist spokesman, and introduced a Bill for the abolition of capital punishment on fifteen occasions between 1956 and 1974. All were unsuccessful, but provided opportunities for serious debate on a subject on which too many on both sides of both Houses preferred to rely on their instincts. (Deeply disappointed that Dick Hamer failed to take over his Bills in 1975, Jack Galbally delivered a short and grudging Second Reading speech).

Sir John Vincent Barry of the Supreme Court of Victoria pointed out the variations in conviction rates in Victoria under abolitionist and retentionist governments.

The figures are too small to prove the point decisively, but they are large enough for some sustenance. Stanley Johnson commented:

> Juries, not always ready to trust the government, commit a pious perjury, and bring in fewer verdicts of the capital crime, murder, under a conservative government than under a Labor government. On the court figures therefore the murder conviction rate gives the grotesque appearance of rising under a Labor government and falling under conservative governments.[17]

Henry (later Sir Henry) Bolte began his record term as premier of a Liberal government in May 1955. Representing a rural electorate and impatient with intellectuals and philosophical niceties, the

---

15   Norval R. Morris, *You the Hangman*, Howard League, Melbourne 1952, passim.
16   *Australian Dictionary of Biography*, vol. 17 (2007), by Barry Jones.
17   Johnston, op. cit., p. 7. The chart on the following page is taken from p. 8.

Verdicts in Murder Trials: Victorian Supreme Court

	Number charged with murder	Convicted of murder	Acquitted of murder; guilty of manslaughter	Acquitted altogether or found 'not guily on the ground of insanity'
Labor govt, 17 Dec 1952 to 7 June 1955 (31 months)	28 100%	9 28.6%	7 25%	13 46.4%
Conservative govt, 7 June 1955 to 31 Dec 1958 (42 months)	55 100%	10 18.2%	24 42.6%	21 38.2%
TOTAL	83 100%	18 21.7%	31 37.3%	34 41%

premier has long been a supporter of the death sentence. However, the dominant figure in the early years of the Bolte government was not the premier but the Liberal Leader in the Upper House, Sir Arthur Warner, one of the 'most successful but ruthless self-made industrialists living in the State'.[18] He told the present writer that although committed to public support of Liberal policy on hanging, he was a convinced abolitionist, and insisted, 'There will be no hangings in Victoria so long as I am a member of Cabinet.'

He retired from cabinet for health reasons in July 1962. In August the death sentence on Robert Peters Tait was confirmed.[19]

Tait, born in Glasgow in 1924, spent eight years in a school for retarded children after an accident to his head, then became a miner and a stoker in the Royal Navy His wife left him on account of his homosexuality and alcoholism. He had several convictions for violent crime, always committed while drunk.

In August 1961 he went to the vicarage of an Anglican priest (Rev. George Hall) intending to scrounge money so that he could

---

18   Katherine West, *Power in the Liberal Party*, Cheshire, Melbourne 1965, p. 42. See generally pp. 40–45. Sir Arthur Warner, KBE, (1899–1966) founded and directed Electronic Industries Ltd, GTV-9, and many other companies. As a young man in England he is said to have been a Fabian.

19   *Australian Dictionary of Biography*, vol. 18 (2012), by Mike Richards.

go to Adelaide. The vicar was out, so Tait broke in. He was disturbed by eighty-two-year old Mrs Ada Hall, the vicar's mother. He hit her on the head, and after repeated blows killed her, then assaulted and mutilated her, before leaving and going to a cinema.

He was arrested in Adelaide.

At the trial, the Crown's chief medical witness, Dr Allan Bartholomew, agreed with defence submissions by John Starke, QC, that Tait was 'a chronic alcoholic', 'a masochist', 'sexually abnormal', 'a transvestite', 'a homosexual', and 'a maniac', and that he was suffering 'from a mental disorder or disease of the mind'. Nevertheless he did not fall within the M'Naghten Rules on legal insanity (formulated in 1842) was convicted, and was then sentenced to death.

Cabinet's execution order led to a storm of protest. David Hirt, a Presbyterian theological student, formed the Student's Anti-Hanging Committee, together with John Ridley and Mike Richards

The Anti-Hanging Committee of Victoria, founded a week later, became the recognised outlet for abolitionist advocacy. Val(entine) Doube, a former Labor state minister of health, became president, and the present writer was secretary, retaining the position until the Committee (renamed Council in 1967) disbanded after achieving its goal in 1975.

Members included Bishop Felix Arnott, Bishop Geoffrey Sambell, Peter Hollingworth, John Westerman and Harold Wood (clergy); Professors Rod Andrew, Joe Bornstein, Zelman Cowen, and Sir Peter MacCallum, John Ryan, Janet Clunies Ross, Stephen Murray-Smith, Andrew Brooke and Myra Roper (academics); Maurice Ashkanasy, QC, and Richard McGarvie, QC (barristers); Dame Mabel Brookes (writer and society doyenne), Harold Blair (singer), William Dargie (artist), David Martin (novelist), Roy Grounds (architect); Prudence Myer, Jan Paterson and David Scott (social workers); Clive Stoneham (Opposition Leader); Austin Dowling and Rosemary Hanbury (teachers); David Hirt and John Ridley (students); Frank Sedgman (tennis player); Ralph Renard (lawyer); and Ken Stone (union official). Our patrons were Arthur Koestler and the Earl of Harewood.

The *Herald, Sun,* and *Age* newspapers gave consistent and

unstinting support. Professional groups protested vigorously, as did Church leaders.

There was an appeal to the Supreme Court about whether Tait was entitled to an enquiry into his mental health. The court rejected this 2:1, with Justice T.W. Smith delivering a powerful dissent.

On 31 October 1962, the day before Tait was due to hang, the Full High Court convened in Melbourne to hear an appeal against the Supreme Court's majority judgment that Tait's execution was now entirely in cabinet's hands. I was in court for the hearing. Sir Owen Dixon, the Chief Justice, asked counsel for the Victorian government for an undertaking that the court would be given time to consider the application. The Chief Justice essentially followed Justice Smith's dissent.

On the question of the High Court's jurisdiction, he said, in words I will never forget:

> The difficulty as to jurisdiction simply does not exist. I have never had any doubt that the incidental powers of the Court can preserve any subject-matter, human or not, pending a decision.

The court then granted an adjournment 'so that the authority of this Court may be maintained', and issued an order staying the execution. It was a heart-stopping moment.[20]

Faced with further embarrassing delays, cabinet then commuted Tait's death sentence and he was certified insane. Bolte was enraged by the humiliation imposed by the High Court, and this was, I believe, central to his determination to hang Ronald Ryan.

After the Tait case, the death penalty, according to many abolitionists, was now defunct. When the reported homicides fell to a record low of twenty-two in 1964, abolitionists thought this a significant sign that under abolition the murder rate would not rise. The deputy premier, Arthur (later Sir Arthur) Rylah, however, saw it as a significant sign that the death penalty was essential to keep homicide rates down.

---

20   See Creighton Burns, *The Tait Case*, op. cit., generally, and John D. Feltham, 'The Common Law and the Execution of Insane Criminals' in *Melbourne University Law Review*, vol. 4, no. 4, pp. 434–75.

The Ryan case restored the death penalty to public notice.

On Sunday 19 December 1965, Ronald Joseph Ryan (forty-one) and Peter Walker (twenty-four) escaped from B Division of Pentridge Gaol with almost incredible ease. There was no warder on duty at the time. Ryan took a rifle from a guard-post and menaced a turnkey into opening the side gate. The escapees knocked down the Salvationist chaplain who tried to stop them and ran for Sydney Road (the busy highway linking Melbourne with Sydney) to steal a getaway car. Ryan aimed his rifle at Warder George Henry Hodson (off duty, but who had run out from his lunch on hearing the alarm siren) to prevent him from seizing Walker. Hodson fell, hit by a bullet which in its downward trajectory pierced the innominate artery in the right side of his chest. He died within minutes.

Ryan and Walker then stole a car and eluded pursuit. They remained in Melbourne for some days, holding up a suburban bank on the day of Hodson's funeral. There was widespread fear in the community around Christmas 1965, especially after a truck driver named Arthur Henderson, an associate of the escapees, was found dead with a bullet in the back of his head in a St Kilda lavatory. The pair then escaped to Sydney where they were captured in January 1966.

Ryan and Walker were jointly tried for Hodson's murder before Justice Starke. Melbourne *Truth*'s edition of 12 March 1966, noting Justice Starke's expressed view that the 'unique deterrent' value of hanging was 'poppycock', and his role in the Tait and Stuart (see below) cases, headlined its lead story, 'Don't-Hang Judge for R and W'. Seven jurors later stated publicly that they had considered the death penalty was now obsolete and would have brought in a different verdict if they had realised that Ryan might be hanged. Philip Opas, QC, stressed the ambiguities surrounding the killing. Hodson, a tall man, was within a few yards of Ryan, a short man, when shot. However, the downward path of the bullet suggested that Hodson was shot from a height or at a distance. Most witnesses heard only one shot—and Warder Paterson admitted having fired a shot in the general direction of Ryan and Hodson, although he said that he lifted his highspeed rifle skywards at the last moment. *The Sun* newspaper reported a penal official as saying that a shot had been fired from the observation tower of the gaol. The fatal bullet and its cartridge case were never recovered.

However, the jury found 'no reasonable doubt'. Ryan was convicted of murder and sentenced to death. Walker was convicted of manslaughter and sentenced to twelve additional years. (He already had nine years of his original sentence to serve.)

Walker was subsequently tried for Henderson's murder and convicted of manslaughter only, receiving yet another twelve years. These differing penalties pointed up the lottery nature of the law. If the jury that acquitted Walker of Henderson's murder had sat in Ryan's case, Ryan might well have been acquitted.

Ryan appealed unsuccessfully to the Full Supreme Court against his conviction, and on 12 December 1966 state cabinet confirmed Ryan's death sentence.

It was easy to type-cast Ryan as the ruthless professional killer, invincible and incorrigibly violent. Indeed, the present writer, who was overseas at the time, shared this opinion for some weeks before examining his record carefully. Apart from an undocumented statement that at seventeen Ryan had taken part in a hold-up at a country bank in New South Wales (no arrest or prosecution followed, at any rate), his criminal record began in 1956, at the advanced age of thirty-one.

His crimes began after his marriage to a girl from an affluent family, and all involved 'get rich quick' schemes: false pretences, receiving, forgery, uttering, store breaking and stealing, factory breaking and stealing, running away from a police station, and possession of explosives in suspicious circumstances. A charge of being in possession of a pistol was not proceeded with. He served two months' jail in 1956, returning between June 1960 and January 1964. He was sentenced to six months' jail in July 1964, and another eight years (with no minimum) was added at Melbourne Court of General Sessions in November 1964. He gained his Intermediate and Leaving Certificates by correspondence in prison, and planned to Matriculate. He spent four years and nine months of his life in jail until his fatal escape bid.

Known to police as a 'homing pigeon', easy to apprehend because he was never far from his wife and daughters, he presumably began planning to escape after his marriage broke up and his children no longer visited him. His papers were marked with a notation that he needed special supervision because of his desire to see his family.

Why was Ryan marked out for execution? The Sydney magazine *Nation* asserted that warders had threatened to strike if he were not hanged, but evidence suggests that that warders were deeply divided and that the decision to execute was against the advice of the director-general of Social Welfare, the director of prisons, and the governor of Pentridge.

The special report of the Brotherhood of St Laurence, issued under the names of Rev G. Kennedy Tucker, Bishop Geoffrey Sambell, David Scott, and Janet Paterson, noted:

> It is not unknown or unreasonable for men who feel they have been wrongly prevented from exerting their authority to want to assert it on another such occasion. Was the Premier, and was Cabinet, influenced in the decision by the Tait case? Would Ryan be facing the gallows if Tait had been executed? As no reasons have been given for choosing Ryan from all the other murderers, these questions must be asked when the lengths to which the government was prepared to go in 1962 are remembered—even to being prepared to proceed with the execution when proceedings were before the Courts, until restrained by the High Court of Australia.

The Anti-Hanging Committee's campaign was more vigorous and received more spontaneous public support than in 1962. The premier refused to see a deputation to be led by Archbishop Frank Woods. He explained that cabinet decision was a popular one, judging by his mail bag. By February 1967 the premier had modified his position a little: he said he had known the decision would be unpopular but had determined to stand firm on a principle (undisclosed).

The most vehement support for commutation of Ryan's sentence came from the daily papers, both in Melbourne and Sydney (with the single exception of Sir Frank Packer's *Daily Telegraph*, although his *Bulletin* and television station GTV-9 were as abolitionist as their ownership permitted), followed closely by church leaders (apart from the Lutherans and Salvationists), professionals, university groups, trade unionists, the Australian Labor Party, Democratic Labor Party, and some elements of the Liberal Party. Suburban and country newspapers were generally strongly retentionist, although not to the point of advancing new reasons or evidence.

When the government refused legal aid, the Anti-Hanging Committee raised $3,000 to fly Philip Opas to London to appeal to the Judicial Committee of the Privy Council.

When this appeal failed, Ryan's hanging was set for Tuesday 31 January.

On the previous Sunday a vast mob, estimated at 8,000, demonstrated outside Pentridge Gaol. A minority behaved in a manner appropriate to a Roman carnival or football match, carrying banners that read 'Hang Bolte'. The Anti-Hanging Committee dissociated itself from the demonstration. Next day, a public holiday, saw a dramatic late-night court sitting when Mr Justice Starke granted a stay of execution largely on the basis of an affidavit by a former prisoner, John Henry Tolmie, that he had seen a warder take aim and fire from the Pentridge tower. A further sensation followed on Tuesday night when Tolmie was arrested for perjury. He had been in prison before and after, but not during, the shooting. He was merely repeating what he had heard from other prisoners.

The tragedy for the abolitionists (not to speak of Ryan) was that Tolmie's discrediting was enough to invalidate independent affidavits made by A.J. Cane and W.R. Brooks, who both swore that as prisoners they had seen shooting from the tower. The premier pronounced the 'domino theory of affidavits' by saying, 'We had two other affidavits from people claiming to be in Pentridge with Tolmie when he wasn't there ... We checked on two others corroborating with Tolmie when he wasn't there'. In fact, Cane's statement (made before Tolmie had been discredited) did not mention Tolmie, and Cane told his Brisbane solicitor that Tolmie was not there. Brooks' statement said, 'I don't know anyone called Tolmie.' Cane flew from Brisbane, but Ministers refused to interview him or charge him with perjury so that his affidavit could be tested in court.

Finally *The Herald* printed the report of an anonymous phone call to the effect that criminals planned to blow up Pentridge and rescue Ryan. No further details of this remarkable plan were ever brought to light.

A new date was set for Ryan's execution. At 8.00 am on Friday 3 February he was duly hanged at Pentridge. The unknown hangman used the alias 'Mr Jones'.

This was the first execution for murder by a non–Country Party government since 1924.

Before the execution, Ryan's mother, an elderly widow, asked that his body be released for Christian burial in consecrated ground. Sir Henry Bolte refused, commenting, 'How ghoulish can you get?'

Earlier, after much provocation, Bolte made another original contribution to jurisprudence—the doctrine of the 'official murder'. He told reporters (in indirect speech) on 25 January 1967 that a murder against authority was different from a murder against society. That was why the murder of a policeman was no different from the murder of a warder, customs officers, and other people murdered in the execution of their duty … He did not favour a distinction in law between the murder of public authorities and individual members of society. But there had to be safeguards to protect people murdered in the execution of their duty while acting under the authority of the state and for the people.

He added, gratuitously, 'Do not think that I derive any pleasure out of the decision to hang Ryan.'

The assistant minister of education, John (later Sir John) Rossiter, MLA, decided that the whole fabric of society would be in jeopardy if Ryan did not hang. In explaining the theory of the separation of powers to Professor Richard Samuel, he wrote:

> It was this system of government which was under attack in recent weeks. If the functions of the traditional arms of government become mixed, our form of government will not last and the people will suffer … Experience in several fields convinces me that the veneer of law and order in our Australian community is not very thick.

The observations on the separation of powers are particularly interesting coming from a minister sitting in an executive that had commuted the death sentence passed by the judiciary in thirty-nine of forty cases (97.5 per cent) without causing apparent social convulsion.

The minister of education, John (later Sir John) Bloomfield, MLA, explained that he would not support a royal commission on capital punishment because it would be impossible to find an impartial commissioner and all the relevant information was already known.[21]

In July 1967 the deputy premier observed that the number of Victorian murders in the period January–June 1967 was only fifteen, compared with twenty-two in the comparable period of 1966. It was pointed out in reply that crimes involving firearms (for which Ryan was hanged) were at a record high in 1967. In any case, the final homicide figures for 1967 were far ahead of 1963, 1964, and 1965—years of de facto abolition.

The Anti-Hanging Committee converted itself to a Council in June 1967 and adopted a new constitution.

To many abolitionists the most objectionable feature of the Victorian way of death was the buck-passing involved. Who bore the moral responsibility for sending a man to his death? The judge tells the jury that its sole concern is the verdict of guilt or innocence. They are not to concern themselves about the penalty: that will be determined elsewhere. The judge passes the death sentence because it is the sole penalty prescribed by the Crimes Act: he has no option—the decision to hang is not his. Then the death sentence is considered by state cabinet. But here it is possible for a premier to say, 'Well, I don't have anything to do with this death sentence. The judge and jury said he ought to hang. We only fix the time and place.' The state governor signs the death warrant and exercises the royal prerogative of mercy, but explains that he can only act on the advice of his ministers. The hangman, of course, says, 'I'm only a public servant. It's not my decision. I'm only doing what my superiors tell me.' Thus it is possible for jurors, judge, premier, governor, and

---

21   See Appendix B

hangman all to put their hands on their respective hearts and say, 'It wasn't my decision. I had nothing to do with it.' The lesson is, perhaps, that moral responsibility belongs to King Henry II, the lawmaker whose institution of hanging for murder was inherited in the Victorian penal code.

Henry Bolte's retirement as premier in August 1972 after a record term marked the end of capital punishment in Victoria because his successor, Dick (later Sir Rupert) Hamer, a progressive Liberal, was a convinced abolitionist. To appease conservatives in his party, he invited the Victorian Law Reform Commissioner, Thomas Weetman Smith, a former Supreme Court justice, to advise on whether degrees of murder could be introduced.

In 1974 Justice Smith recommended strongly against it, and in March 1975 Dick Hamer introduced the Crimes (Capital Offences) Bill, providing for full abolition, on which there was to be a free vote.[22]

The Third Reading of the Bill was carried in the Legislative Assembly by thirty-seven votes to thirty-one. The majority comprised nineteen Liberals, seventeen Labor members, and one Independent. (John Rossiter voted 'Yes' and John Bloomfield was absent from the chamber. The attorney-general, Vernon Wilcox, voted 'No'.) The Bill was passed by the Legislative Council by twenty votes to thirteen, and became law on 23 April 1975.

On 3 February 2017, the fiftieth anniversary of Ryan's execution, there was a re-enactment of the jury's verdict and the death sentence by Justice Starke in the court where it had taken place, followed by addresses by Chief Justice Marilyn Warren, Brian Burke (one of Ryan's counsel), the present author, and Mike Richards.[23]

Queensland

From 1830 to 1900, seventy-four men and one woman were hanged in Queensland, and many informal executions of Indigenous

---

22   My speech in the Second Reading debate is printed below as Appendix C.
23   Mike Richards' powerful speech appears as Appendix D.

Australians occurred in the first decades of colonial settlement.

There were nineteen hangings in Queensland in the period 1901–13, the last two being Charles Deem (May 1913) and Ernest Austin (September 1913).

The Australian Labor Party held office 1915–29 and commuted all death sentences until 1922, and then returned to office 1932–57. As described earlier (in Chapter 1) the death penalty was abolished in Queensland in 1922, after an initial attempt in 1916 had been defeated in the Legislative Council.

Queensland became the first jurisdiction in the then British Empire to abolish capital punishment.

There was a rise in the murder rate after 1922 (although there had been de facto abolition for a decade), and then it dropped far below the rate for 1901–13.

These figures were provided by the Queensland government Statistician:

Murders and attempted murders

(per 100,000 population per year)	1903-07	3.6
	1908-12	2.8
	1913-17	2.6
	1918-22	2.6
Capital punishment abolished	1923	1.6
	1924-29	3.2
	1929-34	1.7
	1934-39	1.0
	1939-44	1.2
	1944-49	1.1

The non–Labor governments of 1929–32 and 1957–89 made no attempt to revive the death penalty.

Despite Queensland having pioneered abolition in the British Empire, the death penalty was carried out, subsequently, for a crime committed in Queensland. In June 1944, when many US troops were located in Australia, Private Avelino Fernandez, a paratrooper, savagely beat up a woman in Brisbane, who later died. Tried for murder by a US military tribunal, he was convicted and sentenced to death. Carrying out the sentence was not possible under Queensland criminal law because of abolition, twenty-two years earlier, and was strenuously opposed by the then Queensland government. Unperturbed, US military authorities transported Fernandez to Papua, where he was hanged on the beach at Oro Bay in November 1944.

Western Australia

There were 145 executions after the British first colonised Western Australia in 1829: 45 per cent were European, 40 per cent Aboriginal, and 15 per cent Asian.

Having only 6 per cent of Australia's population when I wrote in 1968, Western Australia had an unbeatable record both in the absolute number (twenty-six) of executions and as a proportion of population since 1901. Yet despite this (or even, perhaps, because of it), Western Australia's homicide rate ran slightly ahead of the national average in the period studied by Stanley Johnston.[24]

Edith Cowan, the first woman to be elected to an Australian Parliament (in Western Australia) and whose image appears on our $50 notes, was the product of a family tragedy. Her mother was murdered by her father, and he was hanged in 1876.

Geographical factors—a huge area, a scattered population, and a sense of isolation—may have contributed to an undue psychological reliance on the gallows as an instrument of protection, as in South Australia. Again, as in South Australia, the ALP appears to have been converted to abolition much later than in the eastern states. There were five hangings during the Labor ministry of John Scadden (1911–16), and four during Philip Collier's first government (1924–30). There were no hangings from 1932 to 1951 and 1953 to 1959 inclusive. The ALP held office for most of that period (1933–47; 1953–59).

The pattern of murder appears to differ from the other states, with

---

24   Johnston, op. cit., p. 9.

a greater incidence of multiple murder in Western Australia. The real counterpart of that mythical beast, the reprieved murderer who kills again after release, is the man who has committed one murder for which he believes he will be hanged and fears no further sanction for killing others—for example, witnesses or police. This is one way (apart from Thorsten Sellin's arguments above on the morbid attraction of the death penalty for some psychotic criminals) in which the high execution rate may be contributing to the multiple murders.

Jeremiah Thomas, aged twenty-two, hanged in July 1960, and Brian Robinson, aged twenty-five-five, hanged in January 1964, were both multiple murderers.

Eric Edgar Cooke, thirty-three, who was hanged in Fremantle in October 1964, had committed at least seven murders. Immediately before his execution he confessed to the murder of Jillian Brewer in 1959 and the hit-run death of Rosemary Anderson in 1963. He was the last person executed in Western Australia.

John Button had been convicted of manslaughter for Anderson's death, sentenced to ten years' jail, and served five—in 2002, his conviction was quashed by the Court of Criminal Appeal. Darryl Beamish, a deaf-mute, was convicted of murdering Brewer and sentenced to death. His sentence was commuted, but he served fifteen years. His conviction was quashed in 2005, and in 2011 the then state attorney-general, Christian Porter, provided $425,000 compensation.[25]

Early in 1965 a sixteen-year-old boy was sentenced to death in Perth. Some attempt was made to modify the law by introducing degrees of murder in 1965, after a committee of legal experts had recommended abolition.

Western Australia abolished the death penalty in 1984, during the premiership of Brian Burke.

---

25   Peter Brett, *The Beamish Case*, Melbourne University Press, 1966, had been a
      powerful appeal to re-open the case.

South Australia

The political division over abolition was originally less distinct than in the eastern states. There were three executions under the coalition government headed by Tom Price, the Labor Leader (1905-09), but later Labor ministries were firmly abolitionist. There were no hangings between 1911-18 and 1930-43 (both inclusive), although non-Labor parties were generally in power due to an electoral maldistribution that favoured rural voters at the expense of Adelaide.

Often a decision to hang depended on the mindset of a premier—for example, Sir Thomas Playford, who held office for an unprecedented term from 1938 to 1965. His cabinet authorised seven hangings between 1944 and 1964, and one more was only averted by extraordinary legal action. As in Victoria, there was evidence to suggest that juries became extremely reluctant to convict. Greatest retentionist support was found in isolated outback areas where the gallows may have seemed a valued protection.

International interest was attracted by the trial and conviction of Rupert Max Stuart for the rape and murder of a nine-year-old girl near Ceduna in December 1958. Stuart, an illiterate Aranda Aboriginal and itinerant fun-fair worker, was sentenced to death. Repeated criticism of methods used in extracting a confession from him (and its contents) led to the appointment in July 1959 of three judges as a royal commission. These included the trial judge and the presiding judge at the appeal. Stuart's leading counsel, J.W. Shand, QC from New South Wales, and later John Starke, QC from Victoria, were sharp in criticism, provoking a defensive reaction from counsel assisting the commission who, in the words of the Sydney *Observer,* seemed 'to represent a third party, the South Australian way of life, against the various wise men from the East'.[26]

In October 1959, because of the long delay, Stuart's death sentence was commuted. In December the commission reported that he had been rightly convicted. A much-disputed point was whether Stuart's

---

26   The whole extraordinary story, with the subsequent trial of Rohan Rivett, editor of the *Adelaide News,* for seditious libel, is brilliantly told in K.S. Inglis's *The Stuart Case,* Melbourne University Press, 1961.

colour was an asset or a handicap in the case. Would an illiterate white man have secured such wide sympathy?

The last person hanged in South Australia was Glen Sabre Valance in November 1964.

In March 1965 Playford was defeated and a Labor government returned after thirty-two years in opposition. Frank Walsh, the premier form 1965 to 1967, was soon replaced by the charismatic reformer Don Dunstan, who served for two periods (1967–68 and 1970–79), and worked to secure fair electoral redistribution and end the conservative monopoly in the Legislative Council.

Repeated attempts by Dunstan to abolish hanging and flogging were thwarted by the Upper House, and the death penalty remained on the statute books until the Criminal Law Consolidation Act 1976. The late date is extraordinary since Steele Hall, who succeeded Playford as Liberal leader, was sympathetic to reform.

Tasmania

Between 1806 and 1900, there were 542 hangings in Van Diemen's Land/Tasmania — an extraordinary number — but only three in the twentieth century, in 1914, 1922, and 1946.

The ALP, generally opposed to capital punishment, was in government 1923–28 and 1933–69. However, the last execution, in February 1946, took place, exceptionally, when Robert (later Sir Robert) Cosgrove was Labor premier.

Frederick Thompson, aged thirty-two, was hanged in Hobart for the murder of Evelyn Maugham, aged seven. Public feeling ran very high, and 1946 was a state election year, which, I was later told, had been a factor.

Roy Fagan, attorney-general 1946–69, had abolitionist Bills passed by the House of Assembly thirteen times, only to be defeated in the conservative Legislative Council. In 1968, when Eric Reece was the Labor premier, he achieved his goal.

The appalling massacre of thirty-five people, with twenty-three more wounded, at the Port Arthur Historic Site by Martin Bryant in April 1996 led to tighter gun laws being adopted throughout Australia. Significantly, it did not lead to a campaign to restore capital punishment, even in Tasmania — not that it could have been applied retrospectively. Bryant pleaded guilty at his trial and was sentenced to thirty-five life terms, without the possibility of parole.

I chaired the Port Arthur Historic Site Management Authority (PAHSMA) 2000–04 and 2005–12, and discussed the issues involved very carefully.

The Northern Territory

Until 1901 the Northern Territory was subject to South Australian law, then under Commonwealth law 1901–78.

There were ten recorded judicial executions between 1893 and 1952: five Aboriginal, two Chinese, two Czech migrants and one British settler.

In the twentieth century, there were five hangings: Jimmie (no other name given) in 1901, Tommy in 1905, Koppio in 1913, and, on 8 August 1952, Jaroslav Koci and Jan Novotny for the murder of Darwin taxi-driver George Thomas Grantham.

The death penalty was abolished in the Northern Territory and the Australian Capital Territory in 1973 under Commonwealth law.

New Zealand

From 1842 to 1957 there were eighty-five executions in New Zealand, and five soldiers during World War I. The last hanging was in Auckland in February 1957.

For decades, politics determined whether murderers were hanged in New Zealand or not. Capital punishment ceased in practice in 1935 with the election of Michael Savage as Labour prime minister. In 1941, it was formally abolished, but reintroduced in 1950 after a change of government.

For the thirteen years preceding 1935, deaths from murder and manslaughter per million of population equalled 9.1; for the thirteen years following 1935, they equalled 8.4 per cent—that is, a decline since abolition of 8 per cent.

No responsible authority in New Zealand has claimed an increase in the murder rate during the abolition period. The reasons for reintroduction were emotional, sensational, and political.[27]

The New Zealand Labour Party was in power 1935–49 and 1957–60.

In introducing the Bill to restore capital punishment in 1950, the then minister of justice, Clifton Webb, said, 'I have satisfied myself that the figures neither prove nor disprove the case for capital punishment, and therefore they neither prove nor disprove the case against it.' The minister did not make clear, therefore, what led him to change the law, unless it was emotional conviction.

There were seven hangings in the period 1950–57.

In October 1961, the Nationalist government of Keith Holyoake allowed a free vote on a comprehensive revision of the Crimes Act (1908). Clause 172, providing that 'Everyone who commits murder shall upon conviction thereof be sentenced to imprisonment for life', was carried by forty-one votes to thirty, with ten Nationalist members crossing the floor to vote with Labour.

Ralph Hanan, the minister of justice and attorney-general, called for outright abolition for murder, and dismissed attempts to introduce any system recognising 'degrees of murder'. He said:

> There is the argument—and a strong argument—that some murders are so grave and so shock the public opinion that the only appropriate penalty is death.... This raises deep spiritual issues which I do not pretend to be competent to answer.... Murder is a grave crime which rightly shocks public opinion, but that does not justify a departure from reason when we are dealing with the offender. We are frequently asked by people, what if a member of your own family were the victim? The only reply I could make to that is that for me the emotional reaction would be the same as for everybody else, but whether it would be reason

---

27   Morris, op. cit., p. 16.

is another question. Reason, I submit, teaches us that capital punishment does not deter. Look at the figures I shall give later on. There is no evidence that it is a deterrent. Reason surely teaches us that in a Christian civilisation we should avoid taking life in retaliation. If capital punishment was a deterrent, reason would say let us have it; but reason suggests that it does not deter, and reason suggests that in a Christian civilisation we should avoid taking life in retaliation; and perhaps reason teaches us also that we should avoid a punishment so final. The difficulty, I think, is that there is a yawning gap in assumptions and outlooks that figures will not bridge.

To those who say that some murders are so grave, and so shock public opinion that the only appropriate penalty is death, I quote Archbishop William Temple, a former Archbishop of Canterbury and a famous divine, respected as one of the world's very great men. Giving evidence to the British Select Committee in 1930, he said: 'A Christian society must seek the opportunity of evoking penitence and building up character through the remaining years of the criminal's natural life, whether or not the State requires the forfeiture of liberty throughout that period.' To that I would add only this: As the question of what is an appropriate penalty is a moral issue, the views of the various Churches upon it should be taken into account, and what they say is entitled to our respect; and evidence will be given to the House by subsequent speakers that the overwhelming majority of Church opinion in New Zealand is against the continuation of capital punishment. That is a frequent argument, and one of my colleagues says, meant that too much sympathy is reserved for the murderers and that not enough thought is given to their victims.

That is a frequent argument, and one of my colleagues says, 'Hear hear.' Let me remind my colleague that two blacks do not make a white; an execution does not repair the damage, cannot restore the victim to his relations; and since there can be no possible mending of that situation it does seem that we are compelled to lay that argument on one side. What we can do, however, is to see that we ourselves create no unnecessary suffering for innocent persons. There can be brought out the intense and probably life-long suffering of the relatives of the murderer. They played no part in the murder, but there can be few things worse than being branded as the wife or child of a man who has been hanged. It is difficult to meet the point that there is too much sympathy for the murderers and not enough thought given to their victims, but there is a further very powerful argument which I would like particularly my colleague who interrupted me a short time ago to note. There are others who are hurt by an execution.

The last series of executions between 1950 and 1957 was a severe ordeal for prison officers and sheriffs; indeed, they were the cause of more than one breakdown in health. We ask decent men to do a job of work, and we must ask ourselves whether we would be prepared to do it. That is perhaps where the question of conscience comes into this argument most forcibly. The question of the taking of human life is regarded by some as the major argument against capital punishment. They are against it on religious grounds. I do not go that far; I subscribe to the principle of the death penalty for treason, for instance…

Our experience since 1935 makes it plain that capital punishment has no special value as a deterrent. Some who favour retention argue that New Zealand is a small country and that the figures for murder are too low for reliable conclusions to be drawn from them. Maybe we should examine New Zealand figures with caution, but I cannot agree that they tell us nothing. Let me give the figures for conviction for murder from 1929 to 1960. From 1929 to 1935, when capital punishment was the law of the land and was enforced, the figures were one, three, four, four, two, one, one. From 1936 to 1950, when there was no capital punishment, the figures were one, nil, two, one, one, one, two, two, nil, four, three, three, six, three, eight. Members will note that there was a rise after the war in the number of convictions for murder, but that was an experience common to all countries. From 1951 to 1957, when capital punishment was enforced, the figures were three, two, three, four, four, one, one. The figures for 1958 to 1960, when with the change of government capital punishment was the law of the land but was not enforced, the figures were one, three, one. It seems to me that two conclusions can fairly be drawn: that the murder rate is very low in this country, and that it remains more or less constant. When we realise that the penalty for murder has changed three times in the period I have been reviewing—in 1935, in 1950, and in 1957—with no effect on the figures, then surely it is plain to us that executing murderers does not achieve anything. The same thing has been found to happen in other parts of the world. It has been proved beyond doubt in Switzerland, Holland and Norway.

Another reason why I maintain we should drop capital punishment for murder is a political one. In the last twenty-five years the penalty has been changing with every change of government. The first result is that the punishment the murderer receives is not necessarily governed by the gravity of his crime. On the contrary, what may determine whether he is to live or die is which party is in power. When the 1957 election results were being broadcast, a murderer sat in his cell in a cold sweat waiting to find out which party would win the election. That is not good law. It is not good sociology. Another bad feature of this chopping and changing is the creating of injustice, as it were, between one murderer and another. Some of my friends who are trying to interject may say that you cannot have any injustice between one murderer and another, but let us consider the cases of murders committed by A and B who would be hanged under the National government, while C and D who may have committed a much worse murder would, under the Labour government, after a term of imprisonment be restored to the community. There cannot be any justification for that...

All I have read and heard makes it clear that we should abolish capital punishment in New Zealand. Let me say to the House and to the country that we should follow the lead given by New South Wales and by other advanced communities and do away with a punishment which so many of our people are convinced belongs to other days and other times.[28]

The Abolition of the Death Penalty Act (1989) was carried when Geoffrey Palmer was prime minister.

/

---

28   *Parliamentary Debates*, New Zealand, 3 October 1961, vol. 328, pp. 2686–88. There was only one execution for treason in New Zealand history, Hamiora Pera, in 1869.

Canada

There were 710 executions in Canada between 1859 and 1962: 697 of men, and thirteen of women.

In Canada capital crimes were a matter for the Dominion courts, not the provinces.

The last executions took place in Toronto on 11 December 1962: a double hanging for two unrelated murders. John Diefenbaker, prime minister at that time, agonised about the decision, having long been opposed to capital punishment from his career as an advocate. All his successors, except Stephen Harper, have been abolitionist.

In 1967, when Lester Pearson was prime minister, Parliament enacted a mandatory sentence of life imprisonment for murder, except where the victim was an on-duty police officer or prison guard, for a five year trial period.

The Liberals leaned towards abolition, while the Progressive Conservatives were generally retentionist. Social Credit members were unanimously retentionist; New Democrats (Socialist), uniformly abolitionist.

The trial period was extended again in 1972.

In November 1976 the death penalty was abolished, narrowly, by 131 votes to 124, for murder, treason, and piracy. Pierre Trudeau argued passionately for the Bill, but in a free vote thirty-seven Liberal MPs voted for retention, and sixteen Progressive Conservatives for abolition. Oddly, the death penalty was retained for military offences such as cowardice and desertion. (Twenty-five Canadian soldiers had been executed during World War I.).

In June 1987 a motion to restore the death penalty was defeated in the House of Commons 148–127, after a major debate. Prime Minister Brian Mulroney, Liberal Leader John Turner, and External Affairs Minister Joe Clark (both former Prime Ministers), and Ed Broadbent, Leader of the New Democratic Party, all voted against the death penalty.

However, Canada did not abolish capital punishment for all crimes, civilian and military, until 1998.

Stephen Harper, prime minister 2004–15, did not attempt

to reintroduce the death penalty, but reversed the policy of not extraditing prisoners to other jurisdictions without an assurance that execution would not be applied.

Public opinion polling in Canada in 2020 put support for capital punishment at 51 per cent, presumably because of recent terrorist attacks.

South Africa

Under the apartheid regime, 2,949 executions (fourteen of them women) were carried out between 1959 and 1989. Nelson Mandela was fortunate not to be one of them. The Nationalist government was secretive about the details of executions, and the total figure between 1948 and 1989 is likely to have been significantly higher.

Jan Christiaan Smuts, prime minister 1919–24 and 1939–48, had been uneasy about the mandatory death penalty, changed the law to give judges discretion and there were many commutations.

The last execution was in November 1989. President F.W. de Klerk declared a moratorium in 1990, the end of apartheid came in 1994, and in 1995 the Constitutional Court declared an end to capital punishment.

However, with exceptionally high murder rates (thirty-four per 100,000), there are growing calls to restore the death penalty. Public opinion polling in 2014 indicated 76 per cent support for restoration, and it is advocated by several political parties.

The United States

With its fifty-one differing jurisdictions (state and federal), the United States position is far too complex and diverse to be more than sketched at here.

The US had 135 executions in 1950, forty-two in 1961, seven in 1965, one only in 1966, and three in 1967. There were none between June 1967 and January 1977.

The electrocution of Julius Rosenberg and his wife Ethel in June 1953 led to worldwide protests about the death penalty as a political instrument. Julius had provided secret information about nuclear weapons, radar, and sonar between 1942 and 1944 to the USSR when it was an ally of the US. Much was already known, and Stalin was sceptical. The couple were convicted of conspiracy to commit espionage. The case against Ethel was threadbare, but prosecutors hoped that her conviction would lead to information about accomplices in return for commutation.

In 1972 the US Supreme Court ruled, in the case of *Gregg v. Furman*, in a 5–4 decision, that the death penalty was 'a cruel and unusual punishment' and therefore in breach of the 8th and 14th Amendments to the Constitution. Thirty-seven states, insistent on retaining the right to execute, redrafted their criminal codes to make them narrower and more specific, for example excluding juveniles from capital punishment and ensuring that jury selection was racially wider.

On 17 January 1977 Gary Gilmore was executed by firing squad in Utah for two murders, having refused to appeal and choosing death in preference to a lifetime in prison. This set a precedent for further executions.

Between 1977 and 2016 there were 1,533 executions in the US, the overwhelming majority in the states of the old Confederacy, with Texas, Virginia, and Oklahoma accounting for 802. Virginia is now abolitionist. Oklahoma was a border state during the Civil War 1861–65. The preferred method of execution was lethal injection (1,249). Some states offered a menu to choose from—electrocution, hanging, gas, or firing squad.

Of approximately 7,000 convictions followed by a death sentence in that period, 185 are now regarded as wrong or unsafe, especially due to use of DNA in testing physical evidence, such as semen or blood stains.

In 1991 public opinion polling indicated that capital punishment was supported by 76 per cent of Americans, but this figure is steadily falling.

From 2017 to 2021 the total number of executions in the US had fallen to ninety-eight.

California is a striking illustration of where the will of the people runs in sharp contrast to expert opinion. When the California Supreme Court declared capital and punishment unconstitutional, this was overturned by a plebiscite, Proposition 17, in November 1972. The death penalty was reaffirmed, narrowly, in 2012 and 2016. The last execution was in 2006, and successive governors have declared a moratorium.

Oregon is even more confronting. The death penalty was abolished by popular vote in 1914 and 1964, and restored in 1920 and 1978. The last execution was in 1997. Successive state governors have imposed a moratorium since 2011.

Delaware, Joe Biden's home state, provides a disturbing example of abolition, followed by restoration. Until 1958 there were five capital offences in Delaware, although nobody had been hanged since 1946. Following a sustained educational campaign by abolitionists and full congressional hearings, the death penalty was abolished in April 1958. There were seven murders in Delaware in the twelve months before abolition, and only one in the year following. However, in June 1961 the murder of a woman in her ninetieth year by an African American provoked the passage of a Bill restoring hanging for first-degree murder through the state Senate within four days of the killing. It passed through the lower house in December, without debate, after the murder of an elderly white couple by another African American, and became law over the governor's veto, owing to the strong rural representation in the Delaware legislature. The accused were not executed, since the law was not retrospective.

The new law, bizarrely, prescribed twenty-two aggravating factors that would determine if the death penalty was applicable, including if the victim was aged more than sixty-two. Why not sixty-one or sixty-three?

A piquant footnote was added by the first murder case after restoration. Ten days after the death penalty was restored, Detective Sergeant William J. Mulrine III, aged forty-nine, an ardent campaigner for restoration, was charged with first-degree murder for shooting his wife to death.

There were sixteen executions in Delaware between 1992 and

2012. In 2016 the Delaware Supreme Court declared the death penalty unconstitutional, but the legislation on capital punishment has not been repealed.

In Maryland, at hearings conducted by the judiciary committee of the state Senate on two abolitionist bills, in February 1968, Theodore Roosevelt McKeldin, the Republican governor 1951–59, said he had allowed four prisoners to be executed (by lethal gas) 'because I didn't have the character to do what I should have done. I am ashamed to say that … I yielded to the public clamour, and may God forgive me.' McKeldin commuted seventeen death sentences during his term.

Ireland

The Irish Republic's last hanging was in 1954. (Brendan Behan's play *The Quare Fellow* deals with this event.) In July 1964 the death penalty was abolished for civil crime. Ironically, in view of the past history of Irish executions, the death penalty was retained for political crimes, such as treason. The death penalty was abolished for all offences in 1990, and after a referendum was carried in 2001, the Constitution prohibited its restoration.

APPENDIX A

The Victorian Crimes Act (1958)

All the provisions in Victorian law relating to the death penalty are found in 'An Act to consolidate the Law relating to Crimes and Criminal Offenders', known as the Crimes Act 1958, as follows:

3. Whosoever is convicted of murder shall suffer death as a felon.

* * *

485. Sentence of death shall be carried into execution at such time and within the walls or enclosed yard of such gaols as the Governor may be writing under his hand direct and not elsewhere by the sheriff or his deputy and shall in all cases whatsoever whether for treason or murder be executed by hanging the offender by his neck until he is dead.

486. The sheriff the gaoler and such officers of the gaol as he requires, including the medical officer shall be present within such walls or yard at every such execution, together with any justices ministers of religion and officers of police who may desire to attend; and such military guard and adult spectators as the sheriff thinks fit to admit.

487. Every person present at any such execution shall remain within the walls or enclosed yard of the gaol until the sentence has been completed, and until the medical officer has signed a certificate in the form set forth in the Ninth Schedule; and the sheriff gaoler and officers of the gaol and such other persons present as may think fit shall before their departure from the gaol subscribe a declaration according to the form set forth in the Tenth Schedule.

488. The body of the person executed shall not be buried nor removed from the gaol within eight hours next after such execution nor till after inquest as hereinafter provided; and every person who within that time produces to the gaoler of such gaol an order from any justice requiring such gaoler to admit the bearer of such order to view the body of such person shall be admitted by such gaoler accordingly.

489. The coroner acting for the district in which the gaol is situated wherein a sentence of death has been carried into execution upon the body of any person shall so soon after as conveniently may be held an inquest upon the body of such person; and on such inquest there shall be an inquiry and finding whether such sentence was duly carried into execution.

490. Whosoever subscribes any certificate or declaration as aforesaid knowing it to contain any false statement, or who buries or removes from such gaol within eight hours the body of the person executed shall be guilty of felony, and shall be liable to imprisonment for a term not more than seven years.

491. Every such certificate and declaration as aforesaid shall be forthwith transmitted by the sheriff to the Prothonotary of the Supreme Court in Melbourne; and shall be entered and kept in his office as a record of the said court, and shall be by him published in the Government *Gazette* on three separate occasions.

492. The body of every person executed shall be buried within the precincts of the gaol in which he has been last confined after conviction, and the sentence of the court shall so direct.

*　*　*

496. The Governor, in all cases in which he is authorised on behalf of Her Majesty to extend mercy to any offender under sentence or judgment of death, may extend mercy on condition of such offender being imprisoned or imprisoned and kept to hard labour or being detained and kept to hard labour as herein provided on public works for life or for such term as he thinks fit and may also if he thinks fit fix a minimum term during which the offender shall not be eligible to be released on parole; and also may direct that such offender shall be kept in solitary confinement for any portion of such time or term not other than or more than those for which solitary confinement may be awarded under this Act; and in every such case the Governor may if he sees fit exercise in addition in respect of such person the powers vested in the court by section four hundred and seventy-seven and the word 'sentence' in the said section shall for this purpose mean the direction given by the Governor in that behalf.

* * *

505. Nothing in this Act shall in any manner affect Her Majesty's royal prerogative of mercy.

* * *

NINTH SCHEDULE, Section 487

I A.B. being the medical officer in attendance on the execution of C.D. at the gaol at .... do hereby certify and declare that I have this day witnessed the execution of the said C.D. at the said gaol and further certify and declare that the said C.D. was in pursuance of the sentence of the .... court hanged by the neck until his body was dead.

Given under my hand this day of .... One thousand nine hundred and .... at the gaol at ....

TENTH SCHEDULE, Section 487

We do hereby testify and declare that we have this day been present when sentence of death was carried into execution on the body of C.D. convicted at the criminal sittings of the Supreme Court held at ....

on the day of .... and sentenced to death and that the said C.D. was in pursuance of the said sentence hanged by the neck until his body was dead.

Dated this .... day of 19

gaol at .... at ....

> Sheriff
> Gaoler
> Turnkey
> Constables
> Justices of the Peace
> Other Spectators

APPENDIX B

The Victorian government's contribution to this book

On 16 November 1967 I wrote to the Victorian premier (Sir Henry Bolte) and the deputy premier and chief secretary (A.G. Rylah) as follows:

I have been commissioned to edit a book scheduled for publication in February 1968 by Messrs Sun Books Pty Ltd, with the probable title Capital Punishment in the 20th Century.

This book will be, in the main, an anthology of material already published elsewhere but not previously assembled in a single collection. Apart from reports of Parliamentary Debates in the U.K. and New Zealand, and excerpts from Royal Commissions in U.K. and Ceylon, we have been given permission to reprint material from Lord Gardiner (the Lord Chancellor), Arthur Koestler, Thorsten Sellin, the late Albert Camus and Sir Ernest Gowers, and many others.

Despite my own abolitionist position, I have tried to give an even balance to the retentionist case. This has not been easy. As you will know, there is very little published or publishable material available in support of the retentionist cause. We do have statements from Mr Percy Biggin, editorials of the *Geelong Advertiser*, *Wimmera Mail-Times* and the *Cheltenham Standard*, and articles by J. Edgar Hoover and Chief of Police E. J. Allen of Santa Ana, but nothing more.

It would be of immense value to the book — and to the retentionist cause — if you would contribute a statement of your views on the question of capital punishment, summarising the relevant evidence.

Even if you cannot spare the time to write even a short statement, we would be grateful for any assistance you might give in suggesting sociological or criminological works which would help us to faithfully record evidence in support of your position on the question of capital punishment.

We are anxious to avoid polemic and to make this book as objective and factual as we can.

On 14 December 1967 Mr J.V. Dillon, Victorian under secretary, replied on behalf of Mr Rylah:

The Chief Secretary has asked me to acknowledge your letter of 16 November 1967 concerning a book you are editing with the probable title of *Capital Punishment in the 20th Century*.

The Minister has noted your request for a statement on his views on capital punishment but desires me to say that as the Government's attitude to capital punishment is well known and has been stated on a number of occasions, there would appear to be little need for it to be reiterated at this time.

A good source of reference material in support of the retention of capital punishment is the House of Lords Debates. I suggest that the debates that would be of particular interest to you would be those on the Criminal Justice Bill in 1948 (Volume 156), and the Death Penalty (Abolition) Bill in 1956 (Volume 198).

On behalf of the premier, the secretary of his department replied on 5 January 1968:

I am directed to advise that as the Government's attitude is well-known there appears to be little point in commenting further.

It is understood that you also wrote to the Chief Secretary whose views in the matter were sent to you on 14 December last.

APPENDIX C

The Victorian death-penalty debate, 1975

In 1975 the premier of Victoria, Dick (later Sir Rupert) Hamer, a progressive Liberal who succeeded Henry Bolte in August 1972, introduced the Crimes (Capital Offences) Bill providing for the abolition of the death penalty, and persuaded his party to have a free vote on the subject.

I was then the member for the state electorate of Melbourne and a shadow minister. On 19 March 1975 I delivered the most passionately argued speech of my life. It had an impact on some waverers, but credit for abolition, which was carried narrowly, belonged to Dick Hamer.

I felt such acute sensitivity about the execution of Ronald Ryan in February 1967 that I never mentioned him in my speech, but a single sentence slipped out in the committee stages of the debate. I never spoke about Ryan in public until the launch of Mike Richards' *The Hanged Man* in 2002.

In 2001, John Campbell, the former clerk of the parliament, described my speech as the most memorable he had heard during his career in the chamber.

I have edited the Hansard record of my speech (19 March 1975, vol. 321, p. 4300) very slightly.

Mr JONES (Melbourne): In a sense … the death penalty is already abolished in Victoria and has been since August, 1972. This is not really a debate about hanging. Whatever the result of this debate today, it is extremely unlikely there will be another Victorian execution. I doubt whether the doughtiest retentionist in this Chamber believes there will be another execution in Australia.

This is really a debate about us, about the members of the Victorian Parliament, giving us an opportunity to declare, not on party lines, just what manner of men and women we are. It is a chance to indicate whether, in the final analysis, we make our judgments coolly and calmly on the basis of evidence which is capable of being weighed and objectively analysed, or whether in discussing the nature of man, objective analysis is useless and we are forced into terra incognita and must blindly decide … on the basis of instinct or gut reaction: 'I really don't care about the evidence but I know how I feel.'

So, the free vote will enable us all to say, 'Here I stand; I can do no other.' This free vote will enable me to cast my vote for abolition, but only incidentally for abolition. Essentially, I cast it against darkness, against obscurantism, against instinct, against pessimism about society, and about man's capacity for moral regeneration.

Often people who argue for retention have a fundamental pessimism about man's capacity for regeneration … However, they have no humility about their own judgment … they have not a scintilla of doubt that their own judgment is absolutely correct … Their confidence in their own judgment and their pessimism about society is an extraordinary paradox.

The Victorian branch of the Australian Labor Party has had an abolitionist plank in its platform since about 1898, and it has commuted all death sentences during its terms in office. In some respects its record is not altogether inspiring. The late John Cain's government failed to bring down legislation to abolish capital punishment on the grounds that it would not be passed in the Legislative Council and might bring what it considered a marginal issue to the centre of political controversy.

Even worse, the Australian Labor Party held the balance of power when the Dunstan and McDonald governments sent seven men and one woman to the gallows over a total period of ten years and ten months. It is true that in those days of long recesses the state parliament was not in session at the times of the executions in 1936, 1939, 1941, and 1951, but it is a matter of great regret that the Labor Party ever let those executions take place. The efforts of the Hon.

John Galbally in the Legislative Council since 1955 have almost made up for the earlier lapse.

The Country Party has, I understand, no specific written policy plank in favour of the death penalty, but its support can be inferred by its history on this issue and by what has been said here today. The Liberal Party had no specific policy plank until 1974, when an abolitionist plank was adopted by the party's state council. The Nationalist Party and the United Australia Party had no retentionist policy either, but they were prepared to accept the status quo. In the past fifty years in Victoria under Liberal or United Australia Party governments there has been one execution for carnal knowledge in 1932 and one execution for murder in 1967.

There has been some argument that the death penalty is not a deterrent to murder. I would make a qualification: I have never said that it is not a deterrent. The question is whether the punishment deters uniquely. The question that should be raised again and again is whether the death penalty essentially has only a deterrent effect for murder. Nobody ever asks whether the death penalty has a uniquely salutary effect on murder but has no comparable effect on other offences.

The last major review of the death penalty in Victoria occurred in 1949 when the Crimes Act No. 5379 was passed. At the time the late Tom Hollway was the Liberal premier of this state. Before that Bill was passed there were nine capital offences in the Crimes Act and one common law offence—the anomalous offence of treason—which was not and still is not in the Crimes Act. The nine offences were murder, provided for in section 3; administering poison or wounding with intent to murder, in section 8; setting fire to or destroying ships with intent to commit murder, in section 10; rape, in section 40; carnal knowledge of a girl under ten years, in section 42; buggery with violence or with a person under fourteen years, in section 65; robbery with wounding, in section 113; burglary with wounding, beating or striking, in section 123; and setting fire to a dwelling-house, in section 187.

Is it argued that the deletion of the last eight offences suddenly led to a terrible avalanche throughout the state of setting fire to dwelling-houses, or buggery with violence, or setting fire to or destroying ships? Is it seriously suggested that the death penalty deters uniquely for murder, but that it has had no demonstrable effect on the other offences? If it is a unique deterrent it would have deterred the commission of the other eight crimes before 1949.

Volume 229 of Hansard indicates that throughout the long debate on the Crimes Bill in 1949 hanging was barely mentioned. Honourable members were totally preoccupied with the question of flogging, whipping, and birching, and clause 2, which abolished the death penalty for eight offences, was passed in the Legislative Assembly on the voices, without a division and without debate. The death penalty for those eight offences passed from the statute book without any tangible evidence being presented. I can imagine honourable members of that time crying, 'What about carnal knowledge? We have to keep it. What about the young girl who will be violated if it is not retained?' — the argument being that if it deters for murder it will deter uniquely for the other offences as well.

Consider, for example, the crime of attempted murder by poison, which would, in practice, include most attempted mercy killings. That crime brought the death penalty prior to 1949, but attempted murder by strangulation, suffocation, drowning, gassing, or electrocution brought only a fifteen-year term of imprisonment. Is it suggested that the effectiveness of the law was to confine all attempted murders to suffocation, drowning, or any other mode that did not involve wounding? Is there anyone who would suggest that, or is the law exposed as an absolute piece of nonsense?

I invite honorable members to consider some of the anomalies in the old Act. Take the question of attempted murder. Morally it is impossible to distinguish between the heinousness of a murder and an attempted murder, whereby with grace and good luck the person shot survives. For example, in the shooting of a policeman in the London Hotel in 1966, with the greatest of good luck the policeman who was shot did not die. Surely the perpetrator of that offence is not to be preferred to the man who drunkenly and recklessly fires and kills an officer, but yet the penalties differ greatly.

Before 1949, 'setting fire to a dwelling-house, any person being within', but without any intention to kill, was a capital offence. That was covered by section 187 of the Crimes Act. For 'destroying buildings by explosives with intent to murder', which is covered by section 9, the maximum penalty was, and still is, fifteen years.

That is the same penalty for sending a letter threatening murder. Is there any sense in that, any rationality? Will any honorable member say that there is no doubt that the presence of the death penalty prior to 1949 was absolutely responsible for people not setting houses on fire? Is it argued that, of course, enormous numbers of houses were being blown up because the penalty was less?

Rape was a capital offence before 1949, and one might expect a vast increase in its incidence after repeal. In the four years from 1945 to 1949 there were eighty-four cases reported to police and forty-eight prosecutions. In the four years after 1949 there were eighty reported cases and forty-six prosecutions.

The Victorian evidence confirms Cesare Beccaria's dictum that there is no demonstrable correlation between the severity of punishment and the crime rate. The current version of the Crimes Act still perpetuates these anomalies. Section 11 (1) provides twenty years' imprisonment for poisoning and wounding with intent to murder, and section 11 (2) provides fifteen years for attempted murder by shooting, strangling, suffocating or drowning. Section 12 provides fifteen years for blowing up a building with intent to murder, and section 13 provides twenty years for setting fire to an occupied building. Can anyone be expected to make sense of this?

In addition, section 8 maintains the archaic offence of petit treason. It says that it is to be 'charged and treated as murder', but does not abolish it. Petit treason is the murder of a master by a servant or of a husband by a wife — but, significantly, not of a wife by a husband.

When the Crimes (Aircraft) Bill 1963 was brought before the Victorian Parliament, the maximum penalty for destruction of an aircraft with intention to kill was set at twenty years, although parallel Commonwealth legislation, since repealed, provided for the death penalty.

There are no new arguments for abolition. They were all set out more than 200 years ago in a book entitled *On Crimes and*

Punishments by the great Italian economist and pioneer sociologist, Cesare Beccaria. As he pointed out, all punishment deters, but there is no statistical evidence that capital punishment deters uniquely, that when the death penalty is dropped for particular offences, as it was in Victoria in 1949 for eight crimes, the crime rate does not appear to change.

Beccaria argued that the greatest deterrents to crime were certainty of detection and certainty of conviction, and that crime rates tended to be determined by factors other than the severity of punishment-factors such as the general stability of society, the existence of a police force, climate, the degree of urbanisation, economic factors, and drinking habits. Beccaria also argued that the 'appropriate penalty' for crime can be worked out statistically: it is the lowest penalty consistent with public safety. There is a critical point in punishment beyond which increasing severity is unnecessary because it has no demonstrable influence on the crime rate.

It might be said that this is demonstrated in the present Crimes Act. No one suggests that anyone planning an attempted murder leafs through the Crimes Act to select a crime with a fifteen-year penalty rather than one with a twenty-year penalty. That is an absurdity. I regret that the Minister of Transport is not present because I wished to point out to him that Beccaria argued strongly against the power of pardon. He insisted that the power of reprieve was undesirable and should be abolished. This seems harsh at first. The point is that reprieve is built into the system because it is realised that the system is unsatisfactory. The Minister claims to be invested with enormous authority and to be acting, as he calls it, as 'an adjudicator'. He is there not as an adjudicator; he is there to uphold the law as it is set out in the statute or to improve the law.

Cesare Beccaria [opposed the power of pardon] which existed for the purpose of covering deficiencies in the law. If, for example, there was a rare case of somebody being convicted of an offence where the punishment seemed to be quite inappropriate, [the executive] might intervene. Beccaria insisted that intervention indicated that there was something wrong with the law, and therefore the law ought to be changed rather than the power of pardon being relied upon. He said,

'Clemency ought to shine in the code and not in private judgment.' In other words, if you have to reprieve all the time because the law comes up with an appropriate sentence, it is an indication that you ought to change the law.

Professor Thorsten Sellin, an eminent American sociologist, who was described by the British royal commission on capital punishment as perhaps the greatest expert in that field, has produced many charts in which he has compared the crime rates over a long period of various States in America that have similar societies, racially, and in urban-rural balance—for example, Michigan, Indiana, and Ohio. He compared their homicide rates per 100,000 of population from 1920 to 1955. One of the three states was abolitionist throughout, one executed the death penalty frequently, and the third exercised it only spasmodically. I defy the most hardened retentionist to examine the chart and tell me which state is abolitionist and which is the retentionist. I ask leave of the House to incorporate the chart in Hansard.

A reasonable man thinking calmly might well conclude that the death penalty ought to be a unique deterrent because it horrifies him. But examination of criminal statistics throughout the world—not just in Victoria—does not bear this out.

There are some classic examples of how close familiarity with the death penalty does not seem to have had that unique deterrent effect. Sir Ernest Gowers found that of 167 prisoners hanged in Bristol in the nineteenth century, 164 had witnessed one or more executions. Until 1939, when guillotinings were public in France, a majority of French murderers had observed one or more guillotinings. David Bennett, who was hanged at Pentridge Prison in 1932, was a lifelong friend of Angus Murray, who was hanged in 1924. Thomas John Ley, a former New South Wales minister of justice and an ardent retentionist, was sentenced to death in England in 1947. Harold Green, who organised a petition for the hanging of 'the Moors murderers', Ian Brady and Myra Hindley, was soon after convicted of child murder. Sergeant William J. Mulrine III, a senior police officer who campaigned for the restoration of capital punishment in Delaware in 1961, murdered his wife ten days after the death penalty was restored.

It is striking that with the much publicised political assassinations and attempted murders in the United States of America — for example, President Truman, John and Robert Kennedy, Martin Luther King, Medgar Evers, James Meredith, George Lincoln Rockwell, Malcolm X, and George Wallace—all, without exception, took place in states in which the death penalty applies, although these men were all highly mobile and in theory might just as easily have been shot down in an abolitionist jurisdiction. But it does not happen. One might have expected that many murderers in the United States of America would have taken their victims into an abolitionist area to kill them, but they did not.

* * *

Before the suspension of the sitting, honorable members were privileged to hear the Minister of Transport and the honorable member for Benambra (Hon. Tom Mitchell). The Minister of Transport gave an interesting and authoritative account of how he considers things. The honorable gentleman said that in 1950 there were eighteen homicides in Victoria; in 1961, sixty-two homicides; 1962, forty homicides, and in 1963, twenty-six. He implied that the controversy over the Tait case reminded people that capital punishment was still the law and caused the decrease in the number of homicides in 1962. He equated the homicide figures for murders, but those figures include many cases that were subsequently described as manslaughter cases, accident cases, and suicides. For example, in 1961, of the sixty-two cases reported as homicides, there were only forty-four charges of murder or manslaughter, and only five convictions for murder. It is true that in 1962 there was an extraordinary fall. The Tait controversy ran from August 1962, to October, 1962, but the greatest fall in the homicide rate occurred before August and after October. If Tait had been hanged, the Minister of Transport might have claimed that there was a certain connection. The fact that Tait did not hang and that the figures were low that year really supports our case rather than the minister's. I do not believe the figures bear out his facts.

Mr DIXON: The minister made the point that the figures could not be used to prove anything.

Mr JONES: I will make a concession for the Minister of Transport and the Minister for Youth, Sport and Recreation (Hon. Brian Dixon).

Beccaria wrote 200 years ago that there was no relationship between the severity of the punishment and the crime rate; that the rate was determined by factors other than the actual incidence of the penalty. However, if the remarks of the minister and of the honorable member for Benambra are examples of the meticulous way in which they examine evidence, one is not impressed. I pass over the examples cited by the honorable member for Benambra, only to point out that in the New South Wales case to which he referred, which was obviously that of Leonard Lawson, the person of whom he complained was not in fact initially convicted of murder, but of rape. He did not escape, but was simply released—wrongfully in the circumstances—because he appeared to be a model prisoner. Unfortunately, that is a perfect example of how someone can be convicted of a crime for which the original penalty is excessive, and

Crude homicide death rates per 100,000 (1920–55)

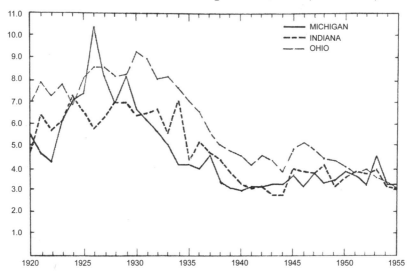

it is then left to cabinet to determine what shall subsequently happen to the person. Members of the Opposition believe this should all be part of the judicial process.

The honorable member for Benambra several times made reference to the one and a half hours of horrifying torture in the case of Lee, Clayton, and Andrews. He failed to remember their eighteen months of horrifying torture under the shadow of the gallows. The point is that the state should tread warily in comparing its position with the position of the murderer and saying, 'The murderer acted thus, so we act thus.'

There appear to be only two logical options open. Contrary to what the Leader of the Country Party said, it is a Yes-No debate. There is no third position. Only two options are open. One is to abolish capital punishment. The alternative is to retain it and use it. Some honorable members seem to believe there is a third choice. That is, to retain capital punishment on the statute book, and not to use it. They attempt to have a bit both ways. This is a morally contemptible and bankrupt position. I have more respect for the outright retentionist than the person who wants to shillyshally and walk a tightrope. This is the dubious position in Victoria today.

Since June, 1955, when the Liberal Party took office, eighty death sentences have been passed. Nine persons are still under sentence of death awaiting commutation. Of the remaining seventy-one, Tait had his sentence confirmed but was later reprieved. Ryan had his sentence confirmed and was executed. Thus, in seventy-one death sentences dealt with by cabinet, seventy were commuted. What on earth can be said in support of a law that comes up with the wrong answer 98.6 per cent of the time—or 97.2 per cent, if the special circumstances of the Tait case are included? Section 3 of the Crimes Act provides: 'Whosoever is convicted of murder shall suffer death as a felon.'

It is not possible to have a subsection that states, 'The above section will not be carried into effect.' It must either be got rid of or enforced.

The Leader of the Country Party (Peter Ross-Edwards) suggested a shopping list of crimes for which he would retain the death penalty, to which the honorable member for Benambra, I thought with some relish, included even more. This appears to me to have no logic. This whole question of degrees of murder was really dealt with prior to the 1949 legislation. The honorable member for Rodney (Eddie Hann) interjected earlier that the 1949 position was absurd. It was absurd because it specified certain types of crime as capital in a way that no honorable members would regard as logical. No one would want the 1949 position brought back. Yet if capital punishment deters uniquely, it should deter crimes other than murder.

Beccaria wrote: 'If I can prove that the death penalty is neither necessary nor useful, I shall have achieved the triumph of mankind.'

On the question of necessity ... some retentionists make a spurious case that certain executions are inescapable, unavoidable, necessary. It is urged that crime is like civil war and that in times of war, civil or international, it is necessary to kill one's enemy in self-defence. This is a poor argument. I can quite accept that where a dangerous armed man is at large it may be necessary to kill him, even though that should be avoided if possible. But if a man were holding a child at gun point, threatening to kill her, and it were possible to have him picked off by a sharp-shooter, I would not hesitate to act or give the order because it would really be a necessity. However, this is not parallel with the situation after the trial, conviction, and appeal processes are concluded. I adopt the words of the great French Nobel Prize-winning novelist, and abolitionist, Albert Camus:

> I stand as far as possible from the position of spineless pity in which our humanitarians take such pride, in which values and responsibilities change places, all crimes become equal, and innocence alternately forfeits all rights.

The point is that after the man is captured, rendered harmless, put in an escape-proof gaol, tried, convicted, sentenced, and has gone through the appeal procedure, it can hardly be said that his death is a matter of necessity; that we can say, 'Unless this man dies, society is in jeopardy.' The reasons for killing a man, which look so pressing at the time, often look hollow and morally dubious in retrospect.

The Minister of Transport said, 'Who is going to raise the question of the prison officers?' I am perfectly happy to raise it. The solution to the prison problem of violence and gaol breaks does not lie in more executions, but in a complete reappraisal of the gaol situation so that prisoners who are highly dangerous need to be kept under certain conditions of maximum security, though not the type contemplated by the new maximum-security gaol in Long Bay. If one goes to European countries that have abolished the death penalty long ago, such as Belgium, since 1963, Sweden since the 1890s, Norway, and Denmark for a similar period, and asks prison administrators, 'But surely you have to cope with refractory prisoners? Is not there some special need for the death penalty for prisoners who kill in gaol?', they look at one absolutely open-mouthed. They say that the answer lies in the way in which the prisons are run, and in which confrontation and escape is avoided.

The problem is comparatively simple, and to suggest that the death penalty is a constructive or helpful way of solving the problem of discipline in prison is extraordinarily short-sighted. Similarly, in England and Canada, strong representations were made that the death penalty be retained for the murder of prison officers. In both cases, the Parliament decided in a free vote against this. The statistics in Great Britain in the five-year period between 1965 and 1970, when there was absolute abolition, and the years since, have confirmed that the death penalty is of no special benefit to the police. It is certainly confirmed in the period in which the Homicide Act operated from 1957 to 1965.

The honorable member for Benambra mentioned Lee, Clayton, and Andrews. I often think of Jean Lee. I saw her once during the trial. She was hanged at Pentridge in February, 1951, with Robert Clayton and Norman Andrews, for an atrocious murder committed in 1949. She was thirty-one years old. Was her death in any way a necessity? The government of the day certainly thought so. Twenty-four years later she would have been fifty-five years old if she had lived. What sort of woman would she be today? It is an idle question to ask. I often wonder whether, if all three had been spared, society would have suffered.

Mr HANN: Why don't you show some compassion for the victims?

Mr JONES: I am glad that the honorable member has asked the question, and he will be sorry that he did. After a victim is dead and buried, the execution does not put roses on the grave; it does not provide any consolation.

Mr HANN: You show no compassion for the victim.

Mr JONES: I do what I can do in the area where it is possible to do something. It is pointless to speculate on what can be done in terms of vengeance. One wishes that the murder was not committed and that the death rate were lower. In fact, in Australia the death rate is fairly static at about one homicide per 100,000 people per annum, and that figure is likely to remain constant while we keep the present type of society.

I often wonder what would have happened if Lee, Clayton, and Andrews had been spared. The triple hanging left a permanent scar in my mind, which will never heal. The execution of Ethel and Julius Rosenberg in New York in 1953, for reasons which in retrospect seem utterly deluded, left another. I often think of the execution in Long Bay Gaol in 1936 of Edwin John Hickey, who was hanged at seventeen years of age for having, when he was sixteen years of age, bashed a conciliation commissioner to death. In retrospect, it seems almost unbelievable. If he had lived, he would be only fifty-six, but he has been dead for nearly forty years. Was his death a necessity? The government of the day thought so, but who would argue in its defence today?

Leo Tolstoy, who was one of the greatest novelists and moralists, thought deeply about that question of necessity in capital punishment after he saw an execution in France. It haunted him all his life. He wrote, inter alia:

> I witnessed many atrocities in the war and in the Caucasus, but I should
> have been less sickened to see a man torn to pieces before my eyes than
> I was by this perfected, elegant machine by means of which a strong,

clean, healthy man was killed in an instant. In the first case there is no reasoning will, but a paroxysm of human passion; in the second, coolness to the point of refinement. homicide-with-comfort, nothing big.

When I saw the head part from the body and each of them fall separately into a box with a thud, I understood—not in my mind, but with my whole being—that no rational doctrine of progress could justify that act, and that if every man now living in the world and every man who had lived since the beginning of time were to maintain, in the name of some theory or other, that this execution was indispensable, I should still know that it was not indispensable, that it was wrong.

Our experience in Victoria, and largely the experience in other countries, is that in many cases the relatives of the victims do not want vengeance. They often reject the concept of 'an eye for an eye and a tooth for a tooth'. Execution simply adds to the total horror. In the case of Mrs Nolte, for whom we all felt great compassion, she ... told me that at first she felt that Lowrey and King should hang. But by the time the death sentence was brought before the Executive Council she did not want them to hang.

There are many cases of victims' families, particularly in Great Britain, where over a long period a large number of executions took place, begging for the death penalty not to be carried out. I wish to quote one case in the United States of America where a nineteen-year-old girl was strangled by a sex killer, and the girl's mother wrote a remarkable letter. The letter was dated 30 November, 1960, and is included in an article entitled 'What about the Victims?' by Arthur Koestler and C.H. Rolph. In the letter, the mother stated:

My daughter was against capital punishment. When she was eight years old she came home from school one day and told me a little boy had thrown a glass of water over her. 'And what did you do?' I asked her. 'At first,' she said, 'I wanted to do the same to him, but I suddenly saw myself doing what he did ... He would have won.' As she grew up, this idea grew into a desire to help the destroyer. If it is to be 'an eye for an eye and a tooth for a tooth', this will soon be a blind and toothless world.

In the Tait case, the Rev. George Hall, son of the victim, Mrs Ada Hall, was prominent in urging commutation. This is often the case where families are deeply involved.

As I have said, this is an historic vote. We have an opportunity to end a particular kind of social excommunication that we call capital punishment where the entire weight of the state rests on the neck of a single isolated, alienated man or woman. It is not out of excessive concern for the murderers but concern for ourselves that I declare my vote for life. Hanging is an evil thing. Let us end it now.

*   *   *

The Legislative Assembly passed the Second Reading of the Bill, after twenty-one hours of debate, on 8 April 1975 by thirty-six votes to thirty, and the Legislative Council followed on 23 April by twenty votes to thirteen.

I was grateful for the encouragement and support of several Liberal MPs, especially Brian Dixon, Athol Guy, Bill Borthwick, and—in the Legislative Council—Peter Block.

APPENDIX D

The fiftieth anniversary of the hanging of Ronald Ryan

Mike Richards (1945–) was the leader of the Student's Anti-Hanging Committee during the 1966–67 campaign against the execution of Ronald Ryan. He became a political scientist, deputy editor of *The Age*, chief of staff to John Cain and Simon Crean, and an influential consultant in Victoria, Tasmania, and New Zealand. He completed his PhD thesis on Ryan's criminality, and subsequently wrote a best-selling biography, *The Hanged Man: the life and death of Ronald Ryan* (Scribe, 2002).

This is a speech given by Mike Richards at the Victorian Supreme Court Library on 3 February 2017 at an event marking the fiftieth anniversary of Ryan's hanging.

* * *

Chief Justice Marilyn Warren, Justice Lex Lasry, distinguished guests, ladies and gentlemen.

Today marks the fiftieth anniversary of an event whose political and social significance is even better understood today than it was at the time.

The anniversary of Ronald Ryan's hanging is being recalled here and elsewhere as a defining moment in Australia's political and legal history: it marks the divisive event that prompted governments around the country that still retained the death penalty to cut the crimson thread running through our law and justice system and finally abolish capital punishment.

In essence, fifty years after his execution, the Ryan hanging is being remembered as a turbulent time in our history, one that inexorably led to a decisive break with a barbaric relic of our colonial past. Ryan's execution was an event that stopped the nation. But, more than that, it was an event that changed the nation.

There has been a great deal broadcast and published in the media this week about those historical and political aspects of the Ryan execution—and other speakers tonight will talk about that, as well.

What about some of the personal stories in this case? I am interested in that question because—in writing my book about Ryan, *The Hanged Man: the life and death of Ronald Ryan*—I learned that the personal repercussions of his execution reached very much further than was appreciated at the time. These repercussions provide additional reasons why the application of the death penalty is profoundly at odds with enlightened legal, judicial, and human rights principles and practice.

Ryan was hanged for the shooting murder of Pentridge prison officer George Hodson during the course of an escape by Ryan and his fellow prisoner Peter Walker in December 1965. For the families, colleagues, and friends of the murder victim—and of Ryan, himself— the grief and anguish were naturally profound and enduring.

Less obviously, for those who had a role to play in the execution drama, the emotional scars run deep, too, and fifty years on, those still with us say they will never get over it. Those scars have been borne by the legal team who defended Ryan and ran his appeals; by prison officials at Pentridge Prison, including the governor of Pentridge, who managed his execution; by anti-hanging activists who protested about it; and by journalists who witnessed it and wrote reports of it, among others.

In fact, the governor of Pentridge, Ian Grindlay, who stood beside Ryan on the gallows, told me in interview that after the hanging he said a prayer for Ryan every day of his life. A journalist from *The Age*, who was in the official execution witness party, subsequently sat at his typewriter in the newsroom, but could not write a word. Several other journalists refused to sign the witness statement.

Some of those who played honorable and commendable roles of

that kind are with us here tonight. Two of them share this platform: barrister Brian Bourke, who was Ryan's legal counsel; and Dr Barry Jones, who led the anti-hanging campaign to save Ryan from the gallows.

But in this place, before this audience, I want to speak about perhaps the most significant personal impact of the hanging on a central but unlikely figure in the case: Supreme Court Justice John Erskine Starke.

Starke was a life-long opponent of the death penalty, and he was deeply involved in two other famous capital cases in Australian legal history. He appeared for Rupert Max Stuart in the royal commission inquiring into his conviction for murder in South Australia in 1958. And he defended Robert Peters Tait at his trial for murder in this Court in 1961. Starke famously appeared before the High Court in 1962 to secure an eleventh-hour reprieve for Tait, less than twenty-four hours before he was due to be hanged.

But—by a quirk of administrative fate—Starke found himself the trial judge in Ryan's case in March 1966.

Now, by another quirk of fate, in 1990—more than twenty years after Ryan's execution—Starke's path and mine crossed in an unexpected way, when my wife and I were guests at a small birthday dinner with friends. Unbeknown to me, the other guests were Sir John Starke and his wife, Beth, who were friends and neighbours of our host.

At that time, I was deep into the research for my book, and I was fully aware of Starke's crucial role as the judge in Ryan's case, but I had always refrained from approaching him, as I believed it was inappropriate and against protocol to engage with a trial judge about a case—even though Starke had retired from the bench several years before.

I found myself at the dinner table sitting opposite the man who had presided at Ryan's trial and was bound to pass the mandatory death sentence according to law if a guilty verdict was reached by the jury.

When Starke spoke to me and asked me what I was up to, I began by telling him I was writing a book about Ronald Ryan and his execution. Then I thought: 'Well, it's now or never!", and so I somewhat tentatively asked if I could come and talk to him about it. Quick as a flash, he said: 'Sure, when do you want to come?'

A fortnight later I duly drove to Starke's house in Jacksons Road, Mount Eliza, to conduct what I hoped might be a helpful interview with him about technical, legal aspects of the trial. I was quite unprepared for what then transpired.

As I approached the front of his house, I could see Starke waiting for me behind his security-screen door. 'Good morning, Judge', I began cheerily. Without a word of greeting, and looking anxious, Starke responded—blurted out, almost:'Do you think I did the right thing on Ryan?'

Stunned and puzzled by the question, I could only reply: 'Judge, what do you mean?' Showing me into his sitting room, Starke—clearly distressed—poured out the anguish he felt at having had to sentence Ryan to death, a sentence mandated by law. More than that, he revealed to me a plan he had devised in his mind to thwart the execution.

He then told me in detail of his attendance at the cabinet meeting in December 1966 to consider Ryan's fate, a meeting of ministers to decide whether to commute his death sentence—as had become the norm in capital cases in Victoria for some years—or allow the hanging to go ahead.

I should briefly explain that it had been the practice in Victoria—but in no other Australian jurisdiction—for the cabinet in capital cases to invite the trial judge to answer questions from ministers about the trial, and especially the verdict. The objective was to ascertain whether there was anything that might be relevant and important to cabinet reaching its decision on commutation.

Bear in mind, prior to the execution of Ryan, the death sentences of all convicted murderers in Victoria since 1951 had been commuted through this cabinet process. Historically, the attendance at cabinet of trial judges in capital cases had been a controversial practice—certainly, in Victoria 100 years before and even in the mid-1960s in the other states—because it arguably gave rise to a perception of a breach of the separation of powers between executive and judiciary.

But Victorian judges had historically gone along to cabinet meetings on the basis that it was an invitation—not a summons—to appear, and naturally they took their responsibilities in capital cases very seriously. Justice Starke had no qualms about accepting an invitation to the cabinet meeting on Ryan's case.

On the day Starke attended cabinet, he knew that one of the questions he would be asked would concern his judgment about the jury's verdict. He told me it was a question that he had dreaded and worried about for many weeks—although his anxiety had been tempered by a lingering, irrational hope since the trial had concluded, that the government would commute Ryan's sentence, after all.

Starke's concern was not whether he had doubts about the validity of the jury's verdict—for in truth he had none—but whether he should feign doubt to the cabinet.

All of Starke's anti-hanging convictions told him that he had an obligation to do whatever he could to avoid an execution that offended him, and which he believed to be morally repugnant. In the weeks and months since the trial had ended, the question that had weighed heavily on Starke's mind and that troubled him still as he entered the cabinet room, was whether—in his words to me—he should 'tell a lie to save a man's life'.

The core of the lie that Starke entertained in his mind—the lie that he told me about in detail—was that, as the trial judge, he would say that he considered the jury's verdict was unsound.

Starke could think of a number of issues upon which he might base and express this fiction. As you know, before his appointment to the Bench in 1964, Starke had been the leading advocate at the Victorian bar, and he knew that while juries exercised their responsibilities conscientiously, the requirement in reaching a verdict 'beyond reasonable doubt' could be challenging and problematic.

Indeed, from his own experience as a criminal barrister, Starke knew that juries sometimes returned guilty verdicts for 'murder' when a finding of 'manslaughter' was a more appropriate one.

Although he firmly believed that the jury's verdict in Ryan's case was sound, Starke rehearsed in his mind the factors he would point to that might plausibly indicate to ministers that the jury's verdict was unsafe.

His hope was that he could put it in a way that might persuade the cabinet to advise the governor of Victoria to exercise the Royal prerogative of mercy and commute Ryan's death sentence to one of life imprisonment.

In the event, when the premier, Sir Henry Bolte, asked Starke if he agreed with the verdict, the judge's innate honesty and integrity won out and he answered truthfully; he could not go through with this obfuscation—his elaborate lie—and he answered that he did agree with the jury's verdict. Later, Starke would worry terribly about his role in sentencing Ryan and agonise whether he could have done more to save him from the gallows.

During the course of my research, I also interviewed Starke's associate, Ron Syme, who told me that—in his chambers early on the morning of the hanging—Starke was inconsolable. He was slumped in his chair, and it took all Syme's efforts to actually get him out of his chambers and into the courtroom for a part-heard case that was due to resume.

*   *   *

Sir John Starke died in 1994 at the age of eighty. I am quite sure that he worried about Ryan and his mandated appointment with the hangman until the day he died.

As we mark this important event in our social and legal history, and think about all those caught up in the tragedy of Ryan's escape from prison, his shooting of prison officer Hodson, and his subsequent execution, there is a special place in my thoughts today for Jack Starke—a peerless advocate, a fine judge, and a great humanitarian—who bore a very heavy burden of public duty and private conscience in having to pronounce a brutal sentence according to law.

APPENDIX E

Abolitionist countries

ARGENTINA: Abolished 1922, reinstated by martial law in 1930. Last judicial execution 1956. More than 300 extra-judicial executions during the military dictatorship 1969–78. Abolished 2009.

AUSTRALIA:
- Commonwealth law. Abolished 1973.
- New South Wales. Last execution 1939. Abolished for murder in 1955 (but retained for treason, piracy and arson in naval dockyards until 1985).
- Victoria. Last execution 1967. Abolished 1975.
- Queensland. Last execution 1913. Abolished 1922.
- Western Australia. Last execution 1964. Abolished 1984.
- South Australia. Last execution 1964. Abolished 1976.
- Tasmania. Last execution 1946. Abolished 1968.
- Northern Territory. Last executions 1952. Abolished 1973.

AUSTRIA: Last execution 1950; abolished for murder 1950 and for all crimes 1968. Originally abolished by Kaiser Joseph II in 1787, restored for political crimes in 1796, abolished in 1919, restored by Engelbert Dollfuss in 1934.

BELGIUM: Since 1863, only one civil execution (1918), but 242 executed for war crimes 1944–50. Abolished for all crimes 1996 and enshrined in Constitution 2005.

BRAZIL: Last execution 1876; (Emperor Pedro II opposed it); abolished 1889 for civilian crimes; entrenched in Constitution 1988.

At least 300 extra-judicial executions during the military dictatorship 1964–85. It remains, in theory, for treason, terrorism, genocide and war crimes.

BULGARIA: last executions 1989; abolished 1998.

CANADA: Last executions 1962; abolished for civil murders 1967, for all murders 1976 and for all crimes 1998.

CHILE: Last execution 1985; abolished 2001.

COLOMBIA: Last execution 1907; abolished 1910, prohibited under Constitution.

COSTA RICA: Last execution 1859, abolished under Constitution 1877.

CZECH REPUBLIC: Last execution 1989; abolished 1990.

DENMARK: Last civil execution 1892; abolished 1933. Forty-six executions 1945–50 for atrocities under Nazi occupation.

ECUADOR: Last execution 1884; abolished 1906.

FINLAND: Last civil execution 1826; some executions for war crimes until 1944. Abolished (civil) 1949, for all crimes 1972, outlawed in Constitution 1984.

FRANCE: Thirty-four executions under the Fifth Republic, the last in 1977. Abolished 1981; prohibited in the Constitution 2007.

GERMANY: Estimated 80,000 executions (narrowly defined) under the Nazi regime 1933–45. Last executions in West Germany in 1949, abolished later that year. Abolished in the former East Germany in 1987; last execution 1981.

GREECE: Last execution 1972; abolished for murder 1975; for all crimes 2004.

HONDURAS: Last execution 1940; abolished 1956.

HONG KONG: Last execution 1966; abolished 1993. (Hong Kong's integration with the People's Republic of China may make this hard to sustain.)

ICELAND: Last execution 1830; abolished 1944.

IRELAND: Last execution 1954; abolished for civil crimes 1964: for all crimes 1990.

ISRAEL: Abolished 1954 — except for war crimes and crimes against humanity. (Adolf Eichmann hanged in 1962 — only Israel's second execution. The first was of Meir Tobianski in 1948, falsely accused of espionage and posthumously pardoned in 1949).

ITALY: Last execution in Tuscany 1769; abolished by Grand Duke Leopold in 1786; restored in 1860 with Italian unification. Abolished nationally in 1889; restored under Mussolini in 1926 (with twenty-six executions). Last execution 1947, abolished again for civil crimes 1948, all crimes 1994 and as part of the Constitution in 2007.

LUXEMBOURG: Last execution 1949; abolished 1979.

MEXICO: Last execution 1961; abolished for civil crimes 1976, for all crimes 2005.

NEPAL: Abolished 1931, then restored. Last execution 1979; abolished 1997.

NETHERLANDS: No civil execution since 1860; abolished 1870. Three executions (1948; 1952) for atrocities during Nazi occupation.

NEW ZEALAND: Last execution 1957; abolished for murder 1961; for treason 1989. Moratorium 1935–41, originally abolished 1941, restored 1950.

NORWAY: Last civil execution 1876; abolished 1905. Restored by Vidkun Quisling in 1942 under German occupation. After 1945, thirty-seven executions of collaborators, including Quisling.

PAPUA NEW GUINEA: Last execution 1954. Unknown number of executions carried out by AIF 1943–44. Abolished by the Australian government 1970. Reintroduced in 1991 but not carried out. Abolished by PNG Parliament 2022.

PERU: Last execution 1979; abolished for civil crimes 1980.

PHILIPPINES: Abolished 1986; restored 1993; abolished again 2006, but there were many extra-judicial killings under Rodrigo Duterte.

POLAND: Last execution 1988; abolished 1988.

ROMANIA: Last executions 1989 (the Ceauçescus). Abolished 1990. Originally abolished in 1864, restored and used under the Fascist and Communist regimes. Ceauçescu's penal code had twenty-eight capital offences.

RUSSIA: Last execution 1996. Remains in the law, but a moratorium is in force.

SERBIA: Last execution 1992, abolished 1995.

SOUTH AFRICA: Last execution 1989; moratorium 1990–95; abolished 1995.

SPAIN: Last execution 1975; abolished (civil) 1978, (military) 1995.

SWEDEN: No execution since 1910; abolished (civil) 1921, (military) 1973, in Constitution 2015.

SWITZERLAND: Last civil execution 1940; abolished (civil) 1942. However, seventeen executions during World War II. Abolished for all crimes 1999.

TURKEY: Last execution 1984; abolished 2004.

UKRAINE: Last execution 1997. Abolished 2000. The unrecognised breakaway republics of Donestsk and Luhansk reintroduced the death penalty in 2014.

UNITED KINGDOM: Last execution 1964; abolished for murder 1965; for all crimes 1998.

UNITED STATES:
- Alaska, abolished 1957.
- Colorado, abolished 2020.
- Connecticut, abolished 2012.
- Delaware, declared unconstitutional 2016.
- District of Columbia, abolished 1981.
- Hawaii, abolished 1957.
- Illinois, abolished 2011 (last execution 1999).
- Iowa, abolished 1964.
- Maine, abolished 1887.
- Maryland, abolished 2013.
- Massachusetts, abolished 1984 (last execution 1947).
- Michigan, abolished 1863 (no executions).
- Minnesota, abolished 1911.
- New Hampshire, abolished 2019 (last execution 1939).
- New Jersey, abolished 2007.
- New Mexico, abolished 2009.
- New York, abolished 2007 (last execution 1963).
- North Dakota, abolished 1973 (no execution since 1905).
- Rhode Island, abolished 1984 (no execution since 1845).

- Vermont, abolished 1965.
- Virginia, abolished 2021.
- Washington State, abolished 2018 (last execution 2010).
- West Virginia, abolished 1965 (last execution 2017).
- Wisconsin, abolished 1853.
- United States Territories, abolished.
- Moratoria in force in California, Ohio, Oregon and Pennsylvania.

URUGUAY: Last execution 1902; abolished 1907.

VATICAN/PAPAL STATES: Last execution in the Papal States 1868, none in the Vatican. Death penalty was available 1929–69, then abolished by Paul VI.

VENEZUELA: Last execution 1830; abolished 1853.

APPENDIX F

Three final notes

The three questions most frequently asked of abolitionists are:

1. What about the poor victim? Why do you only think of the criminal?
This has been answered in Section VII above. It is striking that in Victoria the initiative for securing compensation for victims of criminal attack came from the Anti-Hanging Council.

Sir Henry Bolte undertook 'to consider the matter', but refused to receive a deputation from the council.

Some retentionists appear to take the view that the act of execution is an adequate recompense for the victim and his survivors.

2. How would you (the abolitionist) feel if the murdered person was one of your family?
(a) Obviously most relations of persons murdered would be emotionally distraught and full of vengeance — eager for revenge.

But one ought not to base judgement on emotional distress but on calm detachment. This is why punishment is left to the law — not to surviving relatives.

(b) Nevertheless it is striking how rarely the relatives of murder victims do seek vengeance.

In the Victorian 'Vicarage' murder of 1961, the eighty-two-year-old mother of Rev. George Hall was killed by Robert Peter Tait. When Tait's death was confirmed by state cabinet, Hall protested vehemently. Nevertheless most anonymous letters to abolitionist campaigners usually contain the words, 'How would you feel if it was your mother …'

When asked if she thought Ronald Ryan should hang, the widow of warder George Hodson replied:

> I just really don't know. I had strong feelings on the Tait case and
> believed the sentence should have been carried out then. But it's easier
> to come to these decisions when you are not intimately connected with
> the circumstances. This affects you as you never thought before and your
> line of thinking and reasoning are different.
>
> I will just let things take their course. I couldn't do anything about
> it, one way or the other anyway.

Mrs Michael Gregson, the wife of the man allegedly murdered by
James Hanratty in the 'A6' murder in Britain, was strongly abolitionist
(as was her husband), and appealed for Hanratty's reprieve.

3. Doesn't it stand to reason that death must be the greatest of all deterrents?
As Rosemary Hanbury has noted, the 'common sense' assumption
that death is an immediate and effective deterrent is rebutted in the
matter of road safety. The fact that death is a daily penalty for criminal
or irresponsible road behaviour has been widely and horribly
publicised, but has had little success even in persuading motorists to
use demonstrably effective safety devices (for example, safety belts),
let alone reduce the annual road toll. The same point could be made
about the ineffective threats of death by lung cancer that do not
appear to deter potential or actual smokers.

*   *   *

A final note on the case of Robert Peter Tait (see pp. 265–67). Tait's
insanity in terms of the M'Naghten Rules was of brief duration, and
he was soon returned from the Ararat Asylum to Pentridge. However,
clinical studies (published in *The Lancet*, March 1968) later appeared
to establish that Tait was the first subject ever found to have a XYY-
XYYY mosaic chromosome complement.

Man sees the vanity of laws; he gets rid of them; it is useful, therefore to take him to task. On what will be found the order of the world which he wishes to govern? Will it be on the caprice of each individual? What a confusion there would be! Shall it be on justice? He knows nothing of it.
– Blaise Pascal, *Pensées*, no. 230